The Crime That Pays

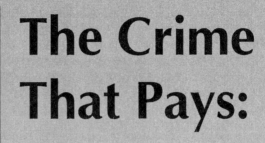

The Crime That Pays:

Drug Trafficking and Organized Crime in Canada

Frederick J. Desroches

Canadian Scholars' Press Inc.
Toronto

The Crime That Pays:
Drug Trafficking and Organized Crime in Canada
by Frederick J. Desroches

First published in 2005 by
Canadian Scholars' Press Inc.
180 Bloor Street West, Suite 801
Toronto, Ontario
M5S 2V6

www.cspi.org

Canadian Scholars' Press gratefully acknowledges financial support for our publishing activities from the Government of Canada through the Book Publishing Industry Development Program (BPIDP) and the Government of Ontario through the Ontario Book Publishing Tax Credit Program.

Library and Archives Canada Cataloguing in Publication

Desroches, Frederick John
    The crime that pays : drug trafficking and organized crime in Canada / Frederick J. Desroches.

Includes bibliographical references and index.
ISBN 1-55130-231-4

    1. Drug traffic--Canada. 2. Organized crime--Canada. I. Title.

HV5840.C3D48 2005   364.177'0971   C2004-906149-6

Cover design by Aldo Fierro
Top cover photo: "Urban Life," by bitter/istockphoto.com
Bottom cover photo: "Addiction Series," by sx70/istockphoto.com
Page design and layout by Brad Horning

06 07 08 09   5 4 3 2

Printed and bound in Canada by AGMV Marquis Imprimeur, Inc.

Canadä

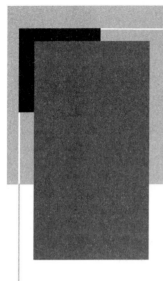

Table of Contents

Preface

This book began out of discussions with a student and former high-level drug trafficker, Mr. J. Serge LeClerc. Serge spent two decades behind bars for his involvement in drug trafficking and organized crime before enrolling in the Honours Sociology program at the University of Waterloo. His knowledge and willingness to assist me in this research was instrumental in getting the project off the ground. I wish to give special thanks to Serge for his generosity and congratulate him on living a crime-free life for the past 15 years.

The purpose of this book is to provide a review of research and theory on higher-level drug trafficking and organized crime. The book focuses primarily on the Canadian experience and presents the results of interviews with 70 convicted drug traffickers. Interviews were also conducted with the Royal Canadian Mounted Police (RCMP) and other drug investigators. The text examines the characteristics of organized crime, the structure and functioning of drug syndicates, motivation, modus operandi, the manner in which the police investigate these groups, and social policy dealing with illicit substances. Chapter 1 discusses the differences between retail and higher-level trafficking, explains the nature of the sample and research methods used in this study, and introduces the theoretical models that are applied in subsequent chapters. Chapter 2 includes a discussion of the history of drug legislation in Canada, current laws that define trafficking and other related offences, conspiracy laws, anti-gang (organized crime) legislation, laws related to the use of informants and agents, and the sentencing and parole of drug offenders. Chapter 3 discusses definitional issues, transnational organized crime, and network and economic models of syndicated crime. Included is a discussion of the criminal background and employment history of the subjects in this study; how drug trafficking compares to legitimate business; the significance of friendship, kinship, race, and ethnicity; the size and composition of drug-dealing syndicates; and an analysis of how drug trafficking operates as independent entrepreneurship. Chapter 4 discusses initial involvement in drug trafficking and applies learning, rational choice, anomie, opportunity, and social control theories. Also discussed are the modes of entry into higher-level drug dealing, how players move up the drug-trafficking ladder, family relationships, the morality and self-concept of dealers, and the dealing lifestyle. The chapter concludes with an analysis of stresses associated with a life of crime and the failure of dealers to quit before they are caught. Chapter 5 discusses the marketing of illicit drugs, relationships among dealers, and partnership arrangements. Also discussed are the risks involved in this crime and how dealers design their modus operandi to maximize security. Chapter 6 also focuses on modus operandi, but examines strategies related to the use of fronts as a marketing tool, the collection of debts, outlaw motorcycle gangs and violence, and the issue of territoriality. Chapter 7 examines the training and operation of undercover officers, the use of informants and agents, the surveillance of offenders, conspiracy laws, and the enforcement of money-laundering legislation. Chapter 8 discusses the implications of research on illicit drug usage and drug trafficking on social policy. Also discussed are the liberalization/prohibition arguments and proposed legislative reforms.

Acknowledgements

I wish to thank the following persons who supported this research project. From Correctional Services Canada: Paul Alves, Diane Brown, Glen Brown, Pat Brown, Judy Campbell, Cathy Gainer, Cathy Haines, Janet-Sue Hamilton, Laura Holthus, Dennis Kerr, Sue Langevin, Matt Logan, Brenda Marshall, Michelle McBride, Judith McGee, Don Menzies, Fay Paris, Leah Place, Heather Scott, Margaret Rattan, and Derek Stone. A special thanks to Kelly Gordon-Kane of Correctional Services Canada, whose assistance went far beyond the call of duty. From the RCMP, I wish to thank: Gary Chaters, Michael Cowley, Costa Dimopoulos, Mark Fleming, Frank Gougeon, Don Loree, Al MacDonald, Steve Martin, Gord Mooney, Paul Nadeau, and Walter Spilkin. From Peel Regional Police, thanks to David Woodland and Doug Rumsley. Ana Freitas, my research assistant was highly resourceful. Thanks also to Dr. Vincent Sacco, Dr. Margaret Beare, Dr. Adie Nelson, and three anonymous reviewers for their helpful comments on earlier drafts of this study. From Canadian Scholars' Press, I wish to thank Althea Prince and Rebecca Conolly for their interest and assistance. I am particularly indebted to my wife, Lisa, to whom this book is dedicated, for editorial comment and support throughout the project.

The financial assistance of St. Jerome's University, The Nathanson Center for the Study of Organized Crime and Corruption, and OIC Research and Evaluation, Royal Canadian Mounted Police, is gratefully acknowledged.

Drug Trafficking
The Crime That Pays

Introduction

All modern nations have laws that prohibit the importation, manufacturing, growth, distribution, sale, and use of a variety of narcotics. The laws that prohibit illicit drugs are typically buttressed with punitive criminal penalties that are meant to deter these types of activities. Nonetheless, illicit drugs are in high demand and the use of prohibited substances is common in most societies. Social scientists, journalists, the police, politicians, and ordinary citizens have long recognized that drug laws act as barriers to legal competitors and limit the trade to those willing to risk criminal sanctions. This results in inflated prices for drugs and potentially huge profits for criminals and criminal syndicates. Just as the prohibition of alcohol in the United States (1919–1932) led to the rise of organized criminal syndicates, drug prohibitions are credited with fuelling the rise of cartels and other large criminal enterprises in modern times.

From a law-enforcement perspective, drug laws are difficult to enforce since drug offences do not have a victim per se. Rather, drug usage involves consenting buyers and sellers, and there is typically no complainant to inform the police and act as a witness. Drug prohibitions criminalize consensual activities and are characterized as *mala prohibita*. As such, these laws typically do not have broad support among the population since they lack a common value consensus. From a social policy perspective, drug laws and drug enforcement polarize the public and often result in widespread violations, defiance, and disrespect for the law. Although some citizens see drug laws as supporting moral values, others view them as divisive, overzealous, intrusive of civil liberties, hypocritical, harmful, and ineffective.

1

The Nature of Drug Trafficking

Drug trafficking is an activity that involves the importation, manufacturing, cultivation, distribution, and/or sale of illicit drugs. Drug trafficking is a hierarchical system in which drugs are moved from smugglers, growers, or manufacturers to wholesalers or middlemen who pass the product down the chain to retailers and the eventual consumer or drug user. In order to conduct business, dealers need a reliable connection, trusted associates who provide a variety of services, and a network of customers who make purchases on a regular basis. By its very nature, drug trafficking involves social networks in which several people engage in an illegal commercial activity for profit on an ongoing basis. Traffickers use the terms "supplier" or "source" to refer to the person above them in the distribution chain and from whom they purchase their drugs. Importers typically have connections in source countries and smuggle drugs such as cocaine, heroin, hashish, and marijuana into Canada. Growers produce marijuana crops often through sophisticated hydroponic operations, while manufacturers produce methamphetamines and other designer drugs in laboratories. The terms "distributor" or "wholesaler" refer to dealers who purchase drugs in large quantities and sell them to other distributors or dealers down the chain. For the purposes of this study, higher-level traffickers are defined as importers, growers, manufacturers, or wholesalers who market large quantities of illicit drugs. Dealers who sell directly to drug users in the retail market are referred to as "retailers," "pushers," "lower-level dealers," or "street-level dealers."

The term "dealing network" describes the ongoing interactions, agreements, and contacts that dealers have with others in the trade (Adler & Adler, 1982:123). Most dealers operate in loosely structured and relatively closed networks of people who know and trust one another and are linked by friendships and/or ethnicity. These groups are referred to by a variety of terms, including "gang," "family," "crew," "syndicate," or "cell." Beyond this small group are users, dealers, suppliers, ex-cons, and others who provide the dealer with associates, illicit drugs, couriers, clients, and act as a source of information on the ever-changing drug scene.

The Structure and Organization of Retail Drug Selling

Most studies of drug trafficking have focused on lower-level dealers who sell directly to the consumer or drug user. These retail level dealers typically are not on anyone's payroll, are not employed or controlled by others, nor are they part of a highly structured or formally organized network or organization. On the contrary, street-level drug sales are largely conducted by independent entrepreneurs, and retail markets are often fragmented, open, fluid, and competitive. Dealing is relatively unsophisticated and dealers make their connections through word of mouth rather than within formally organized networks (Adler, 1985; Atkyns & Hanneman, 1974; Curcione, 1997; Fields, 1984, 1986; Goode, 1970; Hafley & Tewksbury, 1995; Johnson et al., 1992; Lieb & Olson, 1976; Mieczkowski, 1986; Murphy et al., 1990; Redlinger, 1975; Reuter et al., 1990; Weisheit, 1991a, 1991b).

The stereotype of a drug dealer or "pusher," as portrayed in the media, is of someone who sells dangerous, addictive, and consciousness-altering drugs to young people, is motivated by greed and/or addiction, and has crossed a clearly marked moral boundary, severing most ties to the conventional world. Such people are portrayed as self-serving and utterly indifferent to the pain and suffering from which they profit (Murphy et al., 1990). Most studies of drug selling have focused on retail or street-level sales and show that the pusher myth presented by the authorities and the media is not accurate. Drugs are not "pushed" according to popular imagery—they are sold or dealt to friends and acquaintances by a large number of small entrepreneurs who make modest profits. Dealers have little trouble justifying their behaviour and see themselves as businessmen filling a demand or need for a substance that is not usually harmful to people who make their own choices (Carey, 1968; Murphy et al., 1990).

Studies of retail-level trafficking describe a number of patterns and characteristics of offenders and their motives. It appears that most street-level dealers are male, sell small quantities of drugs, deal occasionally while still engaging in legitimate employment, sell to a limited number of friends and acquaintances, and use the relatively small amounts of money earned through drug sales to supplement incomes from work. These dealers may be more accurately characterized as "moonlighters" (Holzman, 1983; Polsky, 1967) because they hold intermittent, unskilled legitimate jobs in the labour market. The primary motive of retail-level dealers is to offset the costs of their own usage and/or addiction. These patterns appear to hold regardless of the socio-economic status of offenders or the types of drugs sold—marijuana, cocaine, heroin, or various designer drugs. In short, most lower-level dealers work independently, do not employ others, have incomes that are surprisingly modest, and take their profit in drugs, which they consume. Research on retail drug trafficking does not support an image of greedy, ruthless, violent offenders as reflected in the pusher stereotype (Atkyns & Hanneman, 1974; Fields, 1984; Goode, 1970; Johnson et al., 1985; MacCoun & Reuter, 1992; Maher & Daly, 1996; Mieczkowski, 1986; Murphy et al., 1990; Preble & Casey, 1969; Redlinger, 1975; Sorfleet, 1976:143; Tunnell, 1993; Waldorf, 1977).

It appears that retail distributors typically develop drug-use patterns first and drift into dealing afterwards. In this way, motivation follows behaviour rather than the reverse and is learned in the course of drug usage. Murphy et al. (1990) found that with the exception of drug-usage sales, the cocaine dealers in their sample were mostly law-abiding citizens who follow conventional values and lifestyles. Most drifted into dealing by virtue of their strategies for solving the problems entailed in using a criminalized substance, and only then developed additional motives centring on money. Subjects did not make a conscious choice to become dealers, nor did they view themselves as such.

> Our subjects were already seasoned users of illicit drugs. For years their drug use coexisted comfortably with their conventional roles and activities; having a deviant dimension to their identities appeared to cause them little strain. In fact, because their use of illicit drugs had gone on for so long, was so common in their social worlds, and had not significantly affected their otherwise normal lives, they hardly considered it deviant at all and did not see themselves as dealers .... Thus when they began to sell cocaine as well as use it, they did not consider it a major leap down an unknown road but rather a series of short steps down a familiar path .... No sharp break in values, motives, world views, or identities was required. Indeed, few woke up one morning and made a conscious decision to become sellers. (Murphy et al., 1990:474)

Research that examines educational and employment experiences of retail drug dealers indicates that many have a low level of school attainment, have worked erratically, and that opportunities for profitable occupations are limited. These findings suggest that for some dealers, anomie theory applies and drug sales can be viewed as an adaptation to a lack of educational and job skills and limited access to decent-paying work. Studies do show that some lower socio-economic-status dealers make a conscious decision to traffick in drugs largely because licit economic opportunities are scarce or non-existent. A small percentage of dealers are motivated by profit and market their product to a large number of clients. However, retail-level drug sales bring them into contact with informants or undercover officers, arrests are common, and prison interrupts their deviant career and significantly diminishes income (MacCoun & Reuter, 1992; Hagedorn, 1994; Carpenter et al., 1988; Tunnell, 1993). In short, most lower socio-economic dealers are involved only sporatically in drug sales, attempt to hold onto a conventional lifestyle, work at poor-paying jobs, and struggle with periods of unemployment and poverty (Carey, 1968; Hagedorn, 1994; Murphy et al., 1990; Padilla, 1992). The majority do not entertain high conventional aspirations, nor do they experience severe strain because of their inability to achieve them (Hirschi, 1969).

Drug officers who have spent years investigating street-level sales report that the dealers they come across fit a different profile than the one suggested by most research studies: a high proportion are non-users and traffick for profit only; most are engaged in frequent sales to a large number of clients; intimidation and assault are common; and drug dealing is a full-time job with very few engaged in legitimate work. These contrasting images may be explained in part by the fact that the police are more likely to come across the most active types of dealers as opposed to those who sell infrequently to their friends. It

is also possible that studies underestimate the number of retailers who are motivated by profit and engaged in dealing on a full-time basis.

There appears to be a combination of motives, often interrelated, that lead individuals to deal drugs: as discussed above, some enter the trade out of financial necessity and a perceived lack of employment opportunities, and others are motivated by greed and the promise of wealth and a luxurious lifestyle. The primary motive for most retail-level dealers, however, is to maintain a consistent supply of drugs and to offset their high costs. Beyond that, dealers also enjoy the additional money—though nominal—that selling provides, the excitement and social interaction associated with dealing, and the status obtained from friends and associates. For the majority of lower-level dealers, however, drug trafficking is simply an adjunct to drug usage and is not a long-term occupational choice (Adler, 1985; Atkyns & Hanneman, 1974; Blum, 1972; Carpenter et al., 1988; Johnson et al., 1990; Langer, 1977; Tunnell, 1993; Waldorf et al., 1977, 1991; Weisheit, 1991a, 1991b). Consistent with these findings, there appears to be little upward mobility in the drug trade and most street-level dealers make no attempt to move into wholesaling or beyond (Carey, 1968; Langer, 1977; Sorfleet, 1976; Tunnell, 1993).

The "Crime Doesn't Pay" Argument

Wilson and Abrahamse (1992) make the case that the common belief that "crime doesn't pay" is substantially correct. Gottfredson and Hirschi (1990) similarly argue that financial returns from crime typically provide at best only a supplemental source of income and that criminal activity is largely motivated for short-term gratification only. They conclude that the "long-term or lasting benefits of crime are profoundly limited" in contrast to honest and stable legitimate employment and "a valid theory of crime must see it as it is: largely petty, typically not completed, and usually of little lasting or substantial benefits to the offender" (Gottfredson & Hirschi, 1990:20). This portrayal of crime and offenders is supported by the research reviewed above that reports on the modest financial success of retail-level drug dealers. The drug economy does not appear to provide enormous opportunities for profit for street-level dealers, and only a few make substantial money at any time during their drug-dealing careers.

Similar results are reported in my earlier study of bank robbers based on interviews with 80 convicted offenders (Desroches, 2002 [1995]). Although most come from the lower socio-economic class and have limited employment opportunities, robbery is not a means of achieving long-term financial goals. On the contrary, the vast majority seek short-term hedonistic pleasures and spend their ill-gotten gains on "partying"—a term used to describe spending on women, alcohol, drugs, and other transitory pleasures. The sums of money obtained from each robbery are relatively modest ($1,500–$2,000), but are deemed sufficient to meet one's immediate needs or wants and are attractive in relation to the poor-paying jobs that are available to those with little education and/or job skills and experience. Even the motive to continue robbing banks (need turns to greed) reflects a short-term pursuit of transitory pleasures. Almost all bank robbers have limited success in crime, are eventually caught, and pay dearly for their escapades with lengthy prison sentences.

In addition, most have few social bonds, little education or job skills, and are already immersed in a deviant/criminal subculture. Because they have so few stakes in conformity, they think that they have nothing to lose through criminal activities and take what most of us would view as extreme risks for relatively small rewards. Even though there is rationality in their decision making, their rationality is subjective and clearly limited or bounded (Cornish & Clarke, 1986a) by time constraints, a mood of fatalism, financial need, alcohol and drug dependency, and other factors that undermine goal-oriented thinking. These findings are consistent with Gottfredson and Hirschi's (1990) thesis that offenders lack self-control, are unable to delay gratification or make long-term plans, and are essentially losers with low aspirations and very limited criminal or legitimate success. They also support Wilson and Abrahamse's (1992) contention that career criminals earn relatively little money, are highly present oriented and opportunistic, and are not governed by rational, utilitarian, decision-making processes.

Successful Criminal Entrepreneurs: Higher-Level Drug Traffickers

Although crime in general may not be highly profitable, some criminal enterprises do offer significant financial rewards. A few theorists have recently argued that the proportion of successful property and market offenders is not trivial, theoretically or practically, and that this phenomenon is often overlooked or dismissed within mainstream criminology (McCarthy & Hagan, 2001; Morselli, 2003a; Tremblay & Morselli, 2000). Higher-level drug trafficking is one such activity that provides opportunities for criminals to achieve an opulent lifestye without the risks inherent in most other crimes. The study of drug wholesaling is a study of criminals who have achieved high incomes and status in their deviant occupation and subculture. This book examines a crime that *does* pay and attempts to shed light on the conditions that contribute to success in this underground economy.

There have been few studies of higher-level drug traffickers, perhaps because they are relatively small in number, have much to lose from being apprehended, and are more careful and secretive. The first systematic study of higher-level dealers was published by Patricia Adler (1985), who observed 65 smugglers and distributors in Southern California. The research grew out of contacts made during her graduate school years, which allowed her to conduct a six-year ethnographic study of dealers who were actively operating their illegitimate business. The sample was predominantly White, middle-class males without prior criminal records who worked in groups that typically ranged from three to eight people. The generalizability of her findings was limited by the nature of the sample and the geographic concentration of the dealers in one locale. Most of her data were gathered in the 1970s.

Reuter and Haaga (1989) interviewed 41 drug traffickers, 29 of whom were classified as higher-level dealers (above the retail level) in U.S. federal prisons. Their sample was also male, but more heterogeneous in relation to race, socio-economic status, and ethnicity. Like Adler, they found long-term supplier/customer relationships, although they were rarely exclusive or centrally directed. Most of the dealers operated primarily in one metropolitan area, but there were no reported barriers to moving outside local areas if dealers were ambitious and entrepreneurial. Barriers to entry into the higher levels of the drug markets were minimal, and most dealers attained their positions without having to undergo lengthy apprenticeships or accumulate large quantities of capital. Their subjects made large incomes (hundreds of thousands of dollars annually), often for many years within relatively small drug syndicates. Reuter and Haaga describe higher-level drug trafficking as an enormously profitable business in which the risks of arrest appeared to be low.

> Men of no obvious skill were able to earn enormous incomes for incurring quite modest risks ... [with] no large initial investments. Capital in this business consists almost entirely of an inventory which is turned over rapidly and the "good will" built up by knowing good suppliers and customers. (Reuter & Haaga, 1989:35)

Although some men had prior criminal backgrounds, others had extensive legitimate work experiences in sales and/or business. Subjects report little use of violence or victimization. The researchers compare higher-level drug dealers to wholesale brokers, independent merchants, or salesmen and conclude that small drug networks provide numerous safety benefits and that a successful drug operation does not require the creation of a large or enduring organization.

Much of the literature on higher-level drug trafficking is subsumed under organized crime. This research, discussed in Chapter 3, also concludes that organized crime syndicates do not resemble the Mafia model—large, violent, monopolistic, centrally controlled bureaucratic organizations. Rather, organized crime tends to consist of a large number of small independent syndicates who often conspire and collaborate for mutual gain.

Research Methodology: An Exploratory Study of Higher-Level Traffickers

The data for this study were gathered through interviews with 70 higher-level drug traffickers: importers, manufacturers, and wholesalers of illicit drugs. All subjects were men serving time in Canadian federal penitentiaries for drug-trafficking offences and were selected from police and correctional files and inmate referrals. Five subjects had recently been released on parole and were interviewed in the community. Offenders were members of 62 drug-dealing syndicates that operated in Nova Scotia, Ontario, Quebec, Alberta, and British Columbia throughout the years 1990–2002. Sixteen interviews were conducted with two members of the same crew. Additional data were gathered through interviews with drug couriers and drug investigators from the Royal Canadian Mounted Police (RCMP). Police interviews and files generated important information about the investigation and acted as a means for testing the accuracy of interview data. Police data were particularly helpful in determining how the investigation was started, how the evidence was gathered, the use of agents and undercover operators, and the connections between the various participants.

The average age of the 70 men was 40 years, and they represented a number of racial and ethnic backgrounds. Most convictions involved conspiracy charges (40/70, 57.1%), followed by importing (15/70, 21.4%), trafficking or possession for the purposes of trafficking (10/70, 14.3%), and manufacturing/cultivation (5/70, 7.1%). Sentences ranged from two to 17 years and averaged approximately seven years. Most subjects specialized in one drug only: 41 sold cocaine; 11 distributed heroin; four manufactured designer drugs; nine dealt in marijuana/hashish; and five sold a variety of illicit drugs. Three-quarters of the sample (52/70, 74.3%) report that they were non-users; eight used drugs (mainly marijuana) recreationally; and 10 men report heavy usage or addiction (seven for cocaine, two for heroin, and one for methamphetamine). There were on average 11 people charged for each of the 62 drug networks in this study, with the number of accused varying from one to 52 offenders. Twenty-five (25/70, 35.7%) subjects sold illicit drugs at the retail level for two to three years on average before moving to wholesale. It is difficult to estimate the average length of time men in this sample engaged in higher-level trafficking since many were cautious about answering this question. Only one subject had been involved for less than a year before his arrest, several reported 10–15 years of successful dealing, and one cocaine importer's career spanned 30 years, including two brief retirements. Most of the 70 respondents operated at the wholesale level for five to eight years and had realized huge profits. For many, their arrest occurred only after the police undertook a sophisticated and proactive criminal investigation that took one or two years to complete.

Only 10 men who were asked refused to be interviewed. Two inmates indicated that they were concerned that the data may be used to assist the police in future investigations; two were advised by their lawyers not to co-operate; one man was concerned that interview materials could be used to adversely affect his parole chances; and five were members of outlaw motorcycle gangs. Biker gangs are tight-knit, regimented organizations that demand a high degree of conformity to norms and exert strong control over individual members. Both the police and inmate sources explained that bikers are highly suspicious and distrustful of authority, and that individual members would not have the authority to grant an interview without getting themselves into trouble with other members. Several career criminals in this sample were invited to join outlaw motorcycle gangs, but declined because they wished to maintain their freedom and independence.

I was very close to bikers—Hells Angels. I could have been a biker, but I like to be myself. I don't want to take orders.

I had no problems dealing with bikers. I had partners who were bikers. I was supposed to be a member, but I turned them down. I don't like to be told what to do. I've been asked, but I don't like the politics. Like they want you to be a runner before you can be a patch member and you have to do things for other guys. I might consider it if I didn't have to do that and just get my patch straight out. That's something I don't want to talk too much about. I'm friends with them and sell to them. I wasn't moving into their territory. I worked with them and I never had any problems.

A patch means a full-fledged membership and I was not interested in that. One of my suppliers was probationary and one was an associate member of a bike gang. I like my independence too much to become a biker.

Inmates who consented to the interview did so for a number of reasons: the topic was highly relevant to their life experiences; the interview provided a break from normal prison routine; they recognized the legitimacy of university research and were willing to co-operate; most stated that the drug business was behind them and they saw no threat in participating in the study; a few thought that it would improve their parole chances by showing that they were co-operative and had nothing to hide; and they trusted the researcher's assurances and/or that of their parole officer that confidentiality was guaranteed. There is little evidence to suggest that subjects in this study exaggerated their accounts, lied, or avoided telling the truth about their activities. Questions dealt with general issues and processes and did not illicit incriminating information such as names, dates, places, Swiss bank accounts, etc. Other researchers have also concluded that drug dealers are forthright in providing valuable data about illegal activities (Jacobs, 1999; Maher, 1997).

Most of those who participated provided highly detailed information about their drug-dealing experiences, incomes, modus operandi, families, lifestyles, and eventual downfall. Twenty subjects were interviewed on a second occasion because of time constraints in the first interview. Interviews lasted an average of four to five hours, and one man was interviewed for 18 hours over a two-day period.

Gaining access to inmates was far more difficult than gaining their participation. It took 18 months to obtain permission from Correctional Services Canada and several more months to gain permission from various regional headquarters across the country. A staff member was appointed as the resource person in each prison through whom interviews had to be arranged. Although some were very helpful, others were indifferent and, in some cases, obstructionist.

The majority of offenders were located in minimum-security institutions because they were largely non-violent, first-time offenders. Most of these men were also classified as low risk to escape because they were eligible for early release on parole; had many ties to the community including homes, families with children, and jobs and/or businesses; and institutional psychological assessments described them as co-operative, exhibiting pro-social attitudes, and not likely to commit institutional offences. Most did not use drugs and, apart from their drug sales, were not viewed as criminal in their orientation or associations.

The sample was chosen from an incarcerated population because it is unrealistic to interview traffickers who are currently engaged in this illegal enterprise. Most are not easily identifiable, nor readily accessible, and approaching them would raise ethical and legal issues as well as compromise ongoing police investigations. It is quite likely that a sample of dealers who have been caught is not representative of all traffickers. Those who are more clever, more careful, and know when to retire are less likely to be apprehended and convicted. Although this is no doubt true, most of the men in this sample were cautious and were caught by sophisticated, time-consuming, and expensive police investigations. Whether or not they differ in other important ways from men who have not been arrested is difficult to know or determine. RCMP drug investigators describe the men in this sample as typical of the higher-level dealers they come across. The most obvious problem with the sample is that outlaw motorcycle gang members are not represented. The men in the study tend to be relatively independent operators and are not part of large and formally structured gangs or cartels. As noted earlier, outlaw motorcycle gangs represent a more traditional organized crime structure, but members of biker gangs declined to be interviewed. Their involvement in the drug trade, however, is believed to be extensive. This is discussed in more detail in Chapter 6.

Higher-level drug trafficking is a sophisticated and complex crime and presents the sociologist with a number of problems. The present study focuses on a wide range of topics, is exploratory in nature, and attempts to answer some of the following questions. What are the characteristics of drug dealers and to what extent do age, gender, race, ethnicity, and prior criminal experiences affect one's entry into trafficking? How successful are most offenders and how long do they operate? How do dealers make contact with suppliers, obtain their drugs, and develop and service clients? What norms govern the relations among dealers; between suppliers and their clients; and between suppliers and their employees? How lucrative are these activities? How are profits spent? Are drug profits invested in legitimate ventures? Do successful drug dealers retire? How do illegal drug businesses compare to legitimate businesses? How do they differ? What are the risks involved in the drug trade? What strategies do dealers use to minimize their risks? To what degree is violence a characteristic of higher-level trafficking? What affects the level of violence used? Does the degree of violence differ in the retail versus the wholesale trade? Is violence a characteristic of certain groups rather than others? What purpose does violence serve? What disadvantages come with the use of violence? How is credit handled in the drug world? What norms govern the use of credit or fronts? To what degree is violence used as a means to collect debts? To what extent is organized crime involved in drug trafficking? How is it best conceptualized? What form does it take? To what degree is organized crime transnational in nature?

From a social policy perspective, the laws that prohibit drug usage and sales and the techniques employed by law enforcement to combat this phenomenon also present the sociologist and others with a number of questions. What techniques do the police use to investigate higher-level drug traffickers? How dangerous is this type of work? What laws are most effective at combatting drug trafficking and organized crime? What limitations do the police face in this endeavour? What impact/threat do police activities have on civil liberties? How effective are the police at limiting the sale and usage of illicit drugs?

Theoretical Framework

Theories that are appropriate to the understanding of drug trafficking include network analysis, opportunity theory, social learning theories, strain/anomie theory, and rational choice theories. Drug trafficking involves a criminal conspiracy that requires offenders to communicate and co-operate with one another for their mutual benefit. Drug dealing involves the movement of drugs through a network of dealers that include manufacturers, growers, or importers, down the chain to distributors and users. Because drug trafficking takes place in an illicit market, there is a need to understand how markets develop, are structured, and function. Although our research focuses on individual participation and earnings, it also examines the structure and organization of illicit drug markets and the networks that make these markets function.

Drug-trafficking networks are often based on criminal associations, friendships, ethnicity, and/or business contacts. Networks not only provide illegitimate opportunity (Cloward & Ohlin, 1960) through contacts with willing collaborators, access to drugs, suppliers, and clients, they also act as a means for evaluating a person's reputation as competent and trustworthy. Networks provide participants with a mechanism for reducing risks, thus making the crime more attractive and increasing a person's willingness to participate.

Social learning theories are also relevant since they assume that criminal contacts, skills, and opportunities are typically obtained through interaction with others (Cloward & Ohlin, 1960; Sutherland, 1947), and these opportunities are strongly influenced by the extent of one's embeddedness in networks of offenders (McCarthy et al., 1998:157). Our data indicate that most higher-level dealers gain their position through direct entry, and that opportunity to do so is based on criminal associates, ethnic networks, and entrepreneurial attitudes and business contacts. In particular, drug trafficking networks allow dealers to keep a safe distance from more dangerous activities such as the handling and movement of drugs. As discussed in detail in chapters 5 and 6, networks limit the flow of information and protect those above and below them in the distribution system. Thus,

the arrest of one participant need not threaten the security of others. In addition, networks often have several branches so that if one is shut down, others continue to function and the flow of drugs is largely uninterrupted.

Robert Merton's theory of anomie (1938, 1968) suggests that certain groups of people—primarily those in the lower class—consider crime as an alternative means for obtaining money when legitimate avenues are blocked. The initial motive for engaging in drug trafficking for all subjects in this study is the pursuit of wealth. Although some dealers in this study enter the market because of the lack of legitimate employment opportunities, most have a history of conventional employment and enjoy a comfortable lifestyle. They opt instead, however, to pursue wealth that is greater than what is available through legitimate channels.

Although most dealers do not face the economic hardships of poverty, other aspects of Merton's theory apply. Higher-level drug traffickers internalize cultural values that support the rational pursuit of money and the weighing of risks to get it. As will be seen in subsequent chapters, dealers are very much like ordinary businesspeople and are deeply committed to the moral order that surrounds the social organization of work and success in our society. In fact, most adhere to conventional versions of how to achieve such status within the drug-dealing world, including the demonstration of a strong work ethic, sound business practices, professional standards, trustworthiness, and organizational and people skills. Similar work-related values drive both illegitimate and legitimate businesspeople, but drug dealing serves as a faster and more efficient method of realizing socially valued goals.

Rational choice theory is applicable to an analysis of drug trafficking since it considers the dealer's perspective in order to understand motives, modus operandi, and decision making. Offenders are viewed as instrumentally rational actors who choose specific behaviours that will maximize benefits while minimizing costs. Crime is chosen as a rational means that offenders believe will be the most effective way to achieve their goals. The expected utility model in economics (Becker, 1968) views offenders as no different from other citizens who select among behavioural options and maintains that individuals behave "as if" they are aware of all possible outcomes and their probabilities, potential costs, and possible benefits. Would-be offenders use this information to choose rationally between various actions, and voluntarily and purposefully choose crime if the expected utility outweighs possible losses. It will be seen that higher-level dealers exhibit a great deal of rationality, are careful to evaluate risks versus rewards, and develop and implement a modus operandi that emphasizes safety and profit.

Summary

In this chapter, we have provided an overview of research on drug trafficking and the theoretical models that shaped the data collection and analysis. The following chapters present the findings from this study and explain motivational factors, important social variables, and answer some of the questions outlined above. Included is a description and analysis of the main social and personal characteristics of offenders; the size and composition of drug-dealing syndicates; the criminal and employment history of dealers; the business and entrepreneurial characteristics of organized crime; and the significance of friendship, kinship, race, and ethnicity in the development of criminal networks. Also discussed are the laws, police strategies used to combat drug usage and trafficking, and social policy implications from this and other research.

Drug Trafficking and Organized Crime
Canadian Legislation and Case Law

Introduction

The first part of this chapter is an analysis of the evolution of Canadian drug laws and social policies. The second section describes and analyzes current Canadian legislation and case law as they relate to drug trafficking, criminal investigative techniques, and the prosecution, conviction, sentencing, and incarceration of higher-level drug traffickers. Included in the latter is a discussion of: the *Controlled Drugs and Substances Act* and the laws relating to possession, double-doctoring, trafficking, cultivation and manufacturing, importing/exporting, and conspiracy; proceeds of crime/money-laundering laws; anti-gang legislation; case law regarding informants and agents; and the *Corrections and Conditional Release Act*.

The History of Drug Legislation in Canada

In 1908, the Canadian federal government passed its first drug laws with the proclamation of an enactment prohibiting the importation, manufacture, and sale of opium (SC 1908, c. 50). Further criminal drug legislation followed in 1911 in the form of the *Opium and Drug Act* (SC 1911, c. 17). The *Opium Act* (1908) represented the first attempt to criminalize drug usage in Canada. Prior to the enactment of this legislation, the Chinese community on the West Coast of Canada lawfully imported large quantities of opium for their own consumption; drug use caused little concern among the population; and opiates were widely available in a variety of legal medicines. Solomon and Green's (1988) historical analysis of the development of early narcotics legislation argues convincingly that the 1908 *Opium Act* was based less on health concerns than on racial and

13

economic factors. The attempt to criminalize opium usage represented a means of social control that targeted the West Coast Chinese community, a segment of the population that was poor, politically powerless, and the object of racial animosity.

Up to the 1880s, Canadian immigration policy encouraged the importation of cheap labour, and Chinese workers earned low wages in British Columbia's mining sector and in the construction of the Canadian Pacific Railway. The Chinese were well accepted and generally praised by employers who viewed them as hard-working, conscientious, thrifty, and law-abiding. By 1885, the railway was complete and the mining boom tapered off, and B.C. experienced an economic downturn. These events created a restricted and competitive labour market resulting in Chinese workers competing directly with Whites for jobs.

> The tolerant attitude to both the Chinese and opium smoking prevailed until the 1880s, when the decline in railroad construction and the gold rush restricted job opportunities in British Columbia. White labour felt it could not compete with the frugal, unmarried Chinese workers. Caucasian businessmen were not blamed. Rather, it was their Chinese employees who became targets of public resentment, for they accepted wages on which a white man's family could not live. As economic conditions worsened, complaints against the Chinese increased. They were criticized as being clannish, heathen, unsanitary, immoral, and disloyal to Canada. (Solomon & Green, 1988:90)

In response to the mounting "Asian problem," the Canadian government passed the *Chinese Immigration Act* of 1885 restricting Chinese immigration, denying Chinese the right to vote, placing restrictions on their ownership of land and businesses, and imposing on them an annual immigrant tax. When racial unrest in British Columbia resulted in the 1907 Vancouver riots, the federal government dispatched the deputy minister of Labour and future prime minister of Canada, William Lyon MacKenzie King, to investigate the damage done to Asian businesses. King received claims for compensation from Chinese opium-manufacturing merchants whose stock had been destroyed in the riot, and was surprised to discover the existence of a large opium industry. Not only were tons of opiates imported into Canada and consumed by the Chinese each year, but various opium preparations were freely distributed by doctors, travelling medicine shows, patent medicine companies, pharmacies, and sold in general stores (Comack, 1985; Small, 1978; Solomon & Green, 1988; Solomon & Madison, 1977, Trasov, 1962).

MacKenzie King undertook a second unofficial investigation of opiate use in his capacity as a concerned citizen and submitted a private report to Parliament. He did not discuss the physiological effects of opium, but instead emphasized the drug's deleterious social and moral impact. He viewed opium as a poison that destroyed the inhibitions of a good Christian upbringing and thus exposed man's natural tendency for depravity. King argued that as a Christian nation, Canada should set an example in the international campaign against opium (Giffen et al., 1991; Solomon & Green, 1988; Solomon & Madison, 1977).

Less than three weeks after King submitted his private study, the *Opium Act* of 1908 was passed in the House of Commons without discussion or opposition. There is little evidence to indicate that British Columbia citizens at that time were concerned about the Chinese's use of the drug, or that a moral stigma was attached to drug use. Rather, drug addiction tended to be viewed as a medical problem or personal vice and did not seriously violate prevailing moral values. Thus the decision to criminally prohibit non-medical opiate use did not rise primarily from concern over its addictive properties, but rather from a redefinition of its moral impact by a small number of moral reformers.

Moral entrepreneurs launched similar crusades against alcohol and tobacco, but failed to pursuade the public and government to take action (Solomon & Green, 1988; Solomon & Madison, 1977; Trasov, 1962). By comparison, the campaign against opium changed both the public perception of non-medical drug use and the criminal law. The anti-opium movement, Solomon and Green argue, was successful because it was directed at the Chinese, a strongly disliked and powerless minority. At the same time, it did not target the large number of Caucasian users dependent on the opium-based products of the Caucasian pharmaceutical companies.

> This crusade succeeded because it was directed against Chinese opium smokers and Chinese opium factories, but at the same time posed no threat to the larger number of predominantly middle-class and middle-aged Caucasian users who were addicted to the products of the established pharmaceutical industry. (Solomon & Green, 1988:88)

Elizabeth Comack (1985) offers a Marxist interpretation of the development of Canadian anti-opium legislation. She argues that when the need for inexpensive labour is high, concern for the immigrant's moral habits—opium smoking—is low. But when conflict arises because of a labour surplus, resentment against immigrants grows and they become targets of criticism and racist sentiment. Comack argues that the opium law was the state's strategy to contain and channel class conflict, and that the 1908 law deflected attention from the problem of class relations by defining B.C.'s troubles

in racist and moral terms. The solution called for strategies of control aimed squarely at Orientals.

In 1920, *Maclean's* magazine ran five racially biased articles on Asians and drug use written by Mrs. Emily Murphy, a magistrate from Edmonton, Alberta. In her book, *The Black Candle* (1922), she claimed that drug use was rampant in some sectors of the country and that it was linked to moral turpitude, spiritual depravity, crime, and insanity. *The Black Candle* led its readers to believe that vile and corrupt Asian and black addicts were spreading addiction among innocent White people. Presumably in a response to this and other lobbying, Parliament passed the *Opium and Narcotic Drug Act* of 1923, added cannabis to the list of prohibited substances, and included a provision for the deportation of aliens convicted of certain drug offences.

In 1920, the newly created federal Department of Health was given responsibility for supervising Canada's drug laws and international treaty obligations and soon created a Narcotics Control Division. The RCMP allied itself with the Narcotics Division and served as its enforcement arm. The division, in turn, acted as spokesperson for the RCMP and periodically proposed enabling legislation when officers faced enforcement and investigative problems. During this time, RCMP officers were given blanket search warrants (called writs of assistance), empowering them to enter any premises for the purpose of a search without the necessity of a judicial overview or sanction. By the early 1930s, federal police and drug officials emerged as Canada's only drug experts and used their experience in drug enforcement to influence legislation, increase powers of investigation and arrest, and expand the roles they played in combatting drug usage.

> The federal police and government drug bureaucracies, which were

established in the early 1920s, aligned themselves with the moral reformers and anti-Asiatic forces in calling for stricter laws. In a series of near-annual amendments, Canada's drug statute was transformed during the 1920s into one of the country's most stringent pieces of criminal legislation. (Solomon & Green, 1988:88–89)

From 1930–1950, the Canadian government continued to expand both the number of prohibited drugs and the range of drug offences punishable by law. Solomon and Green (1988:97) argue that during this time, the centralized federal drug bureaucracy acted as a catalyst by translating domestic pressures, external influences, and its own interests into legislation and shaping Canadian drug policy. The drug bureaucracy's control over drug policy went unchallenged during the next two decades. The public appeared to have accepted their assessment of the dangers of drug abuse, their unflattering portrait of drug users and traffickers, and the necessity for extensive police powers to suppress the problem. Meanwhile, the police and courts used these powers effectively to process substantial numbers drug offenders (Erickson, 1998).

Increasingly severe penalties were the norm for drug laws in the four decades from 1920–1960 and continued in the 1961 *Food and Drug Act* and *Narcotics Control Act*. In the latter legislation, the maximum sentence for trafficking, possession for the purposes of trafficking, and for importing/exporting narcotics was raised from 14 years to life imprisonment and a minimum seven-year sentence was prescribed for the importing/exporting offence. There was little opposition to punitive drug laws while drug users were viewed as outsiders and were primarily from the lower socio-economic class, particular ethnic groups, and remained politically powerless.

Opposition to harsh penalties emerged in the 1960s, however, when significant numbers of young middle-class Canadians began using marijuana and hallucinogenic drugs. Convictions for cannabis offences rose markedly during the 1960s and 1970s until marijuana and hashish offences represented 90% of all drug convictions and the law was widely criticized for making criminals of otherwise law-abiding and respectable youths (Solomon & Green, 1988).

Public concern over the drug issue continued throughout the late 1960s, fuelled in large part by extensive media coverage. Academics, parents, civil libertarians, and prominent political figures criticized the *Narcotic Control Act* as being unduly severe and proposed sweeping changes to the law. The federal government responded to these diverse pressures by appointing a Royal Commission of Inquiry into the non-medical use of drugs. The Le Dain Commission issued four reports in the early 1970s and recommended a harm-reduction strategy based on the gradual withdrawal of criminal sanctions for drug usage. Despite the relatively positive reception of the Le Dain Commission's findings among many Canadians, the government largely ignored their recommendations.

The Canadian government made modest changes in 1969, however, when it gave prosecutors the option of proceeding by way of summary conviction in possession cases—a discretion that had been withdrawn only in 1961. The *Narcotics Control Act* was amended in 1969 to include a "fine only" sentencing option, and in 1972 to allow judges to impose an absolute or conditional discharge. Such discharges were new to the *Criminal Code* and resulted in a finding of guilt without a conviction being registered. The courts, in the meantime, responded to these changes in law and to changing values by imposing the less severe fine and discharge options (Boyd, 1988). Ericson and Murray (1986) suggest that declines in the severity for cannabis possession during this period helped reduce pressure for meaningful law reform.

In the 1970s and 1980s, the courts and legislatures increasingly recognized individual rights in drug cases. During this period, mandatory sentences for importation were removed, the *Charter of Rights and Freedoms* (1982) was declared, and the infamous writs of assistance were abolished. Although these changes were significant, they were far fewer and less radical than the various legal changes that were advocated and debated during this time period.

In 1986, American President Ronald Reagan stepped up the war on drugs. Canada responded shortly thereafter when Prime Minister Brian Mulroney described drugs as an epidemic that undermined our economic and social fabric. Erickson notes that these declarations ushered in a renewed spirit of prohibitionism characterized by greater spending on enforcement, an increase in the number of drug seizures and drug charges, and an increase in jail sentences (1998:219–220). During this time, Bill C-264 (1988) was passed, banning the sale of drug paraphernalia; Bill C-61 (1989) gave the police and courts new powers to seize and forfeit the assets of arrested drug traffickers; and in 1992 the penalties for steroids were increased.

The resurgence of prohibitionism, Ericson (1998) argues, was influenced by the U.S. media-fostered drug panic about cocaine and crack cocaine. Highly negative images of crack addicts in the U.S. and Canadian media helped manufacture a drug panic and create support for an increasingly harsh legal response. Although this renewed prohibitionist approach was provoked in part by an overly fearful image of the dangers of cocaine, the majority of charges for drug offences in Canada continued to be for cannabis usage (64% in 1990).

The history of drug legislation in Canada is a history of repressive laws and relatively zealous law enforcement. Despite some softening in the 1960s and 1970s, drug laws and policies have changed very little in the past four decades. Canada continues to prohibit a vast array of narcotics and relies primarily on repressive measures of law enforcement and sentencing as a mechanism of social control. Unlike the United States, however, Canada did not embrace an all-out drug war, and drug policies in this country are less repressive and more ambivalent than those in the United States. Nonetheless, the Le Dain Commission's goal of gradually diminishing criminal sanctions against users and developing alternative means to discourage drug use and diminish harm has not been seriously attempted. Even with respect to marijuana, little change has occurred despite the government's almost annual discussions about the possibility of decriminalizing this drug.

Current Laws Regulating Drug Usage in Canada

The legislation and case laws governing drug-trafficking offences are perhaps the most complex and wide-ranging of all laws dealing with criminal investigations. In Canada, the *Controlled Drugs and Substances Act* (CDSA) outlines prohibited drugs and penalties for possession, manufacturing, importing, and trafficking in prohibited substances. Other relevant legislation includes sections in the *Criminal Code* related to conspiracy, organized crime "anti-gang" provisions, and proceeds of crime/money-laundering laws. Additional laws govern police investigative techniques, including electronic surveillance, search and seizure, trespassing, the use of agents and informants, disclosure, and entrapment. Many of the laws created by Parliament, including recent anti-gang legislation, are meant to facilitate police investigations and prosecutions of organized criminal syndicates.

Concern with civil liberties and the potential for abuse have led to constitutional challenges to police practices and a variety of case laws that govern and restrict drug investigations. These legal restrictions are largely unique to drug cases because law-enforcement officers are proactive in their pursuit of higher-level drug traffickers. Although the police complain that many judgments based on case laws have severely hampered their investigative capabilities, they also understand the reasons for the judiciary overseeing their practices. Nonetheless, investigators explain that the demands and restrictions that result from case law limit their effectiveness and result in lengthy and expensive prosecutions. Some look with envy to the United States where a wider range of investigative aids are available and the police are not as handcuffed by judicial case law decisions.

The *Controlled Drugs and Substances Act*, 1996

Canadian drug legislation went through many amendments over the years and eventually evolved in 1960–1961 into the *Narcotic Control Act* and the *Food and Drug Act*. In 1997, Parliament replaced these with the *Controlled Drugs and Substances Act* to regulate dangerous drugs and narcotics. The *Controlled Drugs and Substances Act* classifies drugs into eight categories or "schedules," ranging from opiates, cannabis, hallucinogens, and a vast array of prescription drugs. Schedule I includes the most dangerous drugs and narcotics such as heroin and cocaine; Schedule II lists cannabis and its derivatives; Schedule III includes amphetamines and lysergic acid diethylamide (LSD); and Schedule IV includes drugs such as barbiturates and anabolic steroids that may be dangerous but also have therapeutic uses.

Offences

Offences under the *Controlled Drugs and Substances Act* (CDSA) and the *Criminal Code of Canada* (CCC) include:

1. possession of a controlled substance (schedules I, II, III, IV drugs only) (sec. 4, CDSA)
2. double-doctoring (schedules I, II, III, IV drugs only) (sec. 4.2, CDSA)
3. possession for the purpose of trafficking (schedules I, II, III, IV drugs only) (sec. 5, CDSA)
4. trafficking in a controlled substance (schedules I, II, III, IV drugs only) (sec. 5, CDSA)
5. importing and exporting a controlled substance (schedules I, II, III, IV, V, VI drugs) (sec. 6, CDSA)
6. production of a substance (schedules I, II, III, IV drugs only) (sec. 7, CDSA)
7. possession of property obtained by crime (sec. 8, CDSA) (sec. 462.31(1), CCC)
8. laundering the proceeds of crime (sec. 9, CDSA) (sec. 462.31(1), CCC)
9. conspiracy laws (sec. 465, CCC)
10. participation in criminal organizations: anti-gang (organized crime) legislation (sec. 467(1), CCC)

1.   Possession

The *Controlled Drugs and Substances Act* states that anyone who is in possession of a controlled substance in Schedules I, II, III, or IV is guilty of an indictable offence punishable by a maximum of seven years for Schedule I drugs, five years for Schedule II substances, three years for Schedule III drugs, and 18 months for Schedule IV substances.

Sec. 4(3) of the *Criminal Code* defines possession for the purposes of the law and states:

Sec. 4(3) for the purposes of this Act,

(a) a person has anything in possession when he has it in his personal possession or knowingly

(i) has it in the actual possession or custody of another person, or

(ii) has it in any place, whether or not that place belongs to or is occupied by him, for the use or benefit of himself or of another person, and

(b) where one of two or more persons, with the knowledge and consent of the rest, has anything in his custody or possession, it shall be deemed to be in the custody and possession of each and all of them.

Sec. 4(3) deals with the often contentious subject of what constitutes possession and is relevant to stolen property and illicit drug cases. Personal possession includes actual possession, whereas constructive possession occurs when the accused knowingly has an item in possession of another with some control over that item. It does not matter if the person owns or occupies the premises as long as the elements of knowledge and control are satisfied and the goods are for the benefit of the accused or another. Knowledge includes knowing the nature of the item.

To constitute possession for the purpose of the criminal law, in a case of manual handling of the object, there must also be knowledge of what that thing is and both of these elements must be co-existent with some act of control (*Beaver v. Regina*, 1957). To establish possession, the Crown must prove that the accused has a guilty state of mind (*mens rea*) and thus had knowledge of the substance in question and of its nature. It is not necessary for the accused to know the exact nature of the drug that he or she possesses. So long as the accused believes the drug is

prohibited, or is wilfully blind to it being such a drug, then the knowledge necessary to constitute the offence is established (*Beaver v. Regina*, 1957).

Mens rea is typically proven through an accused person's confession, statement, comments, or inferred from other evidence such as where the drugs were found, fingerprints, police observations of the person handling the drugs, and other items such as possession of scales, pipes, and additional narcotics. Similarly, control is seldom proven by direct evidence but must be inferred from other facts proved in evidence. This often includes the statements of co-accused and evidence that the person had access to the drugs such as a key to a storage locker or their location in a girlfriend's home. Inferences of possession have been held to arise, for example, when an accused occupies or controls the premises where drugs are found (*R. v. Caccamo*, 1973; *R. v. Chambers*, 1985; *R. v. Michel*, 1968; *R. v. Tokarek*, 1967); when an accused is the owner and driver of an automobile in which drugs are found (*R. v. Douglas*, 1974; *R. v. Vautour*, 1970); when an accused is present where drugs are found and takes flight (*R. v. Beaulne*, 1979; *R. v. Caldwell*, 1972); when an accused is present and obstructs police (*Fuller v. R.*, 1975); or when the accused is found in close proximity to drugs and there are other inculpatory facts (*R. v. Smith*, 1973).

Sec. 4(3) of the *Criminal Code* states that a person has possession when he or she has it in his or her personal possession or knowingly has it in actual possession or custody of another person or has it in any place for the use or benefit of himself or herself or another person. When one person has illicit drugs in his or her custody or possession with the knowledge and consent of others, then all may be deemed to be in the custody and possession of the illicit substance [sec. 4(3)(b)]. This is known as joint possession and requires an initial finding by the court that one person is in actual or constructive possession of the drugs before others may be found to be in joint possession.

The courts have ruled that consent must be more than passive acquiescence and that proof of consent must include proof of some control of the illicit substance (*McGee v. R.*, 1978). Consent requires at the very least voluntary agreement or permission (*Marshall v. R.*, 1969). Thus, no inference of possession arises from mere presence as a passenger in an automobile where drugs are found, even when the passenger has knowledge of the presence of drugs (*Marshall v. R.*, 1969; *R. v. Harvey*, 1969).

Traffickers will often store drugs in a "safe" place such as a bus station locker or entrust the illicit substances to others. In such cases, the *Criminal Code* allows for a charge of constructive or joint possession even though the accused does not have the narcotics on his or her person. The accused is deemed to be as much in possession as if he or she were actually carrying the drugs if it can be proved that the accused has some degree of control over the substance. To obtain a conviction for possession, the Crown must demonstrate knowledge of the existence and nature of the substance and some measure of control over it. To prove constructive possession, the Crown does not have to establish manual or physical handling of the product.

Possession may also be established by virtue of sec. 21 of the *Criminal Code*, which deals with aiding and abetting and sets out the criminal liability of people who are parties to an offence.

PARTIES TO OFFENCE/Common intention

21. (1) Everyone is party to an offence who
    (a) actually commits it;
    (b) does or omits to do anything for the purpose of aiding any person to commit it; or
    (c) abets any person in committing it.

(2) Where two or more persons form an intention in common to carry out an unlawful purpose and to assist each other therein and any one of them, in carrying out the common purpose, commits an offence, each of them who knew or ought to have known that the commission of the offence would be a probable consequence of carrying out the common purpose is a party to that offence.

(RS, c. C-34, s. 21)

Sec. 21(1)(b) makes an accused as liable as the principal party for actions done for the purpose of aiding the latter to commit an offence. It is not sufficient that the acts had the effect of aiding in the commission of the offence—the purpose must also be proven. Sec. 21(1)(c) makes an accused as liable as the perpetrator if he or she encourages the commission of an offence. Merely being present is not enough unless the accused acts in some way to encourage the principal party to commit the offence. In *R. v. Terrence* (1983), the court upheld the acquittal of the accused, a passenger in a stolen motor vehicle, noting that there was no evidence of control (of the vehicle) and no evidence that he was a party to the offence of the person actually in possession (the driver).

2. Double-Doctoring

Under sec. 4.2 of the *Controlled Drugs and Substances Act*, it is an offence to obtain any of the substances from Schedules I to IV from a practitioner, such as a physician, without disclosing particulars relating to the acquisition of any of the scheduled substances from any other practitioner within the preceding 30 days.

This offence is known as "double-doctoring" or "prescription shopping" and is punishable by imprisonment up to seven years for Schedule I substances, five years for Schedule II drugs, three years for Schedule III substances, and 18 months for Schedule IV substances. The offence of double-doctoring reflects a concern about the abuse of prescription drugs and narcotics, particularly by addicts at times when heroin is scarce.

3. and 4.   Possession for the Purposes of Trafficking and Trafficking

Trafficking within the *Controlled Drugs and Substances Act* is found under sec. 5, which states:

> 5. (1) No person shall traffic in a substance included in Schedule I, II, III, or IV or in any substance represented or held out by that person to be such a substance.
>   (2) No person shall for the purpose of trafficking, possess a substance included in Schedule I, II, III, or IV.

The charge of possession for the purposes of trafficking consists of the offence of possession plus an intention to traffic. The Crown does not need to prove actual trafficking. The onus on the Crown involves proving an intent to traffick and since it commonly occurs that there is no direct proof of trafficking per se, evidence is often circumstantial. Typical evidence used by the Crown includes: the amount and value of the drugs seized; exhibits that indicate sales activities such as scales and debt lists; police observations of the accused associating with known drug traffickers and/or users; and electronic surveillance indicating drug sales activities.

The term "trafficking" is not defined in the *Controlled Drugs and Substances Act*. It is useful, however, to refer to the former *Narcotic Control Act* in which trafficking means (a) to manufacture, sell, give, administer, transport, send, deliver, or distribute the substance or to offer to do any of the above. The definition of "traffick" includes selling the drug, but also means giving or delivering a substance to another person. The Crown does not have to prove that the accused acted to promote the distribution of the drug (*R. v. Larson*, 1972), nor is profit an essential element in the offence (*R. v. Drysdale*, 1978).

Simply offering to sell a narcotic is an offence and the courts have ruled that the accused's *mens rea* is found in the accused's intention to make an offer to sell the prohibited substance with the offer being the *actus reus* (*R. v. Sherman*, 1977). The law also makes it an offence to traffic in a substance that is represented or held out to be a controlled drug or substance under this Act. The case is made upon mere proof of representation, which may be in words or by conduct, and the Crown is under no obligation to establish that the substance was a prohibited substance (*R. v. Masters*, 1973; *R. v. Weselak*, 1972).

People may be found guilty of trafficking by aiding or abetting another person to commit the offence. In *R. v. Arason* (1993), the accused was found guilty of possession for the purposes of trafficking for permitting another person to store a large quantity of drugs in his home. Trafficking is punishable by up to life imprisonment for Schedules I and II drug offences, 10 years for Schedule III substances, and up to three years for Schedule IV drugs.

5.   Importing and Exporting

Sec. 6.1 of the *Controlled Drugs and Substances Act* makes it an offence to import or export controlled substances into or out of Canada. The offence is punishable by a maximum term of life imprisonment for Schedules I and II substances, 10 years for Schedules III and IV drugs, and up to three years for drugs listed in Schedules V and VI. Ordinarily, people engaged in exporting drugs will typically be arrested in a foreign country and charged there with an offence of importing. Only on occasion will an offender be arrested in Canada and charged with exporting. Consequently, importing charges are far more common than exporting cases.

The term "importing" is not defined in the *Controlled Drugs and Substances Act*, but has been broadly construed by the courts so as not to defeat the object of this section, which is the suppression of illicit importation. Generally speaking, to import means to bring illicit substances into the country or to cause to be brought into the country. Consequently, the accused does not have to carry the drugs into the country or be present at the port of entry when the offence was committed. Acts to further the offence are sufficient to bring a finding of guilt to the charge of importing [*R. v. Bell* (1983) 8 CCC (3d) 97 (SCC)]. It has also been held that the offence is committed notwithstanding that the goods have not left the control of the Customs authorities [*R. v. Martin* (1973) 21 CRNS 149 (Ont. HC)].

6.   Production of Substance

The *Controlled Drugs and Substances Act* prohibits the production of substances in Schedules I, II, III, or IV and states:

7.   (1)   Except as authorized under the regulations, no person shall produce a substance included in Schedule I, II, III, or IV.

(2)   Every person who contravenes subsection (1)

(a)   Where the subject-matter of the offence included in Schedule I or II, other than cannabis (marihuana), is guilty of an indictable offence

and liable to imprisonment for life;

(b)   where the subject-matter of the offence is cannabis (marihuana), is guilty of an indictable offence and liable to imprisonment for a term not exceeding seven years.

Sec. 7(2)(c) and (d) stipulate that the production of Schedules III and IV substances is punishable by terms of imprisonment not exceeding 10 and three years respectively.

Production includes the cultivation of crops such as marijuana and has been held to mean the bestowing of labour and attention upon land in order to raise crops (*R. v. Leduc*, 1972; *R. v. Underwood*, 1987). The cultivation of soil and planting of seeds constitutes cultivation even prior to the germination of the seeds (*R. v. Fahlman*, 1968). An act of harvesting alone may constitute cultivation, but the processing of a plant after harvesting is not cultivation (*R. v. Gauvreau*, 1982). Cultivation is a continuous offence that is committed even during the inevitable periods of inactivity involved in raising crops. The mere fact that the crop is left alone to grow constitutes the offence (*R. v. Arnold*, 1989). Possession is an included offence in a charge of cultivation.

Production also includes the manufacture of Schedules I to IV substances. Manufacturing is the production of prohibited substances from raw or prepared materials by giving them new forms, qualities, and properties. Typical is the manufacture of Ecstasy in laboratories from precursor substances.

7. and 8.   Possession of Property Obtained by Crime and Laundering

Proceeds of Crime: Forfeiture of Offence-Related Property
In response to concerns about criminals who accumulate wealth through their illicit

activities, the federal government of Canada enacted Bills C-61 (1989) and C-9 (1991) to deal with money-laundering offences and to seize properties obtained through criminal conduct. The legislation is similar to laws in Australia, Britain, and the United States and aims to increase international co-operation and strip drug dealers of their wealth and power. Bills C-61 and C-9 resulted in several amendments to the *Criminal Code* and is reflected in the *Controlled Drugs and Substances Act*. Sec. 354(1), 355, and 462.31(1) of the CCC and sec. 8 and 9 of the CDSA make it an offence punishable by up to 10 years imprisonment for using, possessing, or transferring property obtained through crime and/or for laundering the proceeds of crime.

Regulations under the *Proceeds of Crime (Money Laundering) Act* came into effect on March 26, 1993. The regulations set out the record-keeping and client-identification requirements for financial institutions and other corporations and people who are susceptible to being used to launder money. These requirements are intended to facilitate money-laundering investigations and prosecutions. The Act provides for a maximum fine of $500,000 and a jail term of five years for failure to comply with the regulations.

Proceeds of crime means any property, benefit, or advantage, within or outside Canada, obtained or derived directly or indirectly as a result of: (a) the commission in Canada of an enterprise crime offence or a designated drug offence; or (b) an act or omission anywhere that, if it had occurred in Canada, would have constituted an enterprise crime offence or a designated drug offence. Laundering refers to the act of transferring, transporting, or in any way disposing of property or any other proceeds of crime. The charge requires an intent to conceal or convert property or proceeds knowing that all or part were obtained or derived directly or indirectly as a result of a criminal offence.

Both the *Controlled Drugs and Substances Act* (sec. 11–23) and the *Criminal Code of Canada* (sec. 462.3–462.5, 489, 490) incorporate provisions for the pre-trial search and seizure and post-conviction forfeiture of any offence-related property and proceeds of crime. Those convicted of a criminal offence may lose their property if the court is satisfied on the balance of probabilities that the property is part of the proceeds of crime (sec. 462.37). The court is also permitted to draw inferences adverse to the offender in forfeiture hearings in which the Crown proves unaccountable increases of the offender's wealth following the commission of the drug offence (sec. 462.39, CCC)

Bills C-61 (1989) and C-9 (1991) have also made it a criminal offence for anyone, including bank employees, to knowingly assist in laundering proceeds of crime and for failing to report money-laundering activities. The United States has had legislation dealing with money laundering for a number of years, and Canadian banks operating in the U.S. have been subjected to the same currency reporting laws as U.S. financial institutions. Canadian law now requires financial institutions to have formal programs in effect that will maintain records of all new and established members and their transactions.

The law allows a judge to issue a warrant authorizing a law-enforcement official to search financial institution records and premises and to seize property believed to be the proceeds of crime. A judge may also issue a restraint order prohibiting the financial institution from disposing of or dealing with any funds or property specified in the order, other than as directed in the order. The Act protects employees against civil or criminal liability when disclosing any facts when the employee reasonably suspects that any property is the proceeds of crime or that any person has committed or is about to commit a crime.

Financial institutions must record all face-to-face cash transactions of $10,000 or more and ensure that clients complete a source of funds declaration form. The regulations also require that financial institutions identify individuals conducting the transaction including his or her name, address, occupation, and the nature of the business in which the person is engaged. Amendments to the *Proceeds of Crime (Money Laundering) Act* requires every person who is engaged in a business, profession, or activity in the course of which cash is received for payment or transferred to a third party [sec. 3(a)] to verify and record the name of individuals exchanging in excess of $1,000 in foreign currency [sec. 6(1)(a)(iii)].

9.   Conspiracy to Traffic: Conspiracy Laws

In the late 1950s the American Bureau of Narcotics and the RCMP intitated a series of high-profile and successful conspiracy prosecutions against upper-level drug traffickers in Canada and the U.S. Up to this time, higher-echelon criminals had remained above traditional enforcement techiques because lower-level personnel handled and transported the drugs. By using conspiracy charges, the police were required only to prove that offenders agreed to commit an unlawful act. In essence, the offence was complete upon proof of an agreement; no other crime needed to have been committed or even attempted (Solomon & Green, 1988:106).

There is no specific offence of conspiracy in the *Controlled Drugs and Substances Act*. The *Criminal Code*, however, makes it an offence punishable by up to life imprisonment to conspire to import, manufacture, and/or traffick in certain prohibited substances. A person can also be found guilty of conspiracy to import even if the act occurs outside of Canada. Sec. 465 of the *Criminal Code of Canada* states:

465. (1) Except where otherwise expressly provided by law, the following provisions apply in respect of conspiracy:

  (c) every one, who conspires with any one to commit an indictable offence ... is guilty of an indictable offence and liable to the same punishment as that to which an accused who is guilty of that offence would, on conviction, be liable.

  (3) Every one who, while in Canada, conspires with any one to do anything referred to in subsection (1) in a place outside of Canada that is an offence under the laws of that place shall be deemed to have conspired to do that thing in Canada.

  (4) Every one who, while in a place outside Canada, conspires with any one to do anything referred to in subsection (1) in Canada shall be deemed to have conspired in Canada to do that thing.

Sec. 465(5) allows for the person to be tried in Canada even if conspiracy occurred outside of the country.

The essential element of a conspiracy is an agreement by two or more people to commit a criminal offence, or to achieve a lawful object by commission of a criminal offence; an intention of two or more people to agree, and an intention to put this common design into effect. It is not necessary that there be proof of an overt act in furtherance of the conspiracy to convict the accused. To convict, there must be an agreement and a common purpose of a single enterprise, and the Crown must establish an intention by the accused to enter into an agreement to commit that offence. Conspiracy rests on the joint decision of two or more people to pursue a common object. Being a participant in a conspiracy requires that a person agree with others to engage in criminal activity. Simply having knowledge of the conspiracy, discussing it with others, or passively acquiescing in a plan of criminal conduct is not of itself sufficient to be convicted as a participant in a conspiracy. A person is a party to the offence of conspiracy, however, if he or she abets or encourages any of the conspirators in their criminal endeavours (*Martin's Annual Criminal Code*, 2005; *R. v. McNamara et al.*, 1981).

Under the law, a husband and wife cannot be found guilty of conspiring together because they are considered in law as one person (*Kowbel v. R.*, 1954). Other case law regarding conspiracy includes the following decisions: when tried separately, the acquittal of one co-conspirator does not necessarily invalidate the conviction of the other (*Guimond v. R.*, 1979); a conspiracy may have several illegal purposes and the Crown can allege in one count a conspiracy to commit several crimes (*R. v. Addison ex p. Mooney*, 1970; *R. v. Krueger*, 1966); it is no defence that an accused, having agreed to carry out the unlawful act with the intention to carry out the common design, later withdraws from the conspiracy, since the offence is already complete (*R. v. O'Brien*, 1954). Conviction for conspiracy does not require that there be proof of an overt act—only that there was an agreement to engage in a criminal enterprise.

Conspiracy law is sufficiently enabling that hearsay evidence may be admitted in the case of co-conspirators under an exception to the hearsay rule. First, there must be admissible evidence against the accused from his or her own acts and declarations that the accused is a participant to the conspiracy charged. In this case, a judge may rule that the acts and declarations of alleged co-conspirators in furtherance of the conspiracy may be used as evidence against the accused. If there is no evidence directly admissible against the accused connecting him or her with the conspiracy, however, the trial judge must direct the jury to acquit (*R. v. Baron and Wertman*, 1976). The judge is not required to view the accused's acts and declarations in isolation, divorced from the context in which they occurred. Hearsay evidence is inadmissible on the initial determination whether the alleged conspiracy or alleged common design existed.

10. Participation in Criminal Organizations: Anti-Gang (Organized Crime) Legislation

The federal government's anti-gang legislation, Bill C-95, was passed in 1997 following a violent clash between the Hells Angels and the Rock Machine motorcycle gangs that resulted in the deaths of more than 150 people in the province of Quebec. The Act indicates in the prelude that the Parliament of Canada recognizes that the activities of criminal organizations pose a threat to public order and to the safety of individuals. The intent of Bill C-95 is to provide the criminal justice system with better means of investigating, prosecuting, and sentencing gang-related crime; to deprive criminals of the proceeds of crime; and to deter criminal organizations and their members from resorting to violence to further their criminal ends.

The Act creates an offence of participating in a criminal organization through the commission of certain indictable offences for the benefit of the organization. An offender who is convicted of an offence shown to have been committed in relation to a criminal organization is subject to an increased sentence (up to 14 years) and periods of increased parole ineligibility. The unlawful possession of explosives in relation to a criminal organization is punishable by imprisonment of up to 14 years.

The Act provides for the forfeiture of any property used to commit offences (e.g., homes, automobiles, boats, aircraft) and the forfeiture of proceeds of crimes committed in relation to criminal organization offences. The enactment provides for procedural changes in relation to the interception of private communications, searches and seizures, and judicial interim release.

Criminal organization is defined in sec. 2 of the *Criminal Code*:

Sec. 2. "Criminal organization" means any group, association or other body consisting of five or more persons, whether formally or informally organized,

(a) having as one of its primary activities the commission of an indictable offence under this or any other Act of Parliament for which the maximum punishment is imprisonment for five years or more, and

(b) any or all of the members which engage in or have, within the preceding five years, engaged in the commission of a series of such offences.

"Criminal organization offence" means

(a) an offence under section 467.1 or an indictable offence under this or any other Act of Parliament committed for the benefit of, at the direction of or in association with a criminal organization for which the maximum punishment is imprisonment for five years or more, or

(b) a conspiracy or an attempt to commit, being an accessory after the fact in relation to, or any counselling in relation to, an offence referred to in paragraph (a).

Sec. 467(1) of the *Criminal Code* states:

467.1 (1) Every one who:

(a) participates or substantially contributes to the activities of a criminal organization knowing that any or all of the members of the organization engage in or have, within the preceding five years, engaged in the commission of a series of indictable offences under this or any other Act of Parliament for each of which the maximum punishment is imprisonment for five years or more, and

(b) is a party to the commission of an indictable offence for the benefit of, at the direction of or in association with the criminal organization for which the maximum punishment is imprisonment for five years or more is guilty of an indictable offence and is liable to imprisonment for a term not exceeding fourteen years.

467(2) A sentence imposed on a person for an offence under subsection (1) shall be served consecutively to any other punishment imposed on the person for an offence arising out of the same event or series of events and to any other sentence to which the person is subject at the time the sentence is imposed on the person for an offence under subsection (1).

On January 30, 2001, the anti-gang legislation was ruled constitutional in the Quebec Superior Court in the trial of 13 bikers (*Globe and Mail*, January 31, 2001). Two weeks later on February 15, 2001, prosecutors scored their first success against criminal bikers under the anti-gang law when four men with ties to the former Rock Machine biker gang were convicted of belonging to a criminal organization (*Globe and Mail*, February 16,

2001; *Kitchener Waterloo Record*, February 16, 2001). On April 12, 2001, prosecutors had their second success with the law when eight Quebec bikers affiliated with the Hells Angels pleaded guilty to gangsterism and other charges (*Globe and Mail*, April 13, 2002; *Kitchener Waterloo Record*, April 13, 2001). It is predicted that organized crime legislation will eventually be tested at the Supreme Court of Canada since bikers and higher-level drug traffickers have the resources to finance a constitutional challenge to the law.

Under the federal government's recent amendments to the anti-gang legislation, members associated with a criminal organization can be sentenced to prison for five years; gang leaders will face a maximum of life in prison for directing others to commit crimes, whether or not their instructions are carried out; and those who knowingly help criminal organizations—such as accountants or landlords—will face prosecution.

The Laws Related to the Use of Informants and Agents

The investigation of higher-level drug traffickers is frequently initiated by information provided to the police by citizens in the community. Civilians who secretly supply information concerning the commission of a crime are known as police informants whose identities are protected under the common law. There are a number of terms used to describe a civilian informant: "informant," "informer," "human source," "confidential source," and "source."

The Supreme Court of Canada has acknowledged the significant contribution that informants make to drug investigations.

The role of informers in drug-related cases is particularly important and dangerous. Informers often provide the only means for the police to gain some knowledge of the workings of drug trafficking operations and networks .... The investigation often will be based upon a relationship of trust between the police officer and the informer, something that may take a long time to establish. The safety, indeed the lives, not only of the informers but also of the undercover officers will depend on that relationship of trust.

Trafficking in narcotics is a lucrative enterprise. The retribution wreaked on informers and undercover officers who attempt to gather evidence is often obscenely cruel. Little assistance can be expected from informers if their identity is not protected. There can be no relationship of trust established by the police with informers without that protection. If the investigation of drug-related crime is to continue then, to the extent it is possible, the identity of informers must be protected. (*R. v. Scott*, 1990)

In criminal matters, the Crown has an obligation to the accused to disclose all relevant evidence whether it supports or contradicts the Crown's case. Under common law, however, the identities of informants are privileged and cannot be revealed without their consent. This rule exists to protect informants against retaliation from those betrayed and to encourage others to assist the police in their fight against crime. The police informant privilege also extends to any information that may reveal an informant's identity or status. This can include a wide range of information such as the person's address, date the information was provided, location where the informant met the police, etc. The courts have ruled that the informant is the only person who knows the details that might reveal his or her identity or status. Consequently, the Crown must consult with an informant prior to the disclosure of any information or document in order to ensure that the details to be disclosed will not lead to his or her identification. From a practical standpoint, this must be done when the information is supplied or as soon as possible thereafter so the police and Crown will know from the outset the exact details that may or may not be disclosed.

The informant privilege applies not only to the disclosure of information and documents, but also to witness testimony at trial. A police officer who takes the stand cannot be compelled to answer questions that reveal the identity or status of an informant. Similarly, civilian witnesses cannot be compelled to reveal whether or not they are informants. Citizens who allow the police to set up surveillance on their property or residence are also protected under the police informant privilege (*R. v. Thomas*, 1998).

The common law rule protecting the identity and status of a police informant is not absolute. In accordance with case law, the rule is subject to an exception imposed by the need to demonstrate the innocence of an accused and is known as the "innocence at stake exception." In *R. v. Scott* (1990), the Supreme Court held that the identity of an informant could be revealed under one of three conditions:

- The informant is a material witness to the crime.
- The informant acted as *agent provocateur* and played an instrumental role in the crime.
- The accused seeks to establish that the search was not undertaken on reasonable grounds.

In theory, these three exceptions seem straightforward, yet they are often difficult to apply in real-life situations. Terms such as "material witness," "*agent provocateur*," and "instrumental role" are not clearly defined. In

addition, it is often unclear when an informant acted as an *agent provocateur* or played an instrumental role. Typically, an informant is considered a material witness to a crime and may be called to testify when he or she is a witness to the offence charged and/or a witness to the defence of coercion, entrapment, or any other line of defence. In short, if the defence can establish that disclosure of information (the identity of the informant or details that might identify him or her) is necessary to prove innocence ("innocence at stake"), then the informant privilege is rescinded.

When an accused seeks to establish that a search warrant was not supported by reasonable grounds, the informant's identity will be revealed only in circumstances when it is absolutely essential and when the accused establishes the "innocence at stake" exception to informant privilege. Such a case might arise, for example, where there is evidence suggesting that the goods seized in execution of the warrant were planted [*R. v. Leipert* (1997) 1 SCR 298]. If the court concludes that disclosure is necessary, the Crown is required to reveal only as much information as is essential to allow proof of innocence. The Crown also has the option of staying the proceedings and dropping the charges, which avoids having to reveal the information sought in the disclosure order (*R. v. Leipert*, 1997). If the Crown chooses to proceed, disclosure of the information necessary to establish innocence will be provided to the accused. Before this happens, however, the informant must give his or her consent. It then becomes necessary for the police to protect the informant as well as certain people with a relationship to or association with the informant [*Witness Protection Program Act*, SC (1996) c.15].

In *R. v. Scott* (1990), the Court ruled that the identity of an informant must be revealed when he or she acts as an agent (*agent provocateur*) and plays an instrumental role in the crime. To determine if an informant is in fact an *agent provocateur*, the circumstances surrounding the crime and the informant's role in the commission of the crime must be closely scrutinized. If the informant acts upon instructions from the police and if he or she goes into the field (the expression used in case law), the informant is usually considered as having played an instrumental role and is defined as an agent. In such cases, his or her identity must then be revealed and the informant is a compellable witness. (See *R. v. Davies*, 1982; and *R. v. Khela*, 1991).

The laws that define and distinguish between informants and agents are based on case law and there is no clear definition of either. It is also unclear when and under what circumstances an informant becomes an agent. Generally, the informant plays a relatively passive role and does little more than provide information to assist the police in their investigation. An agent, on the other hand, not only provides information but enters into a working relationship with the police, often receiving some benefit in return. People need not benefit from giving assistance to the police in order to be defined as agents. They need only take an active part in the investigation. Informants who take their instructions from the police are considered to be *agents provocateurs* by the courts and are compellable witnesses. Even the act of introducing an undercover officer to a suspected drug trafficker means that the informant has played an instrumental role and is now legally considered an *agent provocateur* (*R. v. Davies*, 1982). An informant also crosses the line and becomes an agent if he or she commits or facilitates a crime.

In most cases, an agent is typically a user and/or dealer who has been arrested on drug offences or other crimes and agrees to co-operate with the police in exchange for lenient treatment. At higher levels, agents are often paid large sums of money to assist the police in their investigation. The agent agrees to testify because he or she has been offered a financial incentive and police protection to do so. Police who use informants have an obligation to explain the law and let them know that there are certain behaviours they cannot engage in, otherwise they become agents and compellable witnesses. In addition, the police are under both a moral and legal duty to protect the lives of citizens who act as agents in criminal investigations because they are compellable witnesses and are exposed to the risk of violent retaliation.

Sentences under the Controlled Drugs and Substances Act

Penalties under the *Controlled Drugs and Substances Act* are severe and anyone found guilty of importing or exporting, producing, trafficking, or conspiracy to traffic in substances included in Schedules I and II is liable to imprisonment for life [CC sec. 5(3), sec. 6(3), sec. 7(3)]. Schedule I includes heroin and cocaine whereas Schedule II contains marijuana and other cannabis derivatives. Trafficking in Schedule III substances can bring a 10-year sentence, and the maximum penalty for Schedule IV substances is three years.

Sec. 10 of the Act states that the fundamental purpose of any sentence is to contribute to the respect for the law and the maintenance of a just, peaceful, and safe society while encouraging rehabilitation and treatment of offenders, as well as acknowledging the harm done to victims and to the community. The Act also lists aggravating factors that a judge must consider when imposing a sentence on a person convicted of substance offences, including the use of a weapon, violence or threats of violence, trafficking near schools or other public places frequented by young people, trafficking to those under the age of 18, a previous conviction for a drug offence, and engaging a person under the age of 18 in the commission of a substance offence.

The Corrections and Conditional Release Act: Parole Eligibility

Inmates sentenced to a federal penitentiary (serving a sentence of two years or more) are subject to the *Corrections and Conditional Release Act* (CCRA) and are normally eligible for parole after having served one-third of their sentence (sec. 120). Sec. 125 and 126 of the Act provide for accelerated parole reviews (APR) for non-violent offenders who are not part of a criminal organization and who have been sentenced to a federal penitentiary for the first time. Sec. 126.2 directs the National Parole Board to release such inmates without a hearing if the board is satisfied that there are no reasonable grounds to believe that the offender is likely to commit a violent crime in the community before the expiration of the offender's sentence.

In practice, the inmate is released to a halfway house after serving one-sixth of the sentence and later released on full parole after the expiration of one-third of the sentence. Day parole typically requires that the offender return to a community-based residential facility each night. Full parole allows the offender to be at large in the community under supervision of a parole officer during the final two-thirds of the offender's term of imprisonment.

Accelerated parole reviews (APR) are available to all first-time penitentiary inmates, provided they are not serving a sentence for murder, crimes of violence, or sexual offences as set out in Schedule I of the Act. Also excluded from APR are offenders convicted of certain indictable offences in association with a criminal organization (sec. 467.1, CCC) or any other offence when the court determines that it was a criminal organization offence. In practice, many higher-level drug traffickers are eligible for APR and are released automatically on day parole after having served one-sixth of their sentence. The majority of offenders in this study have not been convicted of crimes of violence and no one was judged to have been involved in a criminal organization.

Under the provisions dealing with gangs, sec. 743.6(1.1) of the *Criminal Code* empowers the court to delay an offender's parole eligibility if he or she has been convicted for a criminal organization offence. In such cases, the court may order that the offender serve one-half of the sentence or 10 years, whichever is less, before being eligible for parole.

Discussion

Higher-level drug dealers are cautious and security conscious and typically insulate themselves from illicit drugs by hiring underlings to handle drug transactions. The police rely on conspiracy laws to arrest higher-level traffickers as evidenced by the fact that the offenders in this sample (40/70, 57.1%) were convicted of conspiracy to traffick or import drugs.

Both the *Criminal Code of Canada* and the *Controlled Drugs and Substances Act* include provisions for charging people involved in money laundering and for the forfeiture of offence-related property. The intent is to reduce the incentive to drug traffickers by making it more likely that they will be prosecuted and lose money and property obtained through crime. Although these laws give the courts significant powers to punish dealers financially, they do not appear to play a significant role in the prosecution of drug traffickers since only 7% (5/70) of subjects in this study were convicted under money-laundering legislation. The forfeiture provisions are more significant since approximately one-quarter (16/70, 23%) report losing money or property through the proceeds of crime. Although a few subjects lost millions of dollars in assets, most lost considerably less. Higher-level drug dealers are acutely aware of these laws and take precautions against losing their assets. Many will use the assistance of lawyers and/or accountants, hide their money outside the country, and protect their assets by putting them in other people's names. Even when money and property are seized, this is often only a small percentage of accumulated wealth. It appears clear that proceeds of crime and money-laundering legislation are not significant deterrents for higher-level drug traffickers since few are convicted under these provisions, the majority (77%) do not suffer forfeitures, and those who do usually have most of their assets safely hidden away.

Anti-gang legislation (participating in criminal organizations) is relatively new, but does not appear to be an effective tool to combat higher-level drug trafficking. Crown attorneys have criticized the anti-gang legislation as placing a heavy burden on them to prove that the accused knew that colleagues had committed crimes in the past five years preceding the current charges. The Crown attorney who successfully prosecuted the four Rock Machine members in Quebec describes the case as exceedingly difficult and time consuming: "The burden for the Crown is so heavy as to the facts we have to prove that the law could certainly benefit from some softening" (*Kitchener Waterloo Record*, February 16, 2001).

The heavy burden of proof also means that pre-trial motions and the trial itself will be lengthy and costly. In Winnipeg, 32 members of the Manitoba Warriors Aboriginal street gang were charged under the federal anti-gang legislation. The case took "an army of lawyers" months to go through pre-trial motions, including constitutional challenges against the law. Costs for the defence lawyers are estimated at over $8 million. The case is described as the longest and most expensive trial in Manitoba history (*Kitchener Waterloo*

Record, September 7, 1999; October 4, 2000). During the lengthy pre-trial delay, most of those arrested were denied bail under sec. 515(6)(d) of the *Criminal Code*, which places a reverse onus on the accused to prove that he or she is unlikely to commit further offences or abscond (see *R. v. Pearson*, 1992). Defence lawyers complained that the law was being used in a racist manner since it unfairly denied Aboriginal gang members their right to bail while awaiting trial. Critics have also argued that the current anti-gang legislation is redundant and unnecessary since the accused were all charged with other offences such as trafficking in cocaine and possession of weapons. In fact, the case was eventually resolved through guilty pleas to drug-trafficking offences and all anti-gang charges were dropped (*Kitchener Waterloo Record*, July 26, 2000).

It is clear from recent experience that anti-gang legislation does not make the prosecution of organized criminals faster, more effective, or less expensive. It is also clear that criminal organization (anti-gang) laws work on the assumption that organized criminal networks are highly structured and hierarchical with clear levels of authority and a division of labour; membership is identifiable; and members know who is part of the gang and interact with one another. These assumptions, however, are based on a Mafia or outlaw motorcycle gang model of organized crime. The present study indicates that many higher-level drug traffickers in Canada are not part of a rigid structure organized along a Mafia hierarchy. Rather, higher-level drug traffickers tend to operate in relatively small and closed criminal syndicates, often deal and compete with other gangs, have a relatively loose and fluid structure, and have modus operandi that change over time, place, and in response to situational and legal factors.

It can be argued that many higher-level drug-dealing syndicates do not meet the criteria set out by Canada's criminal organization legislation. Dealers are not members of a highly structured gang, nor do they work under the direction or authority of others above them in the distribution chain. Higher-level drug traffickers closely resemble independent businesspeople in a wholesale distribution system, and work for their own enrichment and not that of the organization. Many have no sense of membership in a large organization, nor do they know or interact with any more than a small number of people in the distribution chain. The structure and functioning of independent drug syndicates means that prosecutors will have difficulty applying anti-gang legislation to these types of organizations. It appears from this study and the recent judicial experience with Bill-C-95 that this legislation is difficult to implement. Anti-gang legislation may in fact be unnecessary since other laws such as conspiracy to traffic narcotics are more effective.

There are no minimum sentences required in the CDSA, and judges have a wide discretion in imposing what they believe to be an appropriate sentence. Drug trafficking in Canada is punishable by life imprisonment, but this is a maximum sentence that is rarely imposed. The average sentence for the men in this study was 6.5 years and most offenders had a number of mitigating factors that lessened the sentence imposed: they were married, employed, and did not have serious criminal records or crimes of violence. Sentencing in Canada contrasts sharply with many U.S. states where harsh minimum sentences lead to lengthy terms of imprisonment with limited parole eligibility.

Over half of the subjects in this study were eligible for accelerated parole because they were first-time penitentiary inmates with no record of violence. This allowed them to be released into a halfway house after having served one-sixth of their sentence. Many were aware of the relatively lenient sentences imposed by Canadian courts in drug-trafficking cases and also knew that the *Corrections and Conditional Release Act* allows for early parole eligibility. It was common for offenders to claim that they avoided committing their crimes in the U.S. because of the harsh penalties imposed on drug traffickers in that country.

It can be argued that the relatively lenient sentences handed out to higher-level drug traffickers in Canadian courts do not act as significant deterrents to involvement in this type of crime. In addition, parole provisions also diminish the deterrent value of court-imposed sentences. Police complain that our criminal justice system not only fails to deter would-be-offenders, it also denies investigators and prosecutors leverage in recruiting informants/agents and hampers plea negotiations. Police and Crown attorneys have little to offer offenders who know they are likely to be released after 12 to 18 months. Law-enforcement officials in the U.S., however, deal with criminals facing prison terms of 20 years or more and often gain their co-operation by offering substantial reductions in their sentence.

From a rehabilitative perspective, short prison sentences and/or early release on parole can be seen as justified because higher-level drug traffickers in this study are typically non-violent, have strong family relationships and other social bonds, and extensive employment records. Most have significant stakes in conformity and are good bets to lead law-abiding, productive lives.

Summary

Early Canadian narcotics legislation was created in response to perceived threats to the existing moral order and motivated by racist attitudes toward the B.C. Chinese community. In the decades that followed the 1908 *Opium*

Act, various moral entrepreneurs, along with the federal drug bureaucracy, presented Parliament and the public with misconceptions and exaggerated claims of the horrors of the drug problem. The government responded to these lobby groups by expanding the list of prohibited substances and passing progressively harsher laws. Prohibitionists and their punitive policies were rarely challenged until the 1960s when an upsurge in drug use generated renewed public interest and demands for reforms. Members of the academic, legal, and medical communities began to question stereotypes of drug use and users, the overreaching powers of the police, the effectiveness of enforcement, and the law's deleterious effect on offenders. Although some penalties for drug usage were reduced, reformists had little impact on drug laws and social policy. In recent years, international pressure, particularly from the U.S., has discouraged the Canadian government from moving away from a prohibitionist stance and its heavy reliance on law enforcement and deterrence.

Discussions concerning law reform have largely been won by the law-enforcement side, which consistently raises the spectre of organized crime, increased drug addiction, and other social ills. Debates have typically omitted objective assessments of the physiological effects of the opiates themselves, the true extent of the drug/crime problem, and the public health implications. In much of their campaign against substance abuse, prohibitionists have combined scare tactics with moralizing to dissuade young people from using illicit drugs. These tactics have had limited success because users have seen from experience that many illicit drugs can be used in moderation without harming oneself or others.

For the past century, Canadian and U.S. drug-control efforts have relied primarily on a policy of deterrence and the efforts of law enforcement to limit supply. Given that illicit drugs are still readily available, law enforcement and imprisonment are extremely costly, and that drug usage and abuse is an ongoing problem, many professionals and laypeople view the prohibitionist approach as a failure. Scholars, researchers, and treatment specialists, however, continue to play a minimal role in the development of drug policies. Like the U.S, Canada usually ignores its drug professionals when developing laws related to the non-medical use of drugs. Most North American criminologists and drug researchers are generally critical of a harsh prohibitionist policy and tend to favour more tolerant and treatment-based interventions. These involve harm-reduction strategies that attempt to minimize the non-medical use of both illicit drugs and licit ones such as tobacco and alcohol; a focus on health factors rather than on prohibition; the controlled legalized sale of opiates to drug-dependent people; and the decriminalization of at least some illegal drugs. These and other social policy issues are discussed in Chapter 8.

CHAPTER 3

Organized Crime and Higher-Level Drug Trafficking

The Mafia Model of Organized Crime

The traditional view of organized crime is that of a hierarchical organization based on ethnic ties with monopolistic control over a variety of criminal enterprises within specific geographic areas. In the U.S. and Canada, organized crime has been synonymous with the terms "Mafia" or "La Cosa Nostra," an organization alleged to be controlled by a powerful group of Italian-Americans through a national syndicate with international connections. Mafia theorists portray this group as a centralized criminal organization with a well-defined collective identity and division of labour that originated from Sicilian criminal syndicates, and gained much of its power and wealth from Prohibition. Organized crime, it is believed, uses violence to achieve control of illegal markets by driving away competitors while the corruption of law enforcement and politicians buys it protection from investigation and prosecution.

This depiction of organized crime originated in the U.S. in the 1950s and has long been popular with journalists, law enforcement, some academics, and has been endorsed by several governmental investigations and inquiries (Cressey, 1967, 1969, 1972; U.S. Kefauver Commission, 1951; Maas, 1967; U.S. McClelland Commission, 1960; Schelling, 1984; United States President's Commission on Law Enforcement, 1967).

The vast majority of researchers and theorists who study organized crime, however, contend that the popular Mafia/ Godfather image is fictional and inaccurate. Joseph Albini (1971) refers to this traditional model as the "evolution-centralization perspective" because it depicts the Mafia as evolving from earlier forms of Italian criminal organizations, and because the structure is portrayed as a large, tightly controlled, centralized ethnic organization along the lines of the modern multinational corporation. This view—also referred to as an "alien conspiracy" model—is criticized as ideological and serving political interests, lacking in accuracy and empirical evidence, failing to address social class variables, and as conceptualizing organized crime as something evil, alien, and outside of society (Hawkins, 1969; Moore, 1974; Paoli, 2000; Naylor, 2002; Sacco, 1986; Smith, 1976).

One of the first critiques of the alien conspiracy view came from Bell (1953), who argued that organized crime, rather than being the result of an ethnic conspiracy, is instead a ladder of mobility for immigrants and minorities who are denied access to legitimate channels of success. He argued that incoming ethnic groups often moved into market-based crime when legitimate opportunities were blocked, and referred to this process as ethnic succession. Research published in the 1970s by Ianni and Reuss-Ianni (1972), Albini (1971), and Block (1979) also challenged the view that organized crime in the U.S. is characterized by a rigid, formalized, bureaucratic structure. Joseph Albini's work (1971), revealed that even Italian organized crime in the U.S. could be best understood through patron-client relations rather than formal hierarchies. Ianni and Reuss-Ianni (1972) argued that syndicated crime is structured along kinship lines and is based on informal patron-client relationships rather than a bureaucratic organization. A similar conclusion emerged from a historical analysis of organized crime in New York in which Alan Block (1979) described criminal syndicates as fragmented and chaotic. He noted that patterns of affiliation and influence between criminals and people in positions of power in the political and economic world created "webs of influence" that allowed criminals to maximize illegitimate opportunities and were more important than any formal structure.

Reuter characterizes illicit markets as "disorganized" and provides a portrait of syndicated crime that is in stark contrast to the common image of large hierarchical organizations intent on dominating the criminal marketplace through violence and corruption (1983, 1985). He argues that although the American Mafia was once a prominent supplier of bootlegged liquor during Prohibition and a major player in the illegal gambling industry up to the 1960s, they have been unable to control the illicit drug market and are "almost extinguished now as a major actor in the United States' criminal world" (1995:89). Naylor (2002:24) argues that the traditional image of organized crime is not entirely the figment of law-enforcement imagination. There was clearly something that set Italian-American organized crime groups apart from others and for a time assured them an exceptional position in the criminal marketplace. He suggests that the notion that organized crime had a formal structure began with a simple but fundamental error: U.S. law enforcement took a term—"Mafia"—which in Italy referred not to a group but to a form of behaviour (selling protection and connection) by a type of individual (an "entrepreneur of violence" rather than a violent entrepreneur), and transmogrified it into an organization. It compounded the error by making omerta an oath of allegiance among a criminal fraternity when in fact it is a concept endemic to Sicilian society as a whole with its profound distrust of outsiders (Naylor, 2002:24–25). Naylor concludes that the key to Italian-American criminal business lay not in an organizational structure but in a social matrix in which kinship links based on both blood and marriage were reinforced by fictive "family" relations through "godparenting" (Naylor, 2002:25).

The reasons the Mafia stereotype persisted for so long, Naylor suggests, is because of fundamental errors in logic and interpretation: (a) equating an association of criminals with a criminal association; (b) confounding the criminal firm with the criminal industry; and (c) confusing a simplistic fraternal hierarchy with a hierarchical business structure. Although membership provides contacts and an exchange of favours, these are useful but hardly essential for criminal activity (2002:26). Naylor blames police analysts and their "mass-media cheerleaders" for perpetuating this stereotype.

> Why the persistence of the stereotype in the face of the evidence? There is apparently a comfortable symbiosis of objectives between law-enforcement and the mass media. The first institution shows a propensity to hype the target both to enhance self-esteem and to coax more power and money from governments. The second needs to cater to a public in search of vicarious thrills. A coldly calculating cartel uniting stone killers and Harvard MBAs is excellent for selling copy; a jumble of crude, uncoordinated, and trigger-happy wheeler-dealers, some of whom are wired up on their own product, is much less so. (Naylor, 2002:30)

Recent Attempts to Define Organized Crime

In recent years, a consensus seems to have emerged among criminologists that organized crime is a profit-driven criminal enterprise defined by its involvement in illicit market activities. Organized crime produces and distributes illegal goods and services to large numbers of willing consumers. Illicit activities include trafficking in narcotics, running illegal gambling operations, involvement in the sex trade, and smuggling tobacco and alcohol products. These market-based activities produce the highest profit with the least amount of risk because they involve consensual activities with no victims to complain to the police. In addition, since goods and services are provided on an ongoing basis, they generate revenue over an extended period. Thus, organized criminal syndicates pursue illicit commercial activities that are low risk and provide the highest rewards.

One of the pre-conditions for the development of organized/enterprise crime is the existence of laws that prohibit the production and consumption of various goods and services that are widely sought after. These prohibitions represent the state's attempt to legislate morality, but since so many citizens wish to use these prohibited products, the laws lack strong value consensus, are unpopular, and widely flouted. Whereas citizens are opposed to predatory crimes such as assault and robbery, laws that prohibit narcotics, prostitution, or gambling do not have the same degree of support. These prohibitions reduce supply, push up prices and potential profits for illicit entrepreneurs, and encourage an influx of new dealers willing to take the risk.

Currently, most definitions of organized crime depict it as a criminal conspiracy of several people; players are motivated for the purpose of economic enrichment; there is the potential for corruption and/or violence to facilitate the criminal process; and the illicit market activities they engage in operate on an ongoing basis (Beare, 1996; Hagan 1983; Paoli, 2002:55). Organized criminals also operate secretly to avoid arrest and conviction and insulate their leadership from direct involvement in illegal activities through their organization and modus operandi. Beare notes that current definitions of organized crime do not include a formal hierarchical structure as depicted on the charts of Mafia "families"

(1996:15), nor is violence and/or corruption a necessary characteristic of syndicated criminal activities.

It is frequently argued that drug trafficking has much in common with legitimate business and that dealers can be viewed as entrepreneurs involved in "enterprise crime" by supplying clients with illicit products. Despite this "businessman" view of organized crime, criminologists recognize that offenders are opportunistic and will move into any area that offers the chance for enrichment. This includes predatory activities such as robbery, embezzlement, extortion, kidnapping, slavery and sexual slavery, the illicit disposal of industrial waste, and acts of violence.

The Network Model of Organized Crime

Organized crime, like other businesses, needs a structure to provide a constant supply of product to consumers. Cultivating, harvesting, manufacturing, and moving drugs from the fields of Colombia or Afghanistan to the streets of Toronto, Vancouver, and Montreal requires capital, knowledge of the drug trade, reliable and trustworthy associates, as well as suppliers, distributors, and couriers willing to transport drugs across international borders. Some form of organization is clearly needed to operate a large-scale illegal business on an ongoing basis. A number of studies have concluded that organized crime operates largely through network structures in which individuals are organized into small groups or cells and do business with people they know and trust. In the context of enterprise crime, networks represent informal and loosely organized associations of participants who are willing to engage in criminal activities (Arlacchi & Lewis, 1990; Finckenauer & Waring, 1998; Korf & de Kort, 1990; Morselli, 2001; Potter,

1993; Weschke & Heine-Heib, 1990, as cited in Paoli, 2002:67).

Because of the secretive nature of their activities, drug networks tend to be informal, decentralized, and are made up of autonomous units. Most operate as independent entrepreneurs, and relationships among dealers are based on trust and mutual financial benefit. A single person or a few individuals will act as intermediaries between various groups or crews to facilitate the exchange of goods, services, and money. These people become the contact point for moving commodities among distributors in the drug chain. Networks allow like-minded individuals or groups to seek each other out, evaluate one another's criminal capabilities, develop strategies, and engage in criminal conspiracies. Networks are the means by which traffickers gain their connections and develop and expand the distribution of illegal commodities. Dealers use friendship, kinship, and ethnic networks to select partners, employees, suppliers, and distributors. Networks allow traffickers the opportunity to work with people they know and/or people who have been recommended and/or have a reputation as reliable. Friendship between suppliers and distributors provide a degree of loyalty, cohesion, and security. Morselli's (2001) analysis of drug broker Howard Marks's autobiography attributes Marks's success to his ability to develop and utilize networks of others willing and able to collaborate in the smuggling enterprise. Marks was not a member of a cartel, nor was he part of an "organized crime" syndicate. Instead he operated as a "liberal-minded, free willed, and independent illegal entrepreneur" (2001:204). Morselli asks the question: How could Marks endure for two decades as an illegal entrepreneur without having the organizational force and support of a reputed and resource-yielding criminal organization? The answer is that the structure in Marks's organization came in the form of his personal working network.

The concept of social embeddedness is used to grasp the structuring force represented by social networks in curbing, ameliorating, and directing economic action. Such relational structuring of one's business ventures is crucial to generating trust and discouraging malfeasance between co-participants. The network, rather than the market or hierarchy, becomes the principle governance structure designing the economic actions of individuals (Morselli, 2001:204).

Morselli points out that drug networks are held together by long-term mutual benefits and that participants have considerable collective interests in keeping a good thing going. The basic assumption of network relationships is that one party is dependent on resources controlled by another and that there are gains to be had in the pooling of resources (Morselli, 2003a, 2003b). Williams (1998) lists a number of characteristics that make networks particularly well suited for criminal activities.

- Networks can vary in size, shape, membership, cohesion, and purpose. They can be large or small, local or global, cohesive or diffuse, centrally directed or highly decentralized.
- They are capable of considerable expansion through recruitment of new members.
- They have a capacity to extend across national borders either through ethnic linkages or through simple business linkages that enable them to exploit new opportunities.
- Criminal networks develop safeguards against infiltration. In particular, nodes in the network act as built-in insulators protecting core members who are responsible for directing activities.
- They develop a high degree of redundancy and duplication, making

them resilient to disruption and providing a significant capacity for reconstitution in the event that they are damaged by law enforcement.
- Criminal networks are flexible and adaptable and able to expand or contract as circumstances demand.
- They respond quickly to market opportunities and/or law enforcement strategies. (Williams, 1998:154–156; Williams & Godson, 2002:332–333)

Williams argues that networks are far superior to traditional hierarchies in terms of organizational effectiveness and are ideal vehicles for executing transnational criminal activities such as drug trafficking. Networks provide essential links between suppliers and customers and are elusive but effective at achieving goals. Organized criminal networks are "highly sophisticated organizational forms and it is a mistake to refer to [this] as disorganized crime" (Williams, 1998:154).

Transnational Organized Crime

In recent years, criminologists, police, and government agencies have expressed an interest and concern with the emergence of transnational organized crime—criminal networks that transcend national boundaries. The recent growth of transnational crime is evidenced by the increasing international transportation of illicit goods and services such as drugs, stolen vehicles, illegal aliens, sex trade workers, and the smuggling of arms and weapons of war. Worldwide financial and market systems have expanded tremendously, resulting in a huge increase in the magnitude and frequency with which merchandise, money, and people cross national borders. Just as globalization has offered new opportunities for legitimate businesses, it has also encouraged criminal organizations to search out and exploit new markets beyond their home state. The sheer volume of trade and financial transactions allows much smuggling and money laundering to take place undetected.

Often the port of entry comes through contacts with legitimate firms, which are then used to move illicit goods around the world. Because global trade has become so extensive, it is easy for criminal networks to embed and conceal illicit products among licit goods. Modern organized crime has taken advantage of the unintended opportunities provided by decreased government control over the flow of goods, services, and money, including reduced border and custom controls. Technological changes such as the containerization of cargo for transnational shipment has been exploited by criminal syndicates as an increasingly important mode of moving drugs from suppliers to consumers (Lee, 1999:6; William, 1998:156).

In addition to business linkages, ethnic networks that transcend national boundaries offer another port of entry into new markets and facilitate transnational organized criminal activities. Distributors in source countries use ethnic contacts in host countries to open markets for their illicit drugs.

> The capacity of individual criminals or groups in one country to extend their network through linkages with their counterparts in other countries gives organized crime and drug trafficking a transnational character that makes it much more difficult to combat. Criminal networks have become borderless while law enforcement agencies are still constrained by national borders. (Williams, 1998:156)

The predominant image of transnational crime—particularly with respect to cocaine trafficking—is that of a large, hierarchical, cartel-like structure that dominates the market

and is controlled by leaders who orchestrate operations in a manner similar to multinational corporations. Just as international firms have their local subsidiaries, large-scale criminal organizations infiltrate various countries and set up branch outlets. Transnational organized crime is portrayed as a relatively recent development and one that represents a major threat to the integrity of law-enforcement and political institutions (Godson & Olson, 1993; Sterling, 1994).

Naylor challenges the prevailing belief that large cartels control the production and distribution of illicit drugs in source countries. He defines a cartel as a conspiracy in restraint of trade, an illegal clique to restrict quantity, divide up the market, and push up prices. Naylor argues that when the characteristics of the cocaine business in Colombia are critically examined, the so-called cartels were and remain quite unpropitious for the exercise of monopoly power (2002:27). He points out that the *campesinos* who grow coca as part of the traditional peasant economy are independent farmers who number in the tens of thousands and are scattered over a huge area. Next up the chain are thousands of coca-paste manufacturers and scores of refiners spread throughout the Andes. Manufacturers sometimes move their products themselves and at other times use professional smugglers. In most cases, the cocaine is sold to wholesalers in host countries who deal with regional distributors, who sell the product to dealers, and who in turn may resell to several further levels of intermediaries before the product reaches the customer (Naylor, 2002:27).

> At no stage is there a concerted effort to monopolize the business, and far from an integrated organization, cocaine trafficking proceeds through a complex of arms-length commercial transactions .... The reality is that the Medellin "cartel," even at peak,

never attempted to control the price of cocaine by restricting supply. Instead, as an underground government, it represented a cooperative effort by dozens of independant producers to use violence to achieve specific ends vis-à-vis political opponents and to reduce it vis-à-vis each other .... what they represented was not a cartel but a *gremio*, a trade association, standard in Colombian business, set up to engage in political lobbying and to maintain the industry's public image .... there was (is) no effort to restrict product quantity to control price. Indeed, throughout the so-called Medellin cartel's existence, the trend of prices was down, and inside the target market, conditions were a free-for-all. (Naylor, 2002:28)

Other theorists similarly challenge the notion that large-scale criminal organizations control the cocaine market in Colombia. Critics point out that the elimination of the so-called kingpins of the cocaine trade—the leaders of the Medellin and Cali cartels—led to a quick disintegration of their organizations. In addition, the folding of these two groups had very limited impact on the flow of drugs to the United States (Lee, 1999:3; Paoli, 2002:69; Williams, 1998:154). The illegal status of the business seems to prevent the development of a hierarchical organization that can survive after its leaders are eliminated and smaller competitive groups simply move in to meet the demand.

A number of researchers (Block, 1991; Hobbs, 1998a; Rawlinson, 1998) argue that the cartel model is no more than a modified version of the alien conspiracy theory in which transnational organized crime is depicted as "an external threat to western economies by the 'usual suspects' of Russian Mafia, Cosa Nostra, Colombian Cartels, Jamaican

Yardies, Chinese Triads, etc." (Edwards & Gill, 2002:207). Transnational organized crime has been around for a long time in the form of drug and alcohol smuggling and contemporary transnational organized crime does not appear to differ significantly from "old-fashioned" international organized crime (Block, 1999:220; Farer, 1999:xiii).

One of the factors that works against the development of hierarchical, centrally controlled transnational criminal syndicates is the existence of national boundaries. Although the flow of goods across borders has increased significantly with the growth of trade, the movement of people is still tightly curtailed. This makes it difficult for criminal organizations to establish branch offices in foreign countries and station permanent representatives (managers) abroad to handle the business. Not only is it difficult to move people into host countries and keep them from being deported, it is often impossible to monitor agents who must work in covert settings and at great distances from the core. Because of these problems, it is far easier and safer for importers to download their illicit drugs to independent wholesalers who are citizens of the host country and have knowledge of the local situation. It is also wise for suppliers to deal with several distributors in order to maintain a continuous flow of product. In the event that one group is closed down, others will continue to operate and purchase drugs. For these reasons, drug-trafficking ventures in host countries tend to be run by a large number of small, local, and independent groups.

As discussed above, ethnic networks are often the foundation of drug-trafficking syndicates and provide entry into host countries. Ethnically based criminal networks provide additional benefits since they are insular; have strong kinship, friendship, and cultural bonds; and are difficult to penetrate by law enforcement. Police often have few officers from minority communities who understand the language and/or dialects and can infiltrate such tight-knit groups, perform undercover work, and gather the needed intelligence. To the extent that ethnic communities are suspicious of authority, they are less willing to co-operate with police investigations.

Economic Models of Organized Crime

Economic theory provides two closely related models that provide a basis for analyzing organized crime. The market model focuses on the nature of criminal markets, whereas the enterprise model analyzes the manner in which criminal enterprises behave in criminal markets. Both models assume that criminals are rational actors who constantly seek new opportunities to maximize profits. The market model focuses on the dynamics of supply and demand within illegal markets whether they are local or global. Illegal markets provide a constant exchange of goods and services in situations where their production, marketing, and consumption are legally forbidden or severely restricted. Typical markets of this kind include hard drugs, illicit arms sales, trade in economic and sexual slavery, capital originating from criminal activity, and deals involving secret information and intelligence (Williams & Godson, 2002:322).

The enterprise model emphasizes the business dimension of organized crime and the similarity between illicit and legitimate enterprises. Both licit and illicit firms behave in similar ways: they focus on profit, seek out economic opportunities, make rational judgment about their investment of time and money, and attempt to minimize their risks. Williams and Godson argue that although not all criminal organizations engage in a formal planning process, nevertheless their thinking will reflect standard business needs and take into account such factors as new opportunities,

product dominance, profit margin, market needs, the degree of competition, risk management, retirement strategy, and the like (2002:324–325). Despite some differences, both the market and enterprise models focus on market forces, criminal opportunities, and the entrepreneurship of organized crime.

Critics of economic models of organized crime argue that the analogy between legal and illegal firms cannot be pushed too far, and that the comparisons between criminal enterprises and legitimate businesses overlook significant differences. Naylor (2002) and Paoli (2002) outline several characteristics of illicit enterprises that differentiate them from legitimate businesses.

- Legal firms exist in a political and legal milieu designed to help them grow and prosper, whereas illegal firms operate without and against the state and are constantly confronted with regulators seeking to close them down and toss the principals into jail.
- While legal firms aim for profit maximization, the corresponding objective for illegal firms would be risk minimization.
- To reduce costs and increase profits, a legal firm seeks to avoid redundancy by reducing layers of intermediation that separate supplier from ultimate customer. The illegal firm seeks to reduce risk by increasing layers of intermediation between the entrepreneur and the regulatory authorities.
- Legal firms are free to seek clients by advertising their products and services. Because of security concerns, illegal firms are constrained in the manner in which they can market their product. They must structure relationships to limit the amount of information that circulates and to whom. Only a few employees, suppliers, and clients will

have direct knowledge about an illicit firm's organization.

- Legal firms have a life of their own and continue operating even with changes of leadership. Often illegal enterprises do not exist independent of the illegal entrepreneur. Changes in personnel can terminate agreements or produce erratic changes in operations and compromise marketplace stability.

- Legal firms have assets that creditors can use to secure loans. This allows them to access the formal capital market to expand and grow. Creditors will have difficulties collecting debts from illegal firms that must rely instead upon self and underground financing.

- While legal firms are likely to be around for years, illegal enterprises have a time horizon equal to that of the illegal entrepreneur. Illegal firms operate under the constant threat of being closed down and having their assets confiscated. Consequently, they operate in a time line that is much shorter than legitimate business. Money earned is likely to be squirrelled away in safe havens rather than reinvested in the firm.

- Partnerships, trade arrangements, and other contracts between illicit firms are prone to disruption and are thus likely to change frequently and be short term and unstable.

- For a legal firm, property rights are legally defined and there exists a lawful dispute resolution mechanism to ease relations with suppliers, competitors, and customers. For illegal firms, commercial agreements and property rights cannot be ensured through the courts. Exchange of illegal goods and services depends upon the fragile basis of trust developed on the basis of trust relationships. Violence is always a possibility for settling disputes.

- Legal firms will seek out and welcome expansion into new territories if profits are available. Illegal firms may avoid moving into new territories even though profits are there because the risks and dangers are too great. In addition, having to deal with potential informants, expansion, and growth of illicit enterprises increases visibility and attracts additional scrutiny. (Naylor, 2002:19–21; Paoli, 2002:62–66)

The illegality of the products being sold places constraints that limit the growth of large-scale bureaucratic organizations. Because they operate under the constant scrutiny of law enforcement, illicit firms must produce and distribute their products secretly without the benefits of legal protections afforded to legitimate businesses.

Drug Trafficking as Business Enterprise

Drug trafficking has much in common with legitimate business. It is an ongoing activity in which dealers must procure a high-quality product at reasonable prices, compete with other dealers for clients, market their drugs, collect payment, and pay their bills, including the fees, commissions, and/or salaries of people who work for them.

All traffickers in this study view drug dealing as a business that requires knowledge, business sense, and connections. To be successful, traffickers must provide a quality product at competitive prices and maintain a reputation for reliable and trustworthy service. A 42-year-old career criminal serving seven-and-a-half years for conspiracy to import cocaine operated his illicit drug business for several years.

> I referred to this as a business and it was a business. It started small and we

built it up and expanded the business. I had employees and all the problems of handling people's personalities and quirks. You have to keep on top of your employees and as the employer, I had to deal with them. The RCMP have me on tape as referring to the "business." I was in a hotel room and I was talking to someone who should have been taking this more seriously. I was trying to get him to act more cautiously and professionally. They have me on tape saying, "If you're going to be in this business .... "

Like the marijuana growers in rural Kentucky (Hafley & Tewksbury, 1995), dealers in this sample view drug trafficking as a business and do not conceptualize their activities as organized crime. U.S. studies of higher-level smugglers and wholesalers similarly note that dealers view themselves as businessmen and operate in small crews and a variety of partnering arrangements (Adler, 1985:105; Adler & Adler, 1992:264–269; Reuter & Haaga, 1989:36–40).

The Present Study: Criminal Background and Employment History

Subjects in this study tend to fall into one of two types: (a) "businessmen" traffickers (50/70, 71.4%) who live relatively law-abiding lives apart from their involvement in the drug trade; and (b) "criminal" traffickers (20/70, 28.5%) who have extensive criminal involvements and deviant lifestyles. All businessmen drug dealers were employed prior to their arrest and most (37/50, 74%) owned or had previously owned a small business. These dealers typically have lengthy employment histories or business experiences, describe themselves as conscientious workers, associate

with other law-abiding people, begin their criminal career later in life, operate primarily at the wholesale level, and eschew the use of violence. Most have families, homes in middle-class or upscale neighbourhoods, and present themselves as successful businessmen. Partners and associates have similar backgrounds and lifestyles and typically do not use illicit drugs.

Twenty-two of the businessmen traffickers have no prior criminal record, nine have minor convictions, and 19 are serving their second penitentiary sentence for drug trafficking. Of those men with minor convictions, offences include assault, shoplifting, possession of stolen property, possession of marijuana, mail fraud, and producing bootleg alcohol. Most received fines and one man served several months for possession of stolen property. The 19 men with previous drug-trafficking convictions had all spent time in prison with sentences that ranged from six months to 10 years. Three of these subjects had been arrested and incarcerated outside of Canada.

A smaller group of career criminals (20/70, 28.5%) were committed to a deviant lifestyle, became involved in crime at a relatively young age, and all but three report that they never or rarely worked at legitimate employment. Most "criminal" dealers (16/20, 80%) have been convicted of serious offences, including murder, drug trafficking, break and enter, robbery, assault, weapons charges, and theft. Two offenders with minor records are brothers who have never worked, dealt drugs over an eight-year period, and operated an organized criminal syndicate. All 20 criminal dealers earned their income primarily from crime and members of their crew are typically recruited from known criminals (three subjects were associated with outlaw motorcycle gangs). Criminal drug syndicates are generally more willing to use violence in dealing with problems in the drug world.

One surprising finding in this study is that approximately two-thirds (44/70, 62.8%) of the subjects (including 7/20, 35% career criminals) operated small businesses prior to moving into drug dealing. These included: an auto-body repair shop; an auto-mechanic shop; a money exchange; a finance-management company; a fruit and tobacco business; a used car dealership; trucking companies; a fishing boat; a lumber company; clothing-export companies; a beauty salon; food-importing/exporting businesses; a lobster fishing boat; a mushroom-export business; a paint and decorating company; a carpet-cleaning company; a fitness gymnasium; a health club; a diving business; a construction-machinery dealership; and six men who owned and operated liquor establishments. Other subjects operated subcontracting businesses involved in picking worms, cutting lumber, installing roofs, landscaping, pipe fitting, and industrial painting. Several men owned more than one business in their career, and almost all of these owners describe themselves as entrepreneurial, ambitious, opportunistic, and hard working.

These findings differ from most studies of crime that typically depict offenders as young males with lengthy criminal records and poor and erratic work histories in low-paying jobs (Gabor et al., 1987; Feeney, 1986; Haran & Martin, 1977). For example, 80% (64/80) of the offenders interviewed for my study of bank robbery were unemployed at the time of arrest, 91% (73/80) had lengthy and serious criminal records, and almost all report short employment histories.

> Institutionalized in youth and/or adult correctional facilities for years, many are lethargic, lack initiative, and do not enjoy working. Not surprisingly, some describe themselves as lazy while others blame a lack of education and employment skills for their inability to obtain well-paid, satisfying employment. Most report a general disdain for legitimate employment because of the long hours and low pay. (Desroches, 2002 [1995]:89–90)

In contrast, most higher-level drug traffickers in this study not only have substantial work histories, they also invest time and effort in their drug sales (see also VanNostrand & Tewksbury, 1999:64–65; Weisheit, 1990:113). Some even refer to themselves as workaholics:

> In some ways, I'm a workaholic. I love to work .... The [drug] business was my passion. The beauty of this business is that there were always problems to challenge myself—unique problems that no one else had. I took pride that it was such a good business. The thing I miss most in prison is not working.
>
> I have always been aggressive and intense in business. When it came to the drug business and to my legitimate business, I'm on top of it. Every dime and every dollar gets accounted for. You have to be willing to put in the time to be successful.
>
> I treated it as a business and took it very seriously and took pride in the way I ran it—the PR work, the interactions and networking—and I did it with my whole heart.
>
> At that time it was a business and I was applying basic business principles. The way it was presented to me, it was a business and a very lucrative way to make money.

Entrepreneural attitudes, skills, and experience are variables that significantly influence the decision and the opportunity to engage in drug trafficking. A strong work ethic and legitimate business experience also contribute to the relative success of the drug-dealing enterprise. Handelman reports that of 80 leaders of crime syndicates identified by the Russian Ministry of Affairs in 1993, most had occupations listed in police files as "industrial manager" or "business director" (1995:70). Other researchers and theorists (Hafley & Tewksbury, 1995:212; Langer, 1977; Letkemann, 1973; Murphy et al., 1990; Redlinger, 1975; Weisheit, 1990:113) have commented on the "crime as work" nature of drug trafficking and the otherwise law-abiding lifestyle and/or business attitudes of dealers.

> Our respondents came to see selling cocaine as a job—work, just like other kinds of work save for its illegality. For most, selling cocaine did not mean throwing out conventional values and norms. In fact, many of our respondents actively maintained their conventional identities. (Murphy et al., 1990:340)

Reuter and Haaga (1989) interviewed 32 higher-level drug dealers in their U.S. study and similarly noted that being "a good businessman" was a term of praise among drug traffickers, and that many in their sample led conforming lives and had entrepreneurial and business experience:

> The dealers who had important or organizing roles in remunerative schemes tended not to have extensive prior criminal records; many had done well in some legitimate sales-type profession (real estate in at least two cases, and import/export, which provides good training as well as good cover) .... Four of our respondents were owners or managers of bars, nightclubs, or restaurants before becoming dealers. (Reuter & Haaga, 1989:35–36)

Friendship, Kinship, Race, and Ethnicity

Drug-dealing crews in this sample consist of people who have known one another for many years. Because trust is so important, partners and associates are typically chosen on the basis of family ties, friendships, and/or past criminal involvements. Morselli makes the same point.

> The limited selection of accomplices and partners in crime means that one's criminal opportunities for action are embedded within the realms of one's personal network of family, friends, and acquaintances. One's direct contacts' contacts (friends of friends) also entail a latent pool of co-participants available through one's personal network. The network therefore wraps the suitable social basin from which outlaw partnerships, enterprises, and organizations extend from. (Morselli, 2001:209)

Race and ethnicity factor into the structure and dynamics of drug crews since friendship and kinship networks are often culturally based and information networks within ethnic communities allow traffickers to assess a person's character. In addition, there is a tendency among groups to define members of one's own race and/or ethnicity as trustworthy and view others as outsiders.

Over half of the drug syndicates in this study involved people primarily from the same ethnic background. One Sri Lankan subject convicted of importing heroin, for instance, had eight co-accused, all of whom were Sri Lankan. Another subject and his brother immigrated from Guyana as children, established cocaine connections on return visits to Guyana, and operated primarily, although not exclusively, within the Guyanese community in Canada. Another crew of marijuana smugglers was made up of six co-accused, all of Mexican-Mennonite origin. Four had immigrated to Canada and the other two maintained residence in Mexico and fled this country before being arrested. Other drug-trafficking crews consisted mainly or exclusively of people of anglophone, francophone, British, Canadian, Jamaican, Italian, Irish, East Indian, Chinese, or Vietnamese origin. Although many of these groups purchased from and/or distributed drugs to people of other ethnic origins, the composition of their own small crew was restricted by a common ethnic background. Redlinger reports similar findings among street-level heroin dealers who define trust along ethnic lines and limit their associates to other Mexican-Americans (1975:343). Similarly, Hafley and Tewksbury (1995: 216) discovered that business within the marijuana industry in rural Kentucky is primarily, if not always, restricted to involvement of those with whom one is very familiar. Here, too, the recruitment of workers is closely connected to the structure of kinship networks. There is a mistrust of outsiders since their family origins and reputation cannot be adequately determined.

Not all drug-trafficking crews in this study exclude others on the basis of ethnicity or country of origin. Several incorporate people of diverse ethnic backgrounds, but restrict membership to those they know and trust. The limited data available on outlaw motorcycle gangs indicate that membership is restricted to Caucasians, but they, too, purchase from and/or distribute to various racial and ethnic groups. Ethnicity is discussed again in Chapter 4 in relation to opportunity theory.

Size and Composition of Drug-Dealing Syndicates

A large number of studies carried out in different parts of the world appear to support the contention that illegal commodities are provided by criminal syndicates that are relatively small in size; encompass a wide variety of cultural backgrounds; and are independent, autonomous, decentralized, informal, coalitional, and situational. Illicit entrepreneurs appear to operate in loose associations of people that form, split, and come together again as opportunity arises. Some of these "crews" are bound by kinship and ethnic ties, and positions and tasks are usually interchangeable. Relationships between illegal enterprises may involve some co-operation and collusion, but generally these syndicates compete with one another for market share. Rather than being large-scale hierarchical structures centrally controlled by some "godfather"-like figure, organized crime is managed at a local level by independent wholesalers, each working to make a profit and avoid detection and apprehension (Adler, 1985; Adler & Adler, 1982, 1983, 1992; Becchi, 1996; Chambliss, 1978; Chin, 1996; Dubro, 1985; Hobbs, 1998a, 1998b; Jenkins & Potter, 1987; Lewis, 1994; Mieczkowski, 1990; Morselli, 2001; Naylor, 1995, 2002; Paoli, 2000, 2002; Pennsylvania Crime Commission, 1991; Potter, 1993; Reuter 1983, 1985; Reuter & Haaga, 1989; Reuter, MacCoun, & Murphy, 1990). Morselli suggests that the drug-distribution process is a take-and-give procedure more reminiscent of a children's game of hot potato than it is of a formal organization structure and authoritarian control of passage (2001:219).

Most higher-level drug traffickers in this study operate as independent wholesalers who receive narcotics from crews above them in the drug chain and pass them on to individuals or small groups below them in the distribution network. There is no evidence of a Mafia-style monopoly, near-monopoly, or cartel in the Canadian drug market. The organizational structure of higher-level drug trafficking syndicates typically includes the dealer and/or a partner(s), and a handful of paid employees who work in small groups referred to as a gang, organization, family, crew, syndicate, or cell. Even though there were on average 11 arrests for each of the 62 crews in this study, subjects appeared to know and work closely with only three to nine associates. In most drug-trafficking crews, one or two people will be in charge and employ two or three others who are delegated high-risk tasks and work on a commission or a fee-for-service basis. Naylor (2002) argues that being small has significant security advantages for crews working in an illegal arena.

> In illegal markets that are highly segmented, decisions are personalized, information flows constricted, capital supplies short term and unreliable, objective price data lacking, and the time horizons (indeed, the very existence) of enterprises coterminous with those of the enterpreneurs. The operating rule is to reduce risk by downsizing—by multiplying layers of intermediation and therefore reducing direct control over the various stages in the production or distribution chain. This rule applies because regulators go after the biggest first, either to bust them, or sometimes, to collect a form of underground taxation, which will also limit the firm's growth and profitability. All this suggests an ever-greater degree of decentralization and an ever-increasing pool of competitors. It also suggests that most fears of great crime cartels that control markets for illegal goods and services are purely fantasy. (Naylor, 2002:21)

Dorn and South (1990) similarly argue that drug-dealing syndicates remain small because large cartels are likely to attract the attention of police organizations and be targeted for aggressive law enforcement. Because covert police operations are time consuming and expensive, they tend to be mounted against larger rather than smaller drug enterprises. This results in a fragmentation of the illicit market into small drug-dealing syndicates.

> New emphases in law enforcement, such as covert operations and surveillance of cash flow, tend to structure the market into a series of smaller and flexible enterprises .... Smaller is safer as far as drug distribution enterprises are concerned. Within this general tendency, there is considerable variation in organization of drug distribution enterprises .... (Dorn & South, 1990:176)

Paoli (2002:67) and Williams and Godson (2002:324) also argue that the illegal status of narcotics affects the way in which production and distribution are carried out. Small is safer and, consequently, there is no imminent tendency toward monopoly control over illicit markets or the consolidation of large-scale, illegal conglomerates. Although some large criminal organizations exist, the evidence suggests that most organized criminal syndicates are relatively small in size.

Drug Trafficking as Independent Entrepreneurship

Although long-term relations frequently develop among drug traffickers, the association between suppliers and distributors is not an employer-employee relationship in which the upper-level dealer controls his lower-level distributors. Rather, it consists of an ongoing series of transactions in which participants operate as independent businesspeople and maintain a high degree of personal autonomy. Suppliers do not control distributor/clients, nor do they control the drug chain or any given link in a formal authoritarian way. What they do control, however, is access to the illicit product that dealers need to stay in business.

> [Brokers] place themselves so that they control not others, but the information and resources that others need. (Morselli, 2001:206)

Each dealer is free to search out other sources and may in fact be connected to more than one supply network. The normative system that exists and is understood by the players is that clients can change suppliers and take their business elsewhere if they so choose. A common scenario is for a distributor to approach his supplier and negotiate for better-quality product and/or price discounts to match those offered by others. If this offer is refused, the dealer is free to buy drugs elsewhere.

> The drug business is like the legitimate business world. If your supplier is providing an inferior product at too high a price, you'll find a better source to stay in business.

> We're all independent. It's all market value, it's all free market. It's product, price, reputation, and service. Absolutely! And with the people I dealt with, there are no guns and no intimidation.

> You're basically an individual entrepreneur. Even though I supply them with product, they're not working for me. They're working on their own and I'm just their supplier, but there is a lot of loyalty. Believe me, you want to be able to trust people, and you get used to dealing with people.

Dorn and South describe higher-level drug trafficking in Britain in similar terms: it is a competitive market inhabited by a range of small, flexible organizations whose structures vary and reflect their diverse origins and local or regional circumstances (1990:176). Studies of higher-level drug traffickers in the U.S. (Adler, 1985:63–82; Reuter & Haaga, 1989:40–47) similarly describe an open market and informal relationships between suppliers and clients that are sometimes long term but rarely exclusive. Research on street-level drug sales also emphasizes the entrepreneural and competitive aspects of the trade (Dorn & South, 1990; Johnson, Golub, & Fagan, 1995; Mieczkowski, 1988, 1990, 1994; Reuter, MacCoun, & Murphy, 1990). An entrepreneural market is not controlled by a single organization but instead is open to individuals and groups who have the personnel, skills, and products needed to make them competitive. An entrepreneurial model of drug dealing is consistent with opportunity theory since the process of becoming a drug dealer is often an opportunistic extension of a person's life/business experiences and entrepreneurial attitudes and skills.

Summary

Organized crime involves a criminal conspiracy of several people motivated for the purpose of economic enrichment. There is an emerging consensus among criminologists that syndicated crime should be defined primarily by its involvement in illicit market activities— the production and distribution of illegal goods and services. Two different images of organized crime are presented in the criminological literature. At one end of the continuum are hierarchical centrally controlled organizations that resemble modern corporations. American Mafia families and Colombian cocaine cartels are cited as examples of successful and enduring large-scale criminal syndicates. The second image depicts organized crime as consisting of ever-changing criminal networks that connect small groups of independent illicit entrepreneurs. Few studies support the view that cartels or Mafia-style organizations control illicit markets. Instead, research in various countries indicates that the marketing of prohibited goods and services is carried out by small groups of independent criminal syndicates that compete for market share and interact through a system of networks and contacts within countries and across national borders. Although some lasting large-scale criminal organizations may exist, they are not the archetype of organized crime.

A number of studies suggest that organized crime operates largely through network structures in which individuals are organized into small groups and do business with people they know and trust. A criminal network can be understood as an informal association of individuals and groups who participate in illicit activities. Opportunity theory helps to explain entry into higher-level drug trafficking since drug-trafficking networks typically consist of players and would-be dealers linked by friendship, kinship, and/or ethnic background. Connections not only facilitate entry, they allow participants to evaluate one another's reputation, recruit new members, and make easier the flow of information, knowledge, and illicit commodities. Ethnic and business contacts play an important role in the development and expansion of distribution networks into new areas and host countries. Friendship and ethnicity also provide the bonds that protect organized criminal groups from infiltration and betrayal.

Economics theory suggests that market-based illegal activity has much in common with legitimate business. Criminals are viewed as rational actors motivated by financial gain. Economic models focus on market forces, financial opportunities, and the entrepreneurship of organized crime. Despite many similarities, the comparison between criminal enterprises and legitimate businesses overlooks significant differences. The illicit nature of criminal syndicates constrains marketing, limits advertising and expansion, forces dealers to expend resources on security, and encourages redundancy. In addition, illicit firms lack the benefit of legal protections afforded legitimate businesses, are shut out of the financial markets, and often disintegrate after the demise of the illegal entrepreneur.

The present study is based on interviews with a sample of 70 incarcerated higher-level drug traffickers representing 62 drug syndicates operating in Canada throughout the years 1990–2002. The study describes drug dealing as a business and illustrates how entrepreneurial skills are necessary to succeed. Most higher-level dealers act as wholesalers who purchase large quantities of narcotics and market smaller amounts to dealers below them in the drug chain. The arrangement involves an ongoing series of transactions between willing buyers and sellers who operate as independent entrepreneurs.

Higher-level traffickers appear to fall into two categories: (a) "criminal" dealers live a deviant lifestyle, associate with other deviants, and have extensive criminal records and poor employment histories; (b) "businessmen" dealers associate with conventional people, live otherwise law-abiding lives, and have lengthy employment histories. Approximately two-thirds of the men in this study owned small legitimate businesses prior to their involvement in drug trafficking. It appears that business experience, skills, entrepreneurship, and contacts are significant variables that affect the motivation and opportunity to engage in higher-level drug trafficking.

The illicit drug trade in Canada, with the exception of perhaps a few groups such as outlaw motorcycle gangs, is characterized by open competition among a large number of small criminal networks that vary in race and ethnicity, criminal background, types of drugs sold, profits, and modus operandi. The constraints imposed by illegality tend to prevent the development of large, formally organized, hierarchical, and durable criminal enterprises. Instead, illicit markets are run by local criminal groups whose need for caution requires them to be flexible, secretive, and remain relatively small in size. Small drug-trafficking businesses can nonetheless reap millions of dollars in profits.

CHAPTER 4

The Motivation and Lifestyle of Higher-Level Drug Traffickers

This chapter focuses on the motives and decision-making processes that lead offenders to engage in drug trafficking, their reasons for continuing in this activity, and the lifestyles and spending habits of higher-level traffickers. Motivation for both deviant and conforming behaviour is influenced by a complex variety of factors. Some variables are significant and immediate while others are distant and may possibly operate at an unconscious level. Since this is a crime that provides great wealth, the obvious motive for illicit drug trafficking is money. While the need or desire for money is common, most people choose legitimate paths to solve their financial problems. Even those who use illegitimate means may choose other avenues to obtain needed funds. In addition, people who are desperate for cash and who find legitimate financial opportunities blocked may be deterred because of moral prohibitions, a lack of connections, or a fear of apprehension and punishment.

The following chapter analyzes the decision-making process of 70 convicted higher-level drug dealers and the factors that guided them into this particular crime. Variables examined include drug usage, criminal connections, employment and business experience, ethnicity, family bonds, lifestyle, morality and rationalizations, and self-concept. Theories discussed include anomie, rational choice, opportunity theory, and learning and social control theories.

Initial Involvement in Drug Trafficking

Learning Theories of Crime

In accordance with cultural transmission and differential association theory (Shaw & McKay, 1942; Sutherland, 1947),

53

the majority of the subjects in this study were initiated into drug dealing through associations with other criminals either in prison or on the street. Initial involvement in higher-level drug trafficking typically occurs through contact with other dealers. Subjects learn values, rationalizations, and modus operandi from successful criminal role models who introduce them to the game and provide opportunities for entry into this lucrative business. Dealers appear to take one of three paths into higher-level trafficking: moving from retail sales to wholesale; direct entry by way of recruitment; or direct entry through active solicitation.

For some, the move into drug dealing begins at the retail level when subjects sell drugs for profit and/or to deflect the cost of their own usage. Because they have connections, they often supply friends and associates and gradually become a drug retailer without much thought or premeditation. Other retailers realize immediately the value of their connections and decide very quickly to pursue dealing for profit. Twenty-five subjects (25/70, 35.7%) in this study began as street-level dealers. Their move from retail to wholesale drug sales required a conscious decision, planning, deliberate effort, and opportunity, which is typically provided by upper-level dealers.

A more accelerated and direct path into wholesale dealing occurs when subjects are recruited into a drug network. The majority of dealers in this sample (45/70, 64.3%), like those in other studies (Adler, 1985; Adler & Adler, 1983; Redlinger, 1975; Reuter & Haaga, 1989; Sorfleet, 1976), began their criminal involvement through direct entry at relatively high levels as importers and/or wholesalers. Most subjects report that they were approached by a friend or associate who presented them with a chance to make considerable amounts of money. The suggestion is made in the form of a business proposal in which the advantages (wealth) are emphasized and the disadvantages (the risk of apprehension, conviction, and sentencing) minimized. There is no hard sell in the recruitment process and subjects accept the offer willingly if not enthusiastically, even though they may take time to consider the consequences. Their contact's success in making money and evading detection has a major impact on this decision. Recruiters often provide detailed information on safe methods for dealing drugs, clients, and credit in the form of a front. Recruiters also answer questions and concerns, construct rationalizations for the crime, and give reassurances that the risks are low. Drug dealing is portrayed as a business, non-violent, and morally acceptable despite its illegality. A 32-year-old man serving eight years for conspiracy to import cocaine into Canada describes his initial involvement:

> After being laid off, I went into business for myself and started importing clothing from the U.S. and selling them at the Sunday flea markets. The business did poorly and I found myself in debt. I had borrowed $15,000 from a friend and had to tell him that I could only pay him back in very small amounts.
>
> He was a good friend and we had known each other all our lives. He was understanding and suggested that I could repay him by doing what he was doing. He was involved in importing cocaine into the country and suggested that I get involved. He was making a lot of money, but my first reaction was, "No, man. No way!"
>
> I thought about it for a month because the business wasn't getting any better. In hindsight, I didn't look at all of my options. There were other jobs I was qualified for and there were many things I can think of now that I could have done well. I wouldn't have been living in luxury, but we would have got by just fine.

He was importing coke and didn't give me much information at first. He offered to supply me and we would split the profits 50/50. We were not involved in selling, but strictly in importing the cocaine into Canada—no trafficking. We would pass it along to anyone who would buy on a large scale, which usually meant a kilo or more.

I was given information on a means of making income and all I wanted initially was to provide for my family. I looked at it as not hurting anybody and I later learned that drugs do hurt people. I was not committing robberies, but just an illegal form of bootlegging. I told myself that I was doing it for my family.

You have to be from certain entrees and you have to be trusted. I had the opportunity through this one guy I was friends with. He and I came from the same country and we grew up together and we came out of the same community. He had access to certain people and had big connections in Guyana.

The third path into higher-level trafficking is similar to the second and begins with an association or friendship with a supplier. Instead of being recruited, subjects actively pursue opportunities to traffic. Being exposed to the wealth that dealers garner is the main factor motivating them to become drug traffickers. A 33-year-old offender explains:

I met people making a lot of money and living a leisurely lifestyle. People who had a legitimate business like myself, but who made big money on the side— very lucrative. It was all very civil and organized and it was business and kept very professional and there was lots of

money to be made. Any normal person could see it. You meet people who are successful and you can see these are family men and good people. The steps are so simple and easy and rich, and I started to think I can do this. I just approached someone and got started, and you rationalize why it's okay to do this, and I did it for many years.

Entry into upper-level trafficking is not as simple and straightforward as the preceding passages suggest. Not all dealers who start at the retail level, for instance, move up the ladder gradually and not all who begin at the wholesale level move into trafficking quickly and directly. Some street-level dealers in this study—typically non-users—were conscious and deliberate in their choices and moved quickly into wholesaling. Several wholesalers, on the other hand, acted as couriers or performed other services for higher-level dealers before becoming importers or distributors themselves.

Prison and Street Connections

The majority of subjects in this study (51/70, 72.8%) became involved in drug trafficking through friends, relatives, or associates in their community or workplace. Others gained entry through contacts with foreign nationals (9/70, 2.8%) or prison and ex-inmate connections (10/70, 14.2%) (two prison contacts were foreign nationals). One subject who had served time for armed robbery was employed for several years before he engaged in drug importing.

When I was released, I planned to go straight and did so for a while and completed my parole. I served three years of a nine-year prison term and finished the last six years on parole. At first, I worked for a company, then went into the construction business with a partner. We shared a small company for two years, buying and selling heavy construction equipment. It was very profitable, but things went wrong over his drinking and spending. He was a heavy drinker and he would go on binges, and he set up accounts in the company's name and ran up large bills. My wife also ran up some bills and I found myself with some large debts. My mortgage was being called in by the bank and I was looking for money.

I had a Lincoln and tried to sell it to a friend. He was a guy I had known for years who was into crime. He called me a week later and offered me a deal that would allow me to get out of debt. He asked me to provide him with an address so a package with cocaine could be delivered. The package was to be couriered from Venezuela.

The reason I was asked to do this was because I had a good reputation as trustworthy. I had done my pen time without informing on anyone and he knew this. He knew that I could have made a deal for less time, but that I had integrity. We had grown up together and had mutual friends and he knew how I operated.

He also knew that I had run a successful business and that I had a good work ethic. I was not an average criminal who would get up at 4:00 in the afternoon. Most criminals are lazy and not very reliable. He also thought that I was serious enough to be able to handle it.

I told him that I would think about it and called him a week later. The debts led me in that direction. Had the company been viable, then I would have turned him down unless it was a large amount of money and little risk.

Another dealer met his supplier while serving time in an American prison for a weapons offence.

My main supplier was a Colombian from the Medellin cartel. I met my source in jail in Texas in a federal institute and he was a fitness guy like me. He had a master's degree from a U.S. school and he was a finance guy and his job was to move money around for the cartel. He had a conviction for 2,000 kilos.

We spent two years together and we were cellmates and became good friends. We got out around the same time he had the connections in Colombia. At first we started small by importing 60 kilos into Canada each month.

I would send drivers to L.A. to bring it up 60 to 80 kilos a month. I had limited finances and did about 80 a month and I was bringing 20 a week into Canada. I would offload 10 to my Asian people in Vancouver and the other 10 would supply the island for the week.

I realized how much kilos were selling for in Victoria and I was shocked at the profit margin. These guys in Victoria were paying $42,000 to $45,000 per kilo Canadian and I could get it for $14 to $16 U.S. and with the exchange at 20% or around $18,000 Can. I could make $20,000 per kilo.

Rational Choice Theory and Crime

Economists have long held the view that economic crimes are the result of rational decision making reached by men and women who confront a problem faced by many others—a need or desire for money. Implicit in the economic perspective is an actor who views certain illegal activities as rational and productive even though capture, imprisonment, and death may be part of the equation. The expected utility model in economics is based on the assumption that offenders rationally attempt to maximize the monetary and psychic rewards of crime (Becker, 1968). If crime has a higher utility than conforming behaviour—that is, an acceptable chance at not getting caught and a desirable amount to gain—then the individual should decide in favour of committing the crime. On the other hand, if the perceived risk of capture is high and the expected penalty is great, the would-be criminal should be deterred. Rational choice theory is used to analyze the decision-making process as it relates to the various stages of criminal involvement, including initial motivation, the motivation to continue, and the decision to cease criminal involvement. Choice theory can also be used to help explain decisions of a more tactical nature relating to the criminal event itself, including the development of an offender's modus operandi and use of security measures. The rational choice perspective on crime is best suited for utilitarian offences such as theft, burglary, fraud, robbery, and drug trafficking.

The limited-rationality approach (Cornish & Clarke, 1986a, 1986b, 1987) portrays criminal behaviour as the outcome of choices, and asserts that decisions made by offenders exhibit limited or bounded rather than normative rationality. The bounded rationality hypothesis assumes that limitations on people's ability to process information place constraints on decision processes that force them to make simplifications and shortcuts that may appear reasonable at the time, but which can produce inferior outcomes. Offenders are influenced by such factors as drug usage, peer pressure, and emotional or economic desperation. In addition, people are subject to routine and habitual preferences, superstition, prejudices, and emotional attachments that influence the manner in which they engage in crime. Criminal behaviour may be planned and premeditated, but not fully rational in the strict sense that the expected utility model assumes. As discussed in Chapter 1, research on drug trafficking at the retail level does not support an image of offenders as rational, careful, calculating economic planners. For many, their desperate financial situation and drug addiction contribute to behaviour that is often impulsive and poorly executed. Although there is evidence of rational thought and planning, lower-level dealers exhibit limited rationality and take huge risks for very modest rewards.

Higher-level dealers, in contrast, carefully weigh the risks versus the rewards and develop and implement a modus operandi that emphasizes safety and profit. Their behaviour and cognitive processes are clearly instrumental and exhibit a planned, rational, cautious, and utilitarian pursuit of wealth. Though knowledge of risks may be imperfect and participants may underestimate them, most subjects have a reasonable view of what is involved and implement a variety of strategies to reduce the danger. The data from this study indicate that men who enter the drug trade are rational actors, have high financial aspirations, and are willing to face the possibility of apprehension and imprisonment. They give a great deal of thought to their crimes and conclude that dealing drugs at a wholesale level is relatively safe. Because the act is consensual, there are no complainants or witnesses and police are unlikely to be aware that an offence has taken place. By dealing only with people who are known and trusted, there is little chance of anyone informing and/or being an undercover officer. All parties are motivated by the potential for riches and all have a vested interest in ensuring that transactions occur with minimum risk or problems.

Rationality is evident in their assessment of this crime as a shortcut to riches because it requires less effort than working at a job and pays a lot more money. The financial gain from drug trafficking is tremendous and many distributors make $10,000 or more a month. Evidence of rationality is also evident in the modus operandi of dealers and the precautionary methods used to avoid detection and arrest. Security measures usually reflect time, effort, cost, and rational thought. Most dealers take the trouble to learn about police strategies and techniques and take steps to counteract them. In short, higher-level dealers exhibit rational, utilitarian thought processes and behaviours in the development and implementation of their modus operandi. This is discussed further in chapters 5 and 6.

It should be noted that rational choice theory does not explain a person's disposition to commit crime, nor does it take into account the sometimes spontaneous, impulsive, and opportunistic nature of criminal behaviour. Thus, there is always the danger of overemphasizing the voluntary exercise of choice by particular traders and misrepresenting the actual behaviour of criminal entrepreneurs. Indeed, the failure of dealers to adopt rational, utility-maximizing approaches to the calculation of the risks, efforts, and rewards is often the reason for the collapse of criminal organizations (Edwards & Gill, 2002:218).

Anomie Theory and Motivation

The classic strain (anomie) theories of Merton (1938), Cohen (1955), and Cloward and Ohlin (1960) argue that the cultural system encourages everyone to pursue the ideal goals of monetary success and/or middle-class status. Lower-class individuals are often prevented from achieving such goals through legitimate

channels, experience strain, and often select more efficient but deviant avenues to achieve success. Although money is the primary motive, few of the higher-level drug traffickers in this study are financially desperate at the time they decided to engage in crime. Only eight men (8/70, 11.4%) experienced financial setbacks that threatened their customary standard of living and propelled them into drug trafficking, and these resulted from business dealings, job losses, and expenses resulting from divorce or other problems. Anomie theory has limited applicability to the men in this study since the majority were employed and earned sufficient money to support themselves and their families. Most came from middle- or working-class backgrounds and few suffered from poverty. In contrast to bank robbers who are generally poor, in low-paying jobs, unemployed, or looking for work and express an immediate and urgent need for money (Camp, 1968:83–106; Desroches, 2002 [1995]:80–81, 89–92; Feeney & Weir, 1975), most higher-level drug traffickers have jobs and/or businesses and decent incomes. Their motivation is greed, high status, and a wealthy lifestyle.

Agnew (1992) argues that classic strain theories focus on the disjunction between aspirations and expectations and offers a more general theory by emphasizing the disparity between expectations and actual achievements. In the latter case, strain is greater and more distressing because goals are immediate rather than far off in the future. Agnew's theoretical model assigns a central role to the social comparison process and suggests that exposure to the success of others will motivate individuals to attempt to close the gap (1992:52–53). This is true of many of the subjects in this study who admit to being envious of others who are better off than themselves—typically people who became wealthy through legitimate enterprises or through drug dealing. The strain for these men comes not from blocked opportunities but from achievements that fall short of their expectations—they desire the lifestyle and easy money that drug dealing affords.

> It must have been greed—seeing how other people live. I was envious and I wanted what other people had. I should have minded my own business.

> I got into it because I wanted to make money. I was on a mission to make money. I knew businessmen who were rich and successful and had the nice home and cottage and took holidays around the world. I was very motivated and ambitious and I wanted what they had. I'm smart and I figured I could be successful in this game.

> I knew people who were doing this [marijuana grow operations] for several years and I saw the money they were making. They had all the toys—Sea-Doos, the Vet, the Jeep Cherokee.

A Cuban immigrant who had been steadily employed for 10 years was seduced into drug smuggling by his brother-in-law's success.

> He was doing very well and lived in a big house with no mortgage. He and his wife had nice cars and took holidays. I mean, he made it look very attractive. I was doing okay. I had my own business and working hard, but I wanted a lot more. It was greed.

Another dealer was recruited into drug trafficking by a higher-level dealer who lavished money on him.

> He was a friend of mine and he wanted me to work for him. We would go out to the clubs and he would spend

money—no questions asked. Give me some money or buy me some clothes. "Here take it. Don't worry about it." He made it clear that the money was there if I wanted in. It was just too tempting to resist.

Although the primary motive for higher-level traffickers is money—emphasized time and again by dealers in the interviews—wealth is not the only goal or measure of success. The scope of criminal rewards include a variety of personal satisfactions, such as social status, peer and family approval, recognition of one's accomplishments, self-satisfaction with or confidence about one's performance or abilities, and demonstrations of success through conspicuous consumption (Bellah et al., 1985; Bueno de Mesquita & Cohen, 1995; Matsueda et al., 1992). Numerous subjects in this study like taking risks, search for thrills and excitement, enjoy life in the fast lane, and "get off" on the intrigue that comes with their secret criminal lifestyle. Other benefits that are commonly mentioned include the satisfaction and sense of accomplishment from pulling off a deal, and the feelings of power, importance, and control that comes with being a mover and a shaker in the drug world. Many dealers become addicted to the luxuries, power, status, freedom, and financial security associated with drug trafficking. For most, this is an endeavour that affords them a lifestyle that other career choices cannot provide and produces a much higher level of respect than would be available through legitimate employment.

Most of the benefits discussed above are likely to arise in the course of committing the crime and represent secondary gains or by-products of drug trafficking. The thrill, danger, excitement, power, and control that drug trafficking affords likely emerge in the process of committing the crime and are not the reasons that propel many in the first place. It is thus difficult to tease out the motivation to crime and determine whether power tripping and excitement attract people into dealing or whether these pleasures emerge as one successfully pulls off deals and reaps the financial rewards. Regardless of which comes first, euphoric feelings following initial success increase confidence, reinforce motive, and help to explain why subjects continue to offend.

Case Example: Financial Setbacks—the Hotel Owner

This 55-year-old offender has been married for 29 years and has a son and daughter in university. He was convicted of conspiracy to import and traffick in cocaine and was sentenced in both Canada and the United States. His 15 co-accused include several Italian organized crime figures and Satan's Choice members from Montreal. He is serving a 13-year sentence.

I've always been employed and I worked in the textile industry up to age 25. Then I owned my own business in carpet cleaning and janitorial services. From age 30 on I was in the hotel business. I had three hotels in Ontario and Quebec and some apartment buildings in Montreal. The recession came and new hotels were coming in and more competition, and I couldn't fill my rooms. I found that I was losing ground and about to lose everything I had worked for all my life. I was putting my own money into the hotels to keep them alive. I had worked hard for what I had and money was important to me. I had a good life working honestly. I had a beautiful home and drove a Cadillac, and I was losing it all.

Some of the people I grew up with in Montreal were into the drug business and I knew it, but all these years that I knew them, I never thought I would get involved. I didn't think it was right. I had moved to Ontario to get out of the scene. I've always been against drugs, and even as a young man I never took drugs.

But when the recession came in and I was under financial pressure, by accident I was talking to somebody and I told them I was not doing that well. They gave me a hint that if I wanted to get into drugs, that I could make some easy and fast money. The person who got me into it was a long-time friend. It was my decision. He had a restaurant of his own and we just chatted. It happened so fast. When you are in trouble, sometimes you make the wrong decisions and you take the shortcut.

With the people I knew, it was easy to start. I was introduced to his Colombian contacts in the U.S. Then I approached people who were interested in distributing. I had another friend who turned out to be a rat, but who knew a lot of people in the business and he made other introductions. I knew some people on my own from growing up in Montreal and from the hotel business.

I operated a couple of years before I got caught. I was arrested and charged in Canada, and then I was hit with some charges in the United States. It was a sealed indictment given to a grand jury in the U.S. by a partner who didn't want to go to jail. I looked at my options and decided to plead guilty in the U.S. and in Canada.

I made a deal for 13 years concurrent for Canada and the U.S. I was in court in the U.S. for one day with my lawyer to plead guilty and be sentenced. It was all prearranged and I was sent back to Canada. The deal was that I was to be sentenced in Canada and do my time here. Both courts sentenced me to 13 years. I agreed to it because the U.S. [has] stiffer sentences for drugs. There is zero tolerance, and you do 85% of your time down there.

This third party should have been in the same situation, but he decided to talk and make a deal for himself. From my understanding, he got $150,000 and a change of name, and I don't know where he is.

When he got arrested, he decided to turn us in. We were all arrested at the same time and we were all out on bail. He just decided to make a deal and sold us down.

Most of my involvement was getting it into Canada. I had it brought in through the Indian reserve near Cornwall. I would have the Indians smuggle it because they are not searched when they cross the border or else they take it by boat across the lake. Once we got the drugs over the border, I'd have someone bring it to Montreal for distribution. It became routine after that. This would be done every month or every two months: 20, 30, 40 kilos.

I came from little Italy in Montreal and all the families there came from the same town in Sicily. My friend comes from my hometown in Sicily. There were others who were Italian and the rest were French and English. The informant was French. I speak French and Italian and English. The police knew that my connections in Montreal were organized crime, but I was not part of organized crime. They would receive the cocaine and sell it to the Hells Angels.

I would have to travel to Miami to meet with the people down there. They were Colombians. I would tell them I was at the Park Plaza Hotel and they would look me up and we would have the meeting, like any other business meeting. There are no guns and it was just the details of the deal. A guy wants to know "What if this?" and "What if that?" If there is something you cannot do, then you just tell him so he knows where you stand. We'd discuss price, delivery, and how many kilos we needed.

Being honest is very important. I was well liked because they knew I was a businessman and not a gangster. I was not a muscle and it was obvious that I was in it for the money. I would meet them and make the deal as soon as possible. I had their trust and they were sending stuff whenever I asked. That builds up over time. It didn't happen in the first weeks.

They are not stupid. They have been in the business a long time and they can size you up and they knew that I had no problem with drugs. They even asked, "Amigo, do you party with that shit?" I said no and they said they didn't like to do business with people who used the product. They can tell too if someone is a user and has trouble with drugs—the way people behave and the way they look. I came across as a businessman.

I usually went by myself, but one time I brought another guy with me to Miami. He was a representative from Hells Angels and they were paying for the whole shipment, so he wanted to come down as an observer. He went to the meeting and didn't say too much. It was understood that it was given to me and I had the responsibility and he was there to observe and to protect their interest. After a while, the Hells Angels were paying in advance. They knew the type of person I was. The biker was one of the ones arrested and he got seven years.

I could buy kilos for $15,000 to $20,000 Can. and they sold for $35,000 Can. or even as high $40,000. The drugs would usually take three weeks to get through, but sometimes you may have to wait two months because things don't go right.

I was worried about being in contact with the stuff. If I knew it was in a hotel room, I would be scared to go into that room and I wouldn't. I never used it, I never handled it, and never even touched it. Keeping a distance makes it a little safer, but it doesn't really matter. The police use conspiracy laws and I was ignorant about that.

I tried to score and make enough to get out. It was too much pressure and I was about to get out before we were caught. A lot of work and a lot of risk. A lot of trust and one guy screws up and you have a lot of trouble. If you give someone $300,000 and they don't come back, what do you do? It was very stressful and I was a bundle of nerves. I couldn't sleep at nights over this.

I give it to a guy on the Indian reserve and I have to trust him. I might have a guy who holds it in the U.S. until somebody picks it up. The guy I give the money could run off with it. It is a dishonest business and you have to rely on everybody being honest. I wouldn't recommend it to my worst enemy. Not an easy job.

The time spent on this varies, but it became a full-time job. You can put 40 hours a week into it, driving to Montreal, and you have to talk to somebody because you can't use the phone. I had to set up the deals, so I had to fly to Miami and it takes me two days.

Even when you are not doing anything, you are thinking and worrying. If you want 20 kilos and he wants $100,000 down payment, you have to send him the money and then you worry about that.

I was caught with $200,000 U.S. and the RCMP seized and kept it under the proceeds of crime. They also seized one of our shipments— 40 kilos. I didn't lose anything else because I had legitimate businesses and income. Everything that I owned was legit.

I am not unhappy with the end result because I'll get out after one-sixth of my sentence on accelerated parole. I have no problem being on parole because I will have no problem being clean. I'm lucky I didn't end up in the U.S. and their sentences. God forbid, there won't be another time. I made one mistake and won't make another or I'll be here the rest of my life. I have a family. That was my biggest pain. I felt bad about my children knowing, but they love me and they know that I'm not a bad father and it is a mistake that I made and they forgive me.

Opportunity Theory and Entry into Higher-Level Drug Trafficking

Most drug traffickers in this study are initiated into this crime through higher-level dealers who provide them with a supply of drugs and the opportunity to learn the tricks of the trade. These contacts represent illegitimate opportunity structures (Cloward, 1959; Cloward & Ohlin, 1960) and are significant situational determinants of crime. The majority of subjects used one of two main ports of entry into higher-level drug trafficking: by way of ethnic-based networks and through employment and business opportunities.

Ethnicity and Opportunity: Contacts in Source Countries

There is a strong connection between ethnic background and the types of narcotics that offenders import and/or traffic. Most of the 34 (34/70, 48.5%) non-European subjects in this study have ethnic and/or family links to source countries for illicit drugs. Cocaine originates mainly from South America and typically makes its way into Canada from countries south of the border. The majority of subjects (16/19, 84.2%) whose home country is in the Caribbean, South and Central America, or Mexico traffic primarily (or exclusively) in cocaine: one person dealt in heroin; and two Canadian citizens of Mexican-Mennonite origin imported marijuana from Mexico through the United States. It is common for drug syndicates in source countries to actively solicit kinship and/or ethnic connections in Canada to expand their business.

Heroin has its origins in Southeast Asia and Pacific Rim countries, and offenders with ethnic and family links to this part of the world are more likely to deal in this substance. Of the 12 men with ties to Asia and the Pacific, nine (9/12, 75%) dealt heroin and three (3/12, 25%) trafficked in cocaine. The remaining three (3/34, 8.8%) non-European subjects originate from Ghana and Israel: the former was convicted of importing cocaine from the United States; one Israeli sold heroin; and the other Israeli sold a variety of narcotics.

People of European background make up half (36/70, 51.42%) of the sample with the single largest ethnic categories being anglophone and francophone (28/70, 40%). These two groups are more likely to have been born in Canada, all 36 are Caucasian, and they traffick in a wider variety of drugs. The majority (21/36, 58.3%) sold cocaine; seven grew, imported, and/or sold marijuana or its by-products; four manufactured designer drugs; and four sold more than one illicit drug.

Among the 34 men with non-European backgrounds, almost all chose partners, suppliers, and/or distributors primarily or exclusively from their own ethnic group, illustrating the significance of ethnicity in the networking that occurs among drug traffickers. A 40-year-old Cuban-Canadian convicted of conspiracy to import cocaine from the United States had 22 co-accused. He describes the role that ethnicity played in his organization:

> I only knew four or five of those arrested. The network developed through friends. I met my partners in my social circle, which was mainly Spanish people. You have a tendency to trust your own people more than others. Maybe that's why I was approached. They were Cuban, too, and you just meet people through others and you get to trust them since they're friends with your friends. Your friends vouch for them, so you trust them. Our source was from Florida in the Cuban community down there.

Race is frequently intertwined with ethnicity and its significance is difficult to determine. Most subjects of European background are Caucasian and many non-Europeans are visible minorities. Dealers typically refer to ethnicity and/or a person's home country rather than their race when discussing partners and associates in the drug world. In some cases, however, it appears that race does play a significant role in the networking of drug dealers. Two brothers originally from Guyana were convicted for their involvement in a large cocaine smuggling and distribution ring. Their case illustrates the importance of both race and ethnicity in their initial involvement, smuggling enterprise, and distribution network. Both started selling at a retail level and moved up to wholesale when the older brother travelled to Guyana to seek a higher-level supplier. In addition, most of the distributors and many of the couriers used in Canada were from the Guyanese community. Both made it clear that they would deal only with friends and associates from their own ethnic background and race. The younger brother is explicit about the need to trust the people he deals with.

> You have to be very careful who you trust in this game. I trust myself, my family, and my close friends. Most of my close friends are Guyanese like myself, but a lot of them are Jamaicans or from Barbados. A lot of them are Caribbean. I don't deal with anyone that I don't know or didn't grow up with.

The older brother similarly emphasized how race/ethnicity is used to establish trust.

> Race and ethnicity are important 'cause you don't want to deal with outsiders. At least within your own kind, you know who is who 'cause everybody knows everyone. Or even back home [Guyana], you can have your friend check out so and so. Yeah, so we never go out of the race. We used White people as couriers and that was about it. If a White guy was looking to buy from me, we'd think that he's a cop. First of all, he would never get to me. Just on race alone, I would see that as a dividing line that protects me. I dealt only with people from the community that I lived in.

A 30-year-old man convicted of conspiracy to traffick in heroin similarly explains the importance of race and ethnicity for his drug-trafficking network.

> I'm Chinese from China and my parents are immigrants. My circle was mainly Chinese. I found my source from the Chinese community. You meet people when you hang out in certain places. My customers are from Chinese backgrounds. A lot of their customers are Chinese, but I know they also had other customers too.

A 25-year-old Canadian-born Jamaican who retailed cocaine before he began importing explains his Jamaican connections and his reluctance to deal with other ethnic groups:

> My partner and I had grown up together and are really close friends. My partner is Black and has a Jamaican background like myself. We hit it off from about age 15. We started dealing at the street level together. We are like brothers and we are connected and think alike. Our supplier is from out of town and he's Jamaican background .... Often he would run out and we'd be looking elsewhere for a source. Every time you go to a different supplier, it turns out to be garbage. There was nobody with the same quality of drugs. That's crossing into racial boundaries. If the Chinese have it, they will give to their people first. That's why I went to Jamaica. We decided to import it ourselves so we could have our own supply and move off the street.

A primary reason for creating a closed and loyal criminal syndicate based on friendship, kinship, and/or cultural ties is to prevent infiltration by police and/or their agents. A cocaine smuggler who worked with his brother, his best friend, and boyhood friends from the same town and high school was arrested as the result of a currency exchange sting. He states:

That's the only way they could have busted us. Exchanging money was our biggest problem and our downfall. The police could never have penetrated us. We were just too tight an organization. I was involved in the trade for 25 years before being busted. I have no criminal record prior to this beef and I'm 45 years old.

Business, Employment, and Illegitimate Opportunity

As discussed earlier, opportunity theory is relevant to higher-level drug trafficking because one requires connections in order to enter this closed and secretive world. While some traffickers make their drug contacts through known criminals on the street or in prison, others are asked to participate because they have legitimate businesses and knowledge that traffickers need to import and distribute drugs and/or to exchange and launder money. A third of the subjects in this study (24/70, 34%) found their port of entry into drug trafficking through employment and/or business opportunities. Six bar owners and four employees (10/24, 41.6%) made their initial drug contacts in liquor establishments, an environment that allowed them to develop a clientele and learn the ropes of the drug trade.

Eight subjects (8/24, 33.3%) owned import and/or export companies through which they gained experience with transporting goods across national boundaries. In these instances, subjects were approached by established dealers anxious to take advantage of their business expertise and cover. Each used their business to facilitate the smuggling of drugs into Canada, and all eight were convicted of importing or conspiracy to import narcotics.

Of the other respondents (6/24, 25%) whose employment or business provided the opportunity to traffic, one subject made

contacts through his hairdressing salon; another owned a gymnasium in which steroids and other illicit drugs were widely used; a third sold real estate and laundered money for drug traffickers; the fourth subject owned a money exchange and became partners with one of his clients who was a major marijuana importer; the fifth owned a money-managing company and began his career in the drug trade through money laundering; and the sixth person owned his own lobster fishing boat and used it to unload cocaine from a mother ship and smuggle it into Canada.

Case Example: From Fish to Coke

A 45-year-old married man with two children from the Vancouver area serving eight years describes his role in a cocaine smuggling ring.

> At age 20, I owned my own equipment logging business in the forest industry. Then I stumbled into the fish business and sold fish. I started doing my homework in libraries writing letters and faxes and started from scratch. I bought fish from fishermen and shipped them to Europe and Japan. I ran that about 12 years.
>
> The business was good and I was making $200,000 a year—incredible money. I was always willing to work and I would say that I'm a workaholic, but the Japanese economy went into recession and we all hung in there too long and I went into debt.
>
> I've always known people in the drug business. The trading business is where you know what kind of cargo people are shipping. I knew the margins and you know when people are making more than they should. It's always been around and I knew of it. I knew some friends from my youth who were into it.

I never considered it before because I was married with kids and I had a business. I ran into some people I had done some trade with and my forte is to move things from A to B around the world. I was approached and asked if I could do that, and I had a good look at my finances and it was pretty bleak. Not the right answer, but that's the way it happened. I had kids going into university and all the trappings of the good life that took money to support.

When you work the numbers as a businessman and you look at drugs, you go "Whoof!" The numbers and the profit margins are incredible! It's all numbers to a business guy. If you are a business guy, you call it a commodity that makes money. We don't look at this as a drug.

There was a proposition made to me and it outlined what my responsibilities would be. I weighed the pros and cons, and the numbers outweighed the risk factors. It was clear that it was cocaine. My role was to arrange shipping from the U.S. into Canada.

I made a calculation about the risk and decided that the upside was much better than the downside. I was in a real bad financial position, and it made the numbers look even more attractive. The risk seemed manageable to me. I understand how Customs works and if I loaded it as a commodity, we could manage the risk.

From Retail to Wholesale: Moving Up the Ladder

A number of subjects (25/70, 36%) sold illicit drugs at the retail level before moving to wholesale. Retailing involves selling to drug users, whereas wholesalers sell to other dealers. Retailers are also known as street-level dealers because they sometimes sell their product on street corners and similar locations such as crack houses, bars, gymnasiums, schools, and various public places.

Fourteen subjects (14/25, 56%) in this study who moved from retail to wholesale maintained retail clients even though the majority of their business now involved selling drugs to other dealers. The main reasons for doing so were to provide drugs to friends and to maintain wealthy clients who provided a lucrative source of income.

> After a while, I was mainly selling to other dealers. I still did some retail, but at the higher end. I would say about 10% of my business was still retail, but it was a better customer and no addicts.

> I had a client who was a doctor and when he held parties, I would be invited. I put on my best suit and brought my best drugs. I put a lot effort into it and put the drugs in coloured vials to indicate the amounts. I mingled and provided the drugs when wanted. I could triple the amount that I normally made. These were outrageous prices, but they would pay it. He never told anyone who I was. He would come to me and get it and give me the money— a great customer. You cherish these customers and if someone did find out about them, you take evasive action. You never tell anyone about these customers. You don't own people, but you have to protect your clients. If you have [a] good source of money, you try to protect it.

Street-level dealers sell small amounts of drugs often to a large number of clients and, because their behaviour is relatively overt, they are easily identified by the police. Retailers are vulnerable to arrest by undercover officers who attempt to purchase their product. Police can also turn addicts into informants in order to identify and charge street-level dealers. Robbery, assault, and murder are all potential hazards that retailers must face when doing business with people who are addicted, desperate, and sometimes dangerous.

Stages in the Move from Retail to Wholesale

The following analysis employs opportunity and rational choice theory to understand the various factors that precede a retail drug dealer moving to the wholesale level. Opportunity theory suggests that a dealer must have access to and recognize opportunity when it presents itself; alternatively, he or she must search for and/or create opportunities to move up the chain. Opportunity in higher-level drug trafficking requires access to a reliable supplier and contacts with willing and competent distributors. Rational choice theory suggests that dealers rationally assess their involvement in crime, examine relevant variables, conduct a cost-benefit analysis, and conclude that rewards outweigh any perceived risks. The decision to move upwards in the drug chain becomes a rational, calculated, and premeditated attempt to enrich oneself while minimizing the risk of loss, injury, and/or imprisonment. Retailers who become higher-level drug traffickers are influenced by a number of variables and go through several stages in their climb upwards.

1. All subjects who moved from retail to wholesale operated as street-level dealers for a considerable amount of time ranging from one to five years and averaged two to three years.

2. This time element allows retailers the opportunity to discover and develop a higher-level source.

    When you're in it long enough, you get to know more and more people. There are better sources out there. Sometimes you have to be a little bit lucky to find them, and sometimes they may come to you.

    I moved up the ladder in this business. I did my time in the trenches and sold eight balls and got to know people and moved up to a high level at a young age. If you're young, you get into it by selling at a lower level and saving your money, networking, and eventually making the right contacts.

3. Success at the retail level affords dealers the opportunity to establish a reputation as trustworthy and successful. This is often a precondition for higher-level sources being willing to do business with them.

    I was dealing from the age of 14 up to age 25—10 or 11 years. At least five years of that was selling to crackheads on the street. I was young when I started, but I was mature. You only have one or two chances to prove yourself, but that's all you need to establish a reputation. When you start buying more and more from the older guys, they're going to say, "He's a little soldier." They notice because you're making money for them. I didn't use drugs, I always paid my bills, and I had a good reputation. People were willing to deal with me. I eventually moved up and was able to get out of the downtown and away from the crackhead environment.

4. A psychological or cognitive change occurs when individuals realize they can and/or should progress through the ranks. Subjects begin to evaluate their situation and conclude that they have the ability to become a player. For most, there comes a time when they reassess their situation and recognize that the opportunity for advancement is present or can be found if one looks for it. They begin to think bigger than before.

You haven't made the money you want to make and you realize you can't do this street level forever. You realize you are making money for other people and they are getting rich. You start thinking, "Why not me? There is nothing stopping me from moving up with the big boys."

The mindset changes over time. First you start out and your only thought is to make some money. Then you do this for a while and you realize "I'm heading for a fall if I keep doing this." You see guys higher up and you say to yourself, "I can do that."

5. Dealers who contemplate moving from retail to wholesale drug trafficking begin to realize that they are becoming more deeply involved in a life of crime, committed to drug dealing as a living, and hooked on the accompanying lifestyle.

6. Important motivational components in the move from retail to wholesale are ambition, confidence, and greed. Offenders wish to build up their business and have developed confidence in their abilities to deal at a higher level.

I was ambitious and there were things that I wanted to have and this was an easy way.

A lot of guys don't mind selling small because they can deal with that kind of thing. They don't have it in them to go big. They don't have the organizational skills to organize it. And they are scared to do a lot of time, but the time goes with the money.

Most guys stay at the same level. They don't have the ambition. I know personally that some of my friends do it to survive and to get by, but when you go past survival, then that's when you start planning a bit better. Then you are doing it as a business and when you do it as a business, it's different. A lot of guys do it just to survive, to pay the rent, to get a car, to support a lifestyle. I was ambitious.

7. Moving into wholesale often requires sufficient funds to purchase large quantities of product. This means that the retailer must have the ability to earn a profit and the discipline to save money for the investment.

Gradually I put money aside and invested it and started to sell to other dealers.

I began by saving some money and investing it. I was able to buy a lot more cocaine at a much better price.

It takes a while to save up to get to the higher level. I moved up the drug ladder from selling an eight-ball, which is 3 1/2 grams or 1/8 of an ounce, to the point where I'm dealing 8 or 9 kilos a week on a regular basis.

Some street-level dealers move to a higher level by partnering with other retailers with whom they pool their funds in order to make large purchases.

Derek and I were a team and we put our money together to buy more and get a better deal on price. We started with $10,000 and built that up to $250,000 in investment. We built up the business and we were both sitting on fortunes.

We were all friends, we were all about the same age, and all six of us were Black. We just decided that we can all trust each other, so we pooled our money and went for it. We sat down and talked about it and decided to go ahead. We took it off the streets and out of the park and moved it indoors. One apartment turned into many apartments, and the business started to grow quickly.

8. The time spent in retailing exposes dealers to a network of street-level sellers whom they subsequently tap as distributors. Having connections allows them to recruit some of these dealers as customers.

Once I had developed this source, I approached some dealers I knew.

They knew who I was and that I could be trusted. There were four or five guys who were fairly intelligent guys and didn't use drugs. I approached them and did some PR work, and they realized that I was making some moves and looking for some guys to move the product. I had a great source and could sell it to them at a better price.

9. The most significant variable that precedes a move up the ladder is an increased concern with security, coupled with a heightened awareness of the dangers inherent in street-level dealing. Retailing is relatively overt behaviour, drug dealers are likely to become well known in the neighbourhood, and it is often a matter of time before the police make an arrest. By moving off the street, they reduce the number of people with whom they deal, become less visible, and insulate themselves from users and addicts.

When I was at street level, I didn't care about safety. I was young and foolish. As I got older and more concerned, I began to care about safety. I was lucky or good enough not to get caught and eventually move up.

At street level, you have a high profile and that is stupid and dumb. I wanted a low profile.

I did this from the age of 17. I stopped doing the small stuff and started providing for other dealers because the risk was too great on the street.

It was more a safety concern than a money motive. Once the safety is there, the money is going to come.

I moved up because I didn't want to be seen by police and the undercovers. I knew I could get caught if I stayed on the street.

The risk was big time on the street and that's where everybody gets caught. I decided I had to move up. My main concern was security.

When I sold in bars, I had maybe 50 clients. After I started selling to other dealers, I had only five clients—a lot safer and a lot less work.

Street-level dealers also witness the arrest of other retailers and begin to realize that they, too, may be heading for a fall. A close call underlines the threat:

In a couple of crack houses, I had to jump out windows and run for my life. The police are in the front room, yelling "Get on the floor," and my buddy is out the window and I'm right after him. That was a close call, and right after that I stopped for eight months. Later we talked about it and decided we had to move off the street into a higher level of dealing.

Retail-level dealers in this study are undeterred from crime because of a close call with the police. A close call does, however, make them more cautious and, in some cases, it is the key factor persuading them to seek safety in higher-level drug trafficking. Retailers are also motivated to move upwards in order to reduce the possibility of robbery, assault, injury, and death at the hands of other dealers, clients, and/or criminals. Several describe incidents that convinced them to become wholesalers:

After the violent robbery on the street, that is when I realized that I had to move to a different level. This is not for me. I've got the rest of my life to live. I can make more money with less risk.

There was competition among the (street-level) dealers over clients and there was a lot of jealousy. If you are in a certain area that people consider their own or if people are not making any money, there would be threats and fist fights and guns pointed at people. I decided to move out of that scene.

10. A final reason for leaving the street-level scene is to escape problems encountered with users and addicts. Dealing with users is a lot of work and trouble, and most dealers grow tired of being paged at all hours, having people come to their home, and with the problems associated with debt collection.

It was easier to deal with dealers than addicts—a lot easier and less work.

When I moved out of retailing and started dealing in large quantities, it made my wife happier because we moved to the country and no longer had junkies coming to the door at all hours of the night.

It seems reasonable to assume that retail drug traffickers who move into wholesale are likely to differ from dealers who remain on the street. Interview data suggest that those who move up the ladder have several characteristics that differentiate them from those who stay at the retail level: they are likely be more cautious and security conscious; have a more long-term commitment to crime; are more ambitious and propelled by greed; are motivated for profit and are less likely to be users; and have sufficient self-discipline to save money for investment purposes. Entrepreneurial, interpersonal, and organizational skills are also assets in knowing how to judge and interact with others and establish trust, loyalty, and security. Dealers who exhibit these qualities are more likely to attract suppliers and be offered opportunities to move into upper-level trafficking.

You run it just like a business. You need discipline and you have to be willing to work at it. It doesn't just fall in your lap. It takes time and perseverance and ambition. I worked at it and I was ambitious. Most guys on the street don't have what it takes to move upwards.

Always pay your bills on time. Always! That's like one of the major things. Personally, I know a lot of guys that aren't like that. To me, I always pay on time and the money is always correct.

Most street-level guys are users and that stops them from moving up.

A lot of [street-level] dealers don't know how to run a business. That's

why they never go anywhere. I hate people that are late. To me, if I'm late, then it shows that I have no respect for you. Most of these guys can't get out of bed in the morning. I hate people when their money is short. It happens all the time.

In summary, the main motive for moving from retail drug sales to wholesaling is to increase one's profit, minimize the risk of violence and arrest, and avoid the problems that users and addicts represent. Wholesaling is perceived as less trouble, less dangerous, and more remunerative.

Case Example: Street Smarts

This 30-year-old subject pled guilty to conspiracy to import and traffick in cocaine and received a 10-year sentence. His younger brother was also convicted and is serving an eight-year sentence. The subject has a Grade 12 diploma and completed a two-year program in a community college. He lives in a common-law relationship and has one child.

I operated in dealing from age 17 until I was 28 when I was arrested, so, like, 11 years. I've never used drugs. No, I don't even smoke cigarettes. I don't drink either. Not even marijuana. I don't believe in anything that alters my state. I don't even like coffee. I don't need to take any kind of substance.

It started like this. I was age 13 when I came to Canada from Guyana. Personally, I had all of these dreams about what Canada would be, and the reality and the dreams were slightly different. I came here with my mom and she has seven kids and she is by herself, you know. We grew up in a jungle by Dufferin and Lawrence/ Bathurst in the Lawrence area. They call it the jungle.

It's not a very nice area. It's, like, mostly Black and there is a lot of crime. She was working three jobs, and I felt guilty asking her for stuff. I felt guilty asking her for anything for school. Everything was expensive.

So, I remember when I was about 17 I knew someone who wanted to buy some crack, and I knew someone that sold it in my neighbourhood. This guy was selling it for 200 bucks and I talked him down to $150 and I went and sold it for $300. That grew into my business. It's basically supply and demand. I had a lot of friends and I would just get it from one guy and give it to the next and make some cash on the side.

I went to the library when I first started and they have these "How to" manuals, like how to start your own business. I learned that first you need to have a good business plan and you have to have cash flow projections and all this stuff. I just read about it 'cause I like business and I tried to stick to it.

The first thing you've got to do is think to yourself that it is a business and run it like a legal business. You buy low and sell high, and in between you try not to cross anyone and always have good-quality stuff and don't ever rob anyone, and every client is important. Everybody's money is important. It's just like running a business—exactly—except it's illegal. Just make money and that's it. You try to keep the customers happy and always pay your bills on time.

Street-level dealing is more dangerous. I had a bad experience when I started out. There is a building at Keele and Lawrence where people used to go for drugs. One night, myself and this guy, we were selling and this guy came in and we had our backs turned to him 'cause we were talking. We didn't see him at the time and he said that he had a gun and he said, "Give me your dope."

I didn't even want to argue. I said "Give it to him. Who cares?" So we give him our stuff and he says, "Don't turn around or I'll shoot." I just said "Duck!" and me and my friend hit the ground and he shot and it was a shotgun and he blew a hole in the ceiling! He just shot anyways. He tried to blow our heads off and he took off. He robbed us and I never got a look at him. I didn't want to see him. I didn't care. That was the last time that I ever went out on the street. I said to hell with that, these guys are crazy. They'll do anything for it.

I don't believe in any sort of violence at all. The way that I look at it, if you need a gun and you're selling drugs, then you shouldn't be selling to the people that you're selling to.

I never had any problems or conflicts—never—in all the years that I sold. I don't want to have a vendetta. If someone doesn't pay me, I just cut that person off and never work with them again. But violence is stupid.

I dealt at the street level for about a year—not long at all. Then I decided to move up. I said to myself that if I'm going to risk going to prison, then I'm going to play for big stakes.

I'm from Guyana, so I went back and met some people there. It is in South America, so it's easy to buy cocaine. These were people that I had known from before. I went to school with them and we were all little kids. I go back and some of these guys are big drug dealers. Basically, there is no economy there and that's it—that's their job. It's either that or you're a bum.

So, I met these guys again and we talked and I said listen, "If you can get it to me in Canada, then I can distribute it." It was simple for me to make contacts there and be trusted. I was one of them. And it was easy for them to see that I could be an outlet and a potential moneybag to them, especially if you're smart and you know what you're doing.

I thought that these guys from Guyana would have connections for getting the drugs into Canada, but if they don't, then I would work on it. I figured we could always work something out if we put our brains together.

When I went to Guyana, I didn't take any of my own money. I told them that I had no money and they had to trust me. I promised that I would pay them off as soon as I moved the product. I told them that if they didn't trust me, there wouldn't be a deal. Trust is the basis of any business deals, so it started with a front.

One thing that I emphasized was quality. Quality is important when there is a lot around. It's worth more than gold. You can always sell it. I always had good quality. They only sent me really good quality.

The first guy sent me five keys just on trust. He didn't even know me. This guy was loaded. He had a Lamborghini. We sat and we had a conversation and we went to dinner. I stayed there for three weeks. It was excellent.

I never brought any drugs into the country myself—never. I would never put myself at risk. I try to keep far away from the product as possible.

Most of the guys that I grew up with are drug dealers. Yeah, but they had moved all over the city. They are all over, but I keep in touch. I play basketball with these guys. I know a lot of people, period. These guys sell drugs, but they are not organized. If you can sit and talk to them and organize everything, then you can run them all. It is easy and everyone comes to you and everything ends up coming to you. You have to have the right background, though. You have to know the right people. It would be hard for someone who didn't have the contacts that I had coming from my neighbourhood. That's true. You have to be from the right background.

It was a business. That is how I looked at it. And it was importing and distributing. I was working both ends. Most of the work is networking. You have to be a very good people person. It's mostly talking to people on the phone. I'm on the phone, and the next line is beeping, and my pager is going off.

I would pay $3,000 Can. to purchase a kilo of cocaine in Guyana and sell if for 30 grand a kilo here or, if I wanted to, I could sell it by ounces and make 47 grand.

In terms of importing, we used numerous ways. We used couriers, we used a boat, we had people drive it across the border. We had baggage handlers and cleaners at the airport. Another thing that we did was ship it up in bottles of rum. We'd send somebody on vacation and they'd come back with a couple of duty-free bottles of rum that is sealed and filled with cocaine.

I had people whose job it was to find couriers because I didn't want to meet the couriers in case they get arrested.

We tried to find respectable couples like [a] father and wife, and send them on a vacation and have them body-pack the drugs into Canada. They'd get a paid vacation and $5,000 each. We used to crush it up into powder, flatten it out, and put it in body-packs on the rest of the body.

We had one courier team with the mother, father, daughter, another daughter, and a son, and they're from Nova Scotia and they used to go get us a lot of cocaine. The mother was, like, 70 years old—70 years old and White. We always look for White people 'cause it's easier at the airport. And the father, he was, like, 70 and a taxi driver, then the kids—they were, like, our age and we used the whole family. Each trip they each got five grand, plus their expenses. That's the going rate. Some of the family members did, like, five or six trips.

It's organized crime. It's not disorganized. It's very organized and I wanted it to be more organized. You don't just fall into it. You have to consciously work on networking. You have to work on everything. Networking is so important, especially when it comes to money laundering.

My use of people was clearly conscious. If I need a stewardess, then I would go to the airport, see them coming out, pick one that is good looking, doesn't appear too bright, and that looks like she can use a bit of company. I'd go spy them out at the airports, and I'd follow them and see where they go, and start talking to them in a grocery store or whatever. A lot of girls think with their hearts and if you get close to them, then they'll do whatever you want. Actually, one of the stewardesses testified against me. I wouldn't do it just for the hell

of it. Everything is for a reason. It all relates to this business and making money, so in that sense, it is clearly organized and premeditated.

I got introduced to some guys who were working as baggage handlers at the airport and I could have gotten major into that, but I didn't pursue that for the reason that the one guy was talking to me a lot. Too friendly. I just got bad vibes from him and I felt like it was a set-up, so I just broke off the talks. We went out to dinner a couple of times and there was just something about him. I just never called him back and I changed my phone number.

I changed cells and pagers every month anyways. Then I give certain people my new number, and then everybody that I didn't want to call never got my number.

We often had couriers get arrested at the airport, so I would just write that off as a loss. It doesn't matter, though, 'cause everything is a gain. I started with nothing, so anything is a gain. I started with squat. I'd say about one in every six couriers would get busted, either that or they chicken out and leave the stuff behind. I've just paid for their holiday and I'm pissed. I never did anything. Just chalk it up to a business expense.

I always kept my distance from the product. I had people who would make deliveries and pick up the money. My brother took care of deliveries. When a courier got through the airport, they came out, then he would be there and he would have some of his friends pick them up in a cab and put them in a hotel, and then take the cocaine off of them and give it to my brother.

One of the guys got caught with five keys and got two years. The most that anybody got was five years.

Social Control Theories and Family Relationships

Most of the men in this sample were raised in loving and supportive families with conventional values and a strong work ethic. Subjects report that their parents are still supportive despite their arrest on drug-trafficking charges. Strong family bonds are also characteristic of relationships with wives and children. The marital status of the sample include: married with children (27/70, 38.5%); common-law with children (11/70, 15.7%); married with no children (1/70, 1.4%); common-law with no children (8/70, 11.4%); divorced/separated (6/70, 8.5%); and unmarried (17/70, 24.2%). The majority of men in this study (47/70, 67.1%) were involved in a marital or common-law relationship at the time of their arrest, and most of them (38/47, 80.8%) also had children. Only three men describe having been raised in dysfunctional homes, were under the care of social welfare agencies, and/or spent time in juvenile custody.

A significant number of subjects report that they were motivated to provide for their families, and that most of the money earned in drug trafficking was spent on their wives, children, and parents. The most common purchase was a new or more luxurious home.

> I wanted money for a house. I spent most of it on my family. I took my wife and three children to Chile for three months, and found out later that the cops followed us the whole time.

> I just focused on money to support my family here and in Vietnam. I sent a lot of money to my parents and others back in Vietnam.

> The money allows for a lifestyle change. You acquire nice things for yourself and your family. You invest some. There are so many things you can spend money on. I did a lot of stuff with my family. I helped out my parents and my cousins.

> The police wanted to take my mom's house away because they said I had bought it for her from the proceeds of crime. Part of the reason I pled guilty was that they wouldn't take the roof from over her head. I agreed to plead, so they left that alone.

Most married dealers describe themselves as otherwise law-abiding people who take their family responsibilities seriously.

> I'm a total non-user. I'm not even much of a drinker, and I don't go to clubs or into the party scene. I have always had a family and spend most of my time with them. Take the kids to school ....
>
> We lived pretty normal. I'm not a big spender at the bars or clubs. When I was at home, I would go to bed at 10:00 and wake up the girls for breakfast. We take family holidays, but usually no more than once a year.

A 35-year-old smuggler complained that his drug-dealing business took him out of the country for weeks at a time. He missed his wife and three children, and was planning to quit dealing because of concerns for his family.

> The worst part was the time I would spend away from home. She wanted me home a lot more.

Another subject similarly describes how his drug dealing took him away from his family and expresses regret that he ignored them.

> I found that the business took me away from my family. I was so caught up and involved in making money. I found that

my values changed. I thought that I was providing for my family by making money and once you do that, you've done your job. They should be happy, but my family was not happy because I would spend less time with them. Ironically, I had a better quality of life before I had all this money.

Although some spouses knew of their husbands' illegal activities and/or were involved themselves, most wives and parents were shocked and upset at their arrest on charges of drug trafficking. Family members are typically unaware of their criminal involvement and assume that their husband's or son's wealth is due to his business success. Many offenders have no previous convictions and describe their families and parents as hard-working, law-abiding people. This makes the shock of their arrest even greater.

My mother was devastated. She's okay now 'cause she sees the light at the end of the tunnel, but at first, she was devastated at my arrest and my brother's arrest.

My family was shocked that I was arrested, but they became very supportive almost immediately. They came to Calgary to visit me four times during the year. They work in the restaurant and lumber business. My common-law left me after my arrest.

I have a very good family and they are very supportive. My wife and children visit me here as much as they can and are waiting for me to come home.

My parents are not too proud, but they still support me. My father-in-law is the most supportive and so is my wife. My wife's family are totally supportive. My parents tried to change me and

warned me, and now it's happened and I have to do my time and stay out of trouble when I get out.

A 50-year-old offender who spent eight years in prison in the United States for drug-trafficking offences disappointed his family when he was rearrested on a multimillion-dollar drug conspiracy.

My family was shocked, but they are still right behind me. I am very tight with my family. They never showed any anger toward me, but they were very upset—just numbed by it all. They thought it was unfair to put Dad back in jail. A little pissed at me because they have to go through it all over again, but very strong support. They are too good. I am not worth it. But I guess my 31 years of marriage counts for something. My wife and I are still a team.

Another repeat offender similarly describes his family's reaction to his second arrest for drug trafficking.

My family took it bad because I made a promise that I would not be away from them again. They know me as a father and that I worked hard. The embarrassment explaining it to my 14-year-old daughter was hard to bear. I've been married 15 years and my wife is still beside me. Another stupid mistake that I made and it has put me through hell. They know I love them and this is the last time.

Social Bonding Theory and Crime

It is clear from the interview data that most offenders feel great affection for their wives/

spouses and children and express deep pain, shame, and embarrassment for having disappointed them through their crimes. For some, the hardest part of doing time is being apart from their families and the embarrassment and suffering they caused to those close to them.

> When I look back, I ask myself, "What was I doing?" It was a rude awakening. I have paid a heavy price being away from my family for four years. That's a vacuum in my life that can't be replaced.

> I was hurting my family—them seeing me all messed up on dope and going to jail. I hurt my parents' feelings and made them worry.

Social control theory suggests that people who lack social bonds are more likely to be deviant because they have few of the social constraints that make others conform. Without emotional attachments, conventional values, involvements, and commitments to the social order, individuals have few stakes in conformity and are prone to drift into crime (Hirschi, 1969). Men who commit robbery, for example, tend to have little income, few job prospects, a lack of family bonds, and minimal involvement in conventional activities (Camp, 1968; Desroches, 2002 [1995]). They are undeterred by the threat of arrest and imprisonment because they view their life situation as one in which they have little to lose.

In the case of higher-level drug dealers, however, social bonds are intact and offenders have much to lose. Social control theory suggests that the possibility of severe sanctions should deter these men since most have wives, children, homes, jobs or businesses, and social standing in the community. Having social bonds means that they have stakes in conformity and risk a great deal through their involvement in crime. Despite having so much at stake, offenders rationally assessed the risks and concluded that arrest and conviction were unlikely outcomes. They may have had a lot to lose, but they were undeterred because they believed that the risk was outweighed by the financial gains.

Case Example: The Ecstasy Lab

The following interview was conducted with a 23-year-old student enrolled in my criminology course. He was on bail at the time of the interview and was later sentenced to two years in a federal penitentiary on charges related to the manufacture of Ecstasy in a drug laboratory.

> I come from a good family. My parents are both professionals and university educated. They were very upset when I was arrested. I called Dad from jail and Mom came up and bailed me out. They knew something was up because I had a cellphone and a car and didn't need money and I was planning to go to school in the summer. They were asking, "How are you going to pay for that?" They had no idea I was doing this.

> In Grade 12, I tried to print something off the Internet related to drugs, and they tried to talk to me about it. There were never any ultimatums, but they never knew for sure what I was up to and I never admitted anything.

> I was charged with possession of marijuana and methamphetamines for the purpose of trafficking, the production of MDA and MDMA (Ecstasy), conspiracy to export heroin, MDA, (MDMA), and possession of hash oil for the purpose of trafficking.

In total there were 17 charges and I pled guilty to six. The police seized 1 1/2 kilos of Ecstacy (E) and 2 1/2 kilos of ketomine (K) in my freezer.

I'm on bail and I have a curfew, and I can't talk to any of my co-conspirators. No cellphone, no illicit substances, and I have to live with my surety, who is a friend of the family. My curfew is from 11 at night to 6 in the morning, and that restricts me from going out.

I have always worked since I was in high school. I had various summer jobs related to computer programming to help support myself through university, but I have always been into the rave party scene and spent a lot of money. Being in school and being part of the rave scene meant that I was always short of money. Money was clearly one of my motives for starting up a drug lab.

There are a total of nine persons charged, including me, but I'm considered the ringleader. Jane is 23 and has been a heroin addict for three years. She was arrested in California and got off for probation in the U.S. She immediately came back to Canada. She sold ketamine and Ecstasy and would do errands for us and courier stuff around Ontario. Alice is a student who was in school in New Zealand and was called back and interrogated and gave a lengthy statement. She was keen to get money because she was partying a lot—like me, being in school and living on a fixed budget and wanting to party. You start to look for another source of money and that is what she was doing. The other co-accused are guys who ranged from 17 to 23 years and most sold drugs at raves.

They're all charged with conspiracy to traffic. I would go to parties and I would give them drugs and they would sell them for me. They are all from different cities and most don't know one another. They would be waiting for me to get there and they would have people lined up and I would turn over 200 or 300 Es to each of them.

Basically, there were three main players: Paul, Wilfred, and myself. Wilfred is an American, 25 years old, and he has some university education. He was heavy into manufacturing a few years before I met him, and was arrested in 1995. I heard from one of his friends that he turned someone over, but I could never find out for certain. Wilfred only wanted to do stuff in Canada, although he lived in the U.S.

I met Wilfred on the Internet on the Web site: hive.lycaeum.org, which is called "The Hive." He had material on a bulletin board. It's a high-traffic site and members discuss everything related to drug manufacturing. Wilfred started asking me vague, guarded questions through the Internet, and I always answered, and we started talking more and more. Most of the communication between Wilfred and I was about technical details, and it was all encrypted so the police have none of it.

We finally decided to meet face-to-face at a party. He seemed to have a lot of money and was driving a Porche. His family was well off and his father owned a manufacturing company and his mother was a lawyer. He sold drugs for a living. He told me he hadn't worked for five years.

Wilfred was different. He was not a user. He enjoyed the hobby of it, but he was pretty focused on getting rich. While I was thinking about chemistry stuff, he was thinking about acquisitions, and together we were dangerous. Wilfred was trying to manufacture E and so was I, but he had a lot of money and more initiative. We hooked up and he began to fund my work.

Wilfred had an import export/ licence and bought ketamine from a Chinese company. He suggested I try to sell it, and that's how I met Paul. I was at a rave and somebody told me Paul was interested in purchasing large amounts of K. I had an endless source from Wilfred and I was looking for someone who could sell it for me and for new locations. Paul is very good at selling stuff and managing money. He wants to be a big criminal figure. When I started, it was hard to sell K, but after Paul got a hold of it, it took off.

Paul doesn't do any drugs and has no patience for people who do. He is a total businessman and he's taking marketing economics at university. He's a promoter and organizes raves, which is a big entrepreneural undertaking. The ketamine was so cheap and cost us 40¢ a gram and we sold a half-gram vial for $15 to $40. Paul was a stickler for keeping the price high even though we got it cheap. Some drugs make more money, and the dealers will work harder to sell them because they make more profit.

Paul and Wilfred never met and didn't want to. All three of us needed each other. Wilfred was so paranoid about selling that he was happy to let us do that. It was well organized and it was so easy to get so big.

Paul has a previous conviction for aggravated assault for stabbing someone when he was drunk. He had a bad alcohol problem and went to jail and AA and hasn't had a drink since. He was sentenced to 18 months and did six. He is 22 and is almost finished his university degree.

Paul keeps a profile as a promoter rather than as a drug dealer. He learned pretty quickly that he has to be careful because both he and his runners got robbed. He works with a Chinese girl and they keep below the radar. He had one main guy and there is one other guy he uses if the main guy gets tired or too lazy.

Paul started dealing with the bikers, and he was all thrilled when it started because they were buying a lot of K from him and promising to buy a lot more. Then it got serious and it was all about money, and Paul got the shit kicked out of him. Now he's scared to death of them. He's in his twenties and the bikers are all 40 and older. They really wanted to find out where he was getting his Ecstasy.

The rave scene in Toronto is big and there are thousands of people every weekend who buy drugs to party. The whole culture is very organized. I remember being in the car with him and it was like stock market deals with him on the phone, buying thousands of these and thousands of this. He emptied out a bag of cellphones and told me to take a few, so I did. He changed them constantly.

Paul would have crews who sold drugs for him. They would get the pills on consignment and two or three runners would work the line outside the parties. They go up and down the line and sell drugs. If you're at one of these parties, you will get asked if you want to buy drugs.

I've been interested in drugs from a young age. I had an Internet connection from Grade 10. I can't really account for the interest in drugs. I also had an interest in science and got first prize in science at school every year. I thought the drug scene cool and E was hot, and I followed it on the Internet and read about people making it, and it sounded challenging.

At university, I went through the library and took chemistry courses. I tried making it and ran out of money and gave it up for a while. Then I met a guy who was about 40 and he wanted to make stuff and didn't have much luck. He had lab equipment and he got into trouble and gave me the rest of his equipment to make chemicals. Around this time, the Hive started up and it has a bulletin board and you can post messages under topic headings.

This was the start of my third year of university. It took about eight months trying on and off to make a miniscule drop of Ecstasy. I would stop from time to time out of frustration and for exams and to party. It was a hobby and a challenge and I tried to make it four or five different ways. A lot of people on the Hive are hobby oriented, and they would try in different ways and get status on line if you can come up with a new way.

I partied a lot and had student loans, and I was still working and getting good money, but needed more. I was always broke at the end of the year. I was desperate at one point to make it pay off because I had blown a lot of my student loan on it. It started to pay off once I was able to make slightly larger quantities. Once I was up to an ounce a week—that was worth $1,500—but I would spend it quickly. I would rent a car to go to parties and blow $600 each weekend.

I didn't have a serious money motive until I hooked with up with Wilfred and Paul. It was a hobby and I wanted to be the guy with good drugs. It's a status thing in the rave culture. About a year before my arrest, the money really started pouring in.

It's safer posting on the Hive than e-mailing people with your questions. The e-mail is not as anonymous and if they have it on their computer and if they get in trouble, you can be in trouble. It may be encrypted, but if they de-encrypt it, then you can be in trouble. You are more likely to get an answer to a question if you post it than if you e-mail someone.

I started off making small quantities and used the sub-basement at residence. You can't go directly from one chemical to the drugs. You make the intermediate or precursor chemical, and then make the final product. It's a two-step thing. I had a lot of failures initially. The first time I made it, it was less than a gram.

The Hive Web site has a lot of detail, and has done more for making that stuff accessible than anything else. You can spend weeks doing something and not be able to find out why it doesn't work and spend several thousand dollars. All the talk on the Net was 100-gram quantities and most wouldn't talk about doing that much. It takes a lot of perseverance to learn how to make large quantities. It's time consuming, dangerous, and expensive, and requires tearing up and starting over again and again and being up for periods of 48 hours at a time.

I've had people come into the rooms where I was doing this and after four hours, they would get sick and would have to go to the hospital. Once I found that after working with cyanide, my fingertips went numb. One time a couple of years ago, I had a bad rash, which I believe was mercury poisoning. Another time, I got a massive head rush and stumbled out of the lab and passed out. Using sulphuric acid is dangerous. I would work with big drums of chemicals and try to pour them by myself, and sometimes they spill out.

I wanted to produce the stuff in large scale, but the most common method cannot be scaled up. You can't go above 300 grams because you can't keep a 50-litre bucket cool enough. The larger the buckets, the more difficult to cool and produce the product. There is a lot of little things that you need to do right. Is the apparatus air-tight? Is there water on the glass? If you don't stir something enough, it can burn up, or if you stir too much, you have another problem. I would get up for school and then be up all night and go to parties, and then try to make it between all of this. I was a heavy methamphetamine user and I would forget things. Once I fell asleep and burnt $20,000 worth of product—that's the wholesale price.

The knowledge is not that sophisticated because anyone can learn it if they can stick to a project long enough. It's more complicated than

photography and a lot of university students are interested because it's academically challenging. The appeal is there.

Buying the chemicals was a problem. It was unusual to buy these chemicals and the sales clerk asked what I was using it for. It was sassafras oil and mostly used as a precursor to MDA. I gave him some bullshit answer and paid cash. Later on, the companies who sell the chemicals were getting harassed by the RCMP and now they want information from you and names and a business number.

The idea was to use the money from K to get the lab up and running and do a large-scale production of E. Wilfred was providing the K and helping me obtain chemicals and equipment. He was getting containers of drugs sent over from China. I was gearing up to do 50 drum batches and trying to work out how to do it with two or three tanks and transfer pumps.

I rented a warehouse with over 3,000 square feet of space and 20-foot ceilings. You could fit a tractor trailer in there. The place cost me $1,500 a month rent, plus heating, and I paid cash for that. It turned out to be a bad idea because it smelled and I was coming and going early hours. I was driving a brand new car and it looked fishy. It looked like little was going on. The landlady was worried because the people before had left a lot of waste.

The problem in going big is that it takes a lot longer than you think. The final product is smelly and you're working with mercury. Mercury chloride is extremely toxic and I would use it in small amounts. Storing the chemicals was a problem over time.

Once I figured out how to make greater quantities of Ecstasy, it was: "Holy shit, I can do it!" A lot of very small variables have to be just right, but after you get it right, it's really easy. Now the money was flowing in. This was maybe a year before my arrest.

On the weekend, I would go to a party and take 30 to 50 Es and would walk out with $2,000 or $3,000 and see Paul on Monday, and he would give me $10,000 or $20,000. I also had some friends who sold it and I would get money from them. I kept $5,000 a week for spending, and I gave Wilfred $20,000 a week for investment.

I would estimate that between the three of us, we were making $50,000 a week. Paul took $10,000 for himself and Wilfred and I would split the rest after expenses.

With E, 1 kilo will make 10,000 pills and may end up with 5,000 to 7,500 people. The average purchase is usually one or two pills. A kilo of heroin might produce 2,500 hits. E has greater potential for profit. The marketing and distribution of E is very different. E has dropped in price. It used to be $30 or $35, and last year $25 to $30, and now it's $15 to $20 per tablet to buy it at a party.

I was giving as much money to Wilfred as possible because the places in China wanted half or more up front before they would produce the chemicals. We were preparing to go big time. Once I learned to make it at a large scale and could do it fairly efficiently, I was keen to step up.

My motive was totally greed at that point. I was still involved in the party scene and saw this as a contribution to the whole scene. You don't feel at all that you are having any detrimental effect on anyone. Wilfred was keen to keep going and we were gearing up to make more and move up to the next level. If we had not been caught, I was going into this full-time. I was just about to say screw school. I actually said that I wanted to be a career criminal to a friend of mine over the telephone: "This is my calling." Thankfully, this was not on the wiretaps.

After I had decided I was going to be serious about it and be a criminal, I stopped being so flamboyant. Before, I tried to keep it like I did as a hobby because school and work was the focus. Then when the money began to come in, I asked myself: "Why am I still thinking of this as a hobby? Why not focus and do it right?" I wanted to get as big as I could for a short period and then get out.

When I started making money, I was still a student buying beans and here I have $10,000 on my desk. It was the money that changed me. I started thinking: "Why am I in school when I can do it later?" The period of time for the transition was quick. All of a sudden, you have huge amounts of money. You have this paradigm of looking at the world and then it changes completely. It wasn't gradual—it was sudden.

Wilfred had purchased a pill press and a granulator and a mixer for making pills. That's $50,000 in equipment. We were buying mixers, fillers like starch to keep the powder together, lubricants, and dyes. It's all very expensive and it attracts attention. The companies co-operate with the police.

If you want your own trademark, you need somebody to make the dye that gives the pill its own form like a butterfly shape. When I made it, it was in powder form. A pill press machine will spit out thousands of pills a minute, so you need a lot of substance to operate it. These are big machines and they weigh a ton and take up a large space in a room.

Customers trust pills more than powder. It's harder to fake a good pill and certain logos can be used for marketing. People know from one week to the next that it is the same because of the butterfly. They don't have to know the dealer or look for the same dealer from rave to rave. There are not that many different kinds of E around, and people learn quickly what is good.

Different pills don't necessarily come from different producers. To change the shape of the pill, it is just a matter of screwing in another die. Last year, a JB pill arrived on the scene. JB stands for Jim Bean. Pills are sometimes called beans, so Jim Beans. There are also CKs (Calvin Kleins) and RNs (Rough Necks).

My thing was manufacturing, Paul was the distributor, and Wilfred provided the startup costs, equipment, and the materials. Each of us needed one another.

My last cellphone bill was so up and down. Looking at the time of the calls, I was going all the time. I was looking at properties to buy, cars, stainless steel tanks, capsule machines ....

The rave scene is still fairly young and the laws are not strictly enforced. Alice was caught at a rave and they confiscated 50 pills. The security guard walked by and grabbed them out of her hands. They never charge people and they take it and throw it in the bucket. They occasionally search people at the door. I've had them find drugs on me, and they just take it and they may even let you through and go in.

I was caught for trafficking at a rave, and I was handing over some pills and there was a security guard nearby, and he grabbed the other guy and I took off. I started running and other security guards caught me, and they pushed me out the door and didn't take the drugs. I had $2,000 or $3,000 worth of stuff. I just went to another party, so the evening turned out okay.

There is not much concern about the police. There is an occasional arrest, but there are thousands of people there and a lot of exchanges, so it is not high risk. There is concern, but not an atmosphere of paranoia.

Rave parties can get very large. They vary in size from a few hundred to 10,000 or more. There is one every week. Raves have some really young people and the average age is probably 18 or 19. You get a high school and university crowd. Not many people in their thirties and forties, but you do get them. But there are clubs where 20 to 30 years is the range. Others may have 15 to 20 as the range.

Everything is arranged and distributed on the weekend. There are message boards on the Net, which are very popular. The hullaboloo board gets several hundred posts a day. There are different scenes and styles of music. One is mainstream house techno music. Break beads is a type of music, and jungle music, house, techno, drum and base, trance, hard core, happy hard core, bootie house, and other styles of music. Different parties will focus on different styles of music and attract a different crowd and age group. Small brochures are handed out as you leave a party, or you can pick them up at stores that sell clothes and CDs.

People who take E often use pacificers—baby soothers—because one of the effects of the drug is that it makes you chew your tongue. Before I was doing it so much that my tongue had toughened up. They give away suckers at these parties for the same reason. I went to the dentist and he said my teeth are worn down. The drug makes you grind your teeth. If you're really high, your jaw shakes and your mouth is sore the next day. A lot of people will wear athletic teeth protectors. I find that soothers just make my mouth more sore. Some people have tongue piercing and it irritates your mouth even more. It's nothing serious, but a minor annoyance the next day. Eventually your tongue toughens up.

I would say that 19 out of 20 people at these parties are using drugs, either smoking pot or taking Ecstasy. There is a certain stigma attached to Crystal and K because on K you sit there and don't interact and with Crystal you become antisocial, kind of like a drunk at a bar. There is no stigma attached to Ecstasy because on Ecstasy you are very social and empathetic—[it] makes you nice. That is the drug of choice and most will be doing that. Crystal refers to methaphetamine. There is more of a demand for E, and people with a good supply have a lot of status.

The DJs are listed on the brochures for raves. They have on-line information. There is one at the Molson Centre in Montreal and they expect 15,000 people to attend. They have huge video screens up in the centre with feeds from other parties. One brochure has five parties all in one night and connects Toronto, Atlanta, Seattle, Calgary, and Montreal. In Toronto, it was held at the Better Living Centre and had 12,000 people. The *Toronto Sun* called it a drugfest on city property.

I spent two nights in custody after my arrest and got bail with a $65,000 surety. Paul was picked up a month and a half later, but he had laid low for that time. Wilfred was arrested crossing the border into the U.S. with drugs in his possession and may get 10 to 15 years without parole.

The RCMP thought I was crossing the border because my friend Alice had called me to come down to the U.S. and I agreed. I went to Windsor and gave Wilfred the weekly 400 grams of MDA and money, but the police arrested him crossing the border. I drove around Windsor in case somebody was following us, but they still were able to keep a tail. I remember driving home and there was a car behind me the whole way. I was arrested the next day. I was so glad that I didn't cross the border.

When I got into this, I had no idea how the police worked. The landlady asked me if I was in trouble with the police and told me about two police officers watching some units down below. I was so stupid I didn't realize they were watching me. I should have clued in, but I thought they would be after much bigger fish. I didn't want to believe because I wanted the money, and it was so nice to have a car and the cash.

I didn't go back to the warehouse for two weeks after she said that. The rental agent got me to switch my car because the police asked them to. I should have caught on to that.

If I had told Wilfred about what the landlady said about the police watching the other unit, he would have clued in right away because he's had experience with the police. I didn't tell him because I didn't want to stop. I just stayed low for a couple of weeks and hoped it would blow over. I don't know what I was thinking—it was so stupid.

I told Paul, but he has had no experience with drug investigations. Now he is very paranoid. He was concerned, but didn't suggest I stop. Paul used to call me up and say, "I need one" and I knew he meant 1 kilo. Or he would say, "I have 10 for you" and it was $10,000. I did this without much awareness of police. It sounds so dumb because I wasn't trying to be subversive. I would have seen the surveillance easily if I had been aware.

The police were alerted through one of the lab companies I dealt with. I thought that because they only sold used lab equipment, they wouldn't be so concerned about it. They were totally suspicious and it was obvious because they asked where my lab was located and I gave them a bullshit answer. And he wanted to take it to my car, probably to get my licence plate number. I didn't give them my real name the first time, but later I took back this vacuum pump that didn't work and had to give my name

to get a refund. Apparently there were traces of MDMA on it. They made me wait for a while and gave the police time to follow me. After that I was under pretty tight surveillance. They even installed cameras in my warehouse without me realizing it.

One chemical firm was happy to sell me large quantities of chemicals and they knew what I was doing. I would have my gloves on and they were black and had burn marks, and the guy would say: "Nice gloves. Ha, ha."

There is not much on the Internet that would have warned me about the police or how lab companies collaborate with them. I had no idea that they would have wiretaps or videos. I did think about it, but just didn't want to think about it too much. I didn't think I was that exposed and figured that if I shut down for a while, it would go away. I had no idea how a drug company might proceed if they were suspicious. I guess I didn't want to believe that there is serious risk in doing this.

Morality and Techniques of Neutralization

"I justified it so that it was okay in my heart."
—45-year-old drug trafficker

Sykes and Matza's social control theory (1957) argues that people who commit deviant acts use a variety of justifications or techniques of neutralization that release them from the constraints of internalized values. Most drug traffickers suscribe to conventional value systems and realize that community values condemn drug dealing as morally wrong. Society is ambivalent toward the use of illicit drugs, however, and offenders use these conflicting views as a means of diminishing guilt, responsibility, and the seriousness of the offence. Although subjects regret being caught and incarcerated, few view their conduct as reprehensible or express remorse over their actions. On the contrary, most seem proud of their criminal accomplishments.

The fact that so many legitimate people demand, purchase, and consume drugs is cited by dealers as evidence that the laws are wrong. Most make the argument that tobacco and alcohol are legal despite the widespread harm caused by these substances, and this argument is used to condemn drug prohibitions and the politicians and public who support repressive and punitive policies. Typical comments by dealers include:

You know it's prohibited, but it's something so many people do. You don't really think it's so terrible.

A lot of respectable people use drugs recreationally. Not all users are addicts.

I justified it through the hypocrisy in society. The CEO of some alcohol corporation gets great status despite drunk driving deaths. They are not blamed for it and they even receive big pay bonuses if the business does well.

I always tended to look at it as alcohol during Prohibition, and now it's okay to drink alcohol and now its legal. Really strange ideas in defining what is illegal and what isn't. It throws your views off.

Drugs are not used just by the lower class. Many middle-class and well-to-do people use them. There is more

harm done by alcohol and cigarettes, yet they're legal.

I have no trouble justifying it. It's the same as Prohibition in [the] U.S. The government didn't learn from that. History repeats itself.

If you go through history and pull the skeletons out the closet, you'll find that the shakers and movers have all crossed the line to make their millions. How do you think the Bronfmans, the Seagrams, the Reichmans, and the Kennedys got rich?

Drug traffickers normalize their actions by viewing themselves not as criminals but as businessmen who compete in a market to sell a commodity that law-abiding people desire. They refer to their illegal activity as a business and the illicit drugs as a "commodity," "product," or "unit."

I think it got to the point that I looked at it as a business. You just think of it as a commodity and not a drug. The way I looked at it, I could have been selling paper napkins. It was just a product and all I cared about were the profit margins.

It was all very civil and organized and it was a business and kept very professional, and there was lots of money to be made. Everybody I dealt with treated it as a business.

I see it as a business just like any other business—totally. I don't have any moral qualms about it either. To me, it's no different than selling alcohol. The CEO of Seagrams doesn't get blamed for spousal abuse or drunk drivers killing people on the road. I'm sure he doesn't go home at night and feel guilty for all those people who abuse alcohol. To him, it's a job and a business, and he's just providing for his family.

I see the drug business the same way I look at alcohol. I'm just supporting myself and my family. Why should I go to prison for doing the same thing as distillers do? Sure it's illegal, but that is hypocritical.

Another common technique is to deny or diminish responsibility for one's actions. Even when dealers admit that drugs cause harm, they shift responsibility to the user.

I never forced anybody to use drugs. People have choices and options. People make the wrong choices all the time. It's not my fault if they choose to use drugs.

I never forced this on anyone and never manufactured any victims. It's just like people using barbiturates, red meat, sleeping pills, etc.

They can say it's bad, but people will do drugs anyway. I'm not turning people on. They are going to do it anyway, so why not provide it? If not me, then somebody else will do it. Why shouldn't I benefit from it?

As far as drugs go, everybody has a choice. You don't have to take it. Cocaine is a serious drug. Anybody who chooses to do it, it's their choice and they know what they're doing.
As for users who abuse cocaine, everyone makes their own choices and I don't see that I'm responsible for another person's choices.

There are lots of people who use drugs to get high and have a good time. Am I responsible for those people who abuse drugs? I don't think so.

A dealer who routinely used young girls to courier drugs into Canada through airport Customs felt no guilt when his couriers were arrested and sent to jail.

I don't care basically 'cause they [couriers] are doing it for the same reason that I am—greed. Most of them don't have a substance abuse problem or anything. They are just greedy. They want to make some fast and easy money and that's why they do it. I had people going five, six times. Come on, that's greed. That never bothered me if they got caught. They make their own choices. I don't force them to go. They know the risk.

Other dealers diminish responsibility by shifting the blame onto society for the conditions that give rise to drug abuse.

I don't think I'm a bad guy. There is so much wrong in society. Drug abuse is tied into poverty, racism, family violence. I fail to see how I can be held responsible for all of that.

Other societal problems account for drug abuse. I didn't cause family abuse or poverty.

Some dealers will also deny or diminish the harm caused by their behaviour by arguing that they sold drugs to an upscale clientele who did not abuse the product, or by emphasizing that they did not sell to young people or children.

I've never sold drugs to kids or pregnant women.

Morally, I don't think drugs are wrong. I use them myself in moderation. I'm not selling to children.

I'm a proud person and I have family values, but when it comes to drugs, I believe that adults should be able to make their own choices. I'm against pushing to kids. I did it for the profit, but I wouldn't go that far and push drugs on kids.

I justified selling cocaine by the market I had. There were no kids buying it. My market included all professional people who knew what they were doing. They were all age 35 to 55 and earned $100,000 to $200,000 a year.

Dealers who sold marijuana or hashish argue strongly that this particular drug causes little or no harm. Some even cite medicinal benefits to this herb. Other dealers will argue that cocaine or heroin are not harmful if used recreationally and in moderation. Upper-level traffickers also point to the non-violent nature of the business as a way of diminishing the seriousness of their crimes.

I ran my business totally non-violent and I took pride in that fact.

I tried to justify what I did and thought cocaine was okay because it's a recreational sport.

I justify and rationalize it's okay because lots of people are doing it and nobody is getting hurt.

Dealers report that they tried not to think of the wrongfulness of their actions or the harm that drugs might cause to users and others. This was facilitated by the fact that they primarily sold to other dealers and did not observe the suffering of users or the victims of drug-induced crime. By keeping a distance from the victims of drug abuse, higher-level dealers avoid seeing the damage their product is causing.

You're not in the alleys or gutters and seeing the harm that it does do.

You don't think of it hurting anybody. You don't see any of the suffering that might come from it.

I put up a wall psychologically between myself and the product and the harm done.

I closed my eyes to the crime and made $50,000 and did it so easily, so why not close my eyes again and make another $50,000? Soon you close your eyes all the time.

It's easy to deal at that level because you insulate yourself from the harm. I was not exposed to junkies or street dealing and I never thought of the destruction it causes. It was a business and it worked out well, and you become elastic with your morals if there is lots of money to be made.

Several dealers refused to think about the harmful effects of their actions.

I knew what I was doing was illegal and I put a wall up and tried to think of it more as a business. I tried not to think of myself as a drug dealer, but I knew that behind the wall, I was a dealer.

I was thinking of the money and not of the harm. It's easy to not think about it or to rationalize.

Finally, some dealers rationalized their conduct by arguing that their behaviour was justified because they were supporting their families. This was not a common argument since most dealers had sufficient employment and/or business opportunities to earn money and did not have to rely on crime to make a living.

The Ego and Self-Concept of Drug Traffickers

The majority of subjects in this study have inflated egos due to the wealth, status, power, and sense of accomplishment that comes with being a successful dealer. The following discussion differentiates between dealers with lenghty criminal backgrounds and those who have extensive work and business experience. Although the self-concepts of "criminal" drug traffickers and "businessmen" dealers are similar, there are significant differences.

The Criminal Drug Dealer

Dealers who have lengthy criminal backgrounds tend to associate with other criminals, have often done time in prison, and view themselves as career criminals. These men are likely to be known as successful dealers within their criminal milieu and have high status because of their success. They are motivated in part by the feeling of self-importance that develops from being a major player in this environment. The drug-dealing role includes conspicuous spending on clothing, cars, women, and the "club scene." A 28-year-old offender describes his lifestyle:

Most Black people know I'm a drug dealer without even knowing me personally—without even knowing my name. You can look at me and tell. I would meet girls and they would know right off the bat—"You're a drug dealer"—'cause of my lifestyle. You're 20-something years old, you've got your own house, different cars, money to burn. If you were working honestly

for that money, then you wouldn't have money to burn unless you're, like, a sports star or a rock-and-roll star. There is no way that you can have a nine-to-five job and go out and have money to burn. Going out and treating the whole club to drinks and shit like that—it's impossible. You'd have a bit more respect for your money, so they know. I can tell when a guy is selling.

Dealers with extensive criminal backgrounds are more likely to report living and enjoying a hedonistic lifestyle that includes leisure as opposed to work, and conspicuous and lavish spending on alcohol, drugs, sex, and partying.

It is quite easy to build an ego in this business. When you have money, you can get almost anything you want.

The lifestyle that goes with it is great. I walk into a bar and I'm Hollywood. I would be treated like I was a god. Everyone wants to be your friend.

I've been there in the bars and everybody knows you, and we would go to certain places and we had our own parking places in the front. The owners know who is spending the money. We would get out of our cars and walk past everybody. You never wait in line. I was flamboyant in the early days. This is when I was making the transition.

Offenders know that maintaining a flashy lifestyle brings unwanted attention, but they nonetheless enjoy the celebrity status and ego gratification. A number of older dealers lived an extravagant party lifestyle in their early years of dealing and describe it as a stage they went through. They eventually tired of it and developed a lower profile for security reasons.

You have to get that out of your system if you want to last in this game. But it's hard to give up because it's a celebrity lifestyle, going to the clubs. There is status in making so much money. I command respect when I go into a bar because I'm a high roller. The owner knows who spends the money and "Here he comes." Sends over his best-looking waitress.

Dealers also build an ego on their connections in the drug world since status relates to one's associates. A career criminal boasts:

I was well connected and I had some important people behind me. You travel in certain crowds and people know you are not a person to be messed with.

In prison, dealers occupy the higher echelons within the inmate subculture.

I find that I get a lot of respect from guys in prison. I get great respect because of my crime, because it's such a big money maker. I was the source.

Most criminal dealers view themselves as intelligent and have an inflated ego because of their success in taking risks, operating a successful drug business, making money, outsmarting the police, and avoiding arrest.

I glamorized the lifestyle and I had a glamorous image of myself. I had the money and the women and the world was my oyster. I could do all that I wanted.

It's a euphoric feeling to make $50,000 on a deal. It's a rush and an ego boost. Fuck, I'm good. It's very satisfying and you feel so smug. You look out and see all those schmoes stuck in traffic, and you begin to think you're so much smarter than them.

A number of subjects report that their ego grew extraordinarily large during their drug-trafficking years.

In terms of your ego, it gives you a sense of power. You feel that you're untouchable because of the money. You become arrogant and it's something you can't control. You're all that matters. You can buy anything you want. It affects your character.

At the time I was doing it, I was arrogant and very confident and smug—vain. I was on top of the world. I was the king and I could do anything anytime to anyone I wanted, and there was nothing anyone could do about it. I am a very humble person today.

For some dealers, their extravagant spending brought unwanted attention and their overblown egos made them underestimate the police.

You can get very cocky in this game. You feel invincible because you are in power. You get praise and have beautiful girlfriends, and it's a powerful feeling. People notice and talk about you. That all leads to being busted.

You get an ego from getting away with it for so long. You are supposed to go undetected and not bring attention to yourself. But the way I looked at it, it's one thing for people to think something about you, but different for them to know what you are up to.

Case Example: International Drug Smuggler

From February 19–23, 2001, the *National Post* ran the following advertisement in its "Employment Wanted" section of the classifieds.

Former Marijuana Smuggler

Having successfully completed a ten-year sentence, incident-free, for importing 75 tons of marijuana into the United States, I am now seeking a legal and legitimate means to support myself and my family.

Business Experience: Owned and operated a successful fishing business—multi-vessel, one airplane, one island and processing facility. Simultaneously owned and operated a fleet of tractor-trailer trucks conducting business in the western United States. During this time I also co-owned and participated in the executive level management of 120 people worldwide in a successful pot smuggling venture with revenues in excess of U.S. $100 million annually. I took responsibility for my own actions, and received a ten-year sentence in the United States while others walked free for their co-operation.

Attributes: I am an expert in all levels of security; I have extensive computer skills, am personable, outgoing, well educated, reliable, clean, and sober. I have spoken in schools to thousands of kids and parent groups over the past ten years on "the consequences of choice," and received public recognition from the RCMP for community service. I am well travelled and speak English, French, and Spanish. References available from friends, family, the U.S. District Attorney, etc.

Please direct replies to

Box 375, *National Post*, Classified

The advertisement attracted the attention of a reporter and the story became front-page news for two consecutive days. The author of the ad, Mr. John Davies [fictitious name

used], age 52, allowed himself to be publicly identified in the media and later set up a Web page inviting comments and questions. Mr. John Davies reportedly received hundreds of media calls from as far away as England and New Zealand. He placed the advertisement because he had recently finished serving a 10-year prison term in the U.S. and was looking for employment at an executive level in a legitimate business.

Mr. Davies's Web site describes his childhood in Newfoundland, including physical and sexual abuse in the Catholic public school he attended. It also documents his early involvement in marijuana smuggling between Canada and Jamaica, his "carefree" lifestyle, his drug abuse and resulting health problems, and his two convictions and prison sentences of 19 months in the 1970s and 10 years in the early 1990s.

Mr. Davies fits into the "criminal trafficker" category in this study because he was involved in organized crime from an early age, he has no employment history, has served two prison terms, and his friends and associates are primarily criminals.

An analysis of Mr. Davies's Web site and his advertisement reveals attitudes and beliefs that are typical of higher-level drug traffickers. He does not view his behaviour as morally wrong and strongly supports the legalization of marijuana. He claims that "I took responsibility for my own actions, and received a ten-year sentence in the United States while others walked free for their co-operation." His boast that he did not inform on others is consistent with major values in the inmate/criminal code.

Mr. Davies also views himself as a businessman who provided a product to his clients. His ego is apparent in his quest for employment at an executive level within a legitimate business. His advertisement emphasizes the size, financial importance, and international scope of his drug-dealing enterprise:

Owned and operated a successful fishing business—multi-vessel, one airplane, one island and processing facility. Simultaneously owned and operated a fleet of tractor-trailer trucks conducting business in the western United States. During this time, I also co-owned and participated in the executive level management of 120 people worldwide in a successful pot smuggling venture with revenues in excess of U.S. $100 million annually.

Mr. Davies claims to be well educated and to be an expert in "all levels of security." These claims are not substantiated in the Web page or advertisement, and it appears that he has little formal education or professional qualifications. His expertise appears to be based solely on his involvement in illegitimate enterprises, which began when he was 22 years old. Mr. Davies also reveals that he abused drugs throughout his whole life and suffered from a serious addiction to cocaine. Apart from his marijuana-smuggling business, Mr. Davies does not present any characteristics that would qualify him for an executive-level position in a legitimate firm. He has no business degree, no university education, no employment history, no references from former employers, and no accomplishments in the business world. He believes, however, that he has functioned as a chief executive in managing 120 employees, a fishing boat, and a trucking fleet used in his marijuana-smuggling operation. One of the interviews with Mr. Davies is entitled "I can do anything an MBA can."

Like many higher-level dealers in this study, Mr. Davies views success in the drug business as equivalent to success in the legitimate business world and ignores the significant differences. For instance, there is much less competition in the drug world and profit margins are incredibly high. Many of the dealers in this study operated legitimate businesses with some degree of success.

None of them made millions of dollars, however, and most preferred the easy profits from drug trafficking. Many also report that their legitimate businesses lost money. Mr. Davies similarly reports his failed attempts at legitimate enterprise: "From time to time I attempted to become involved in legal affairs and invariably they ended in a heap of self-sabotage .... "

Mr. Davies's inflated view of himself is due to the financial success he enjoyed in the drug world. Assuming his claims to be true, he made millions of dollars in profits and moved huge quantities of marijuana into the United States. His view of himself as a successful drug dealer is undermined in part by his record: he was twice arrested, convicted, and incarcerated.

The Businessman Drug Dealer

The majority of higher-level drug traffickers in this study have extensive employment or business backgrounds and live relatively law-abiding lives. They typically present themselves as family men and successful entrepreneurs, and keep their drug-dealing identity hidden from all but a small and select circle. They are not widely known as drug traffickers, nor do they experience the celebrity status that goes with the drug-dealing role. Like their more flashy "criminal" cousins, however, they, too, gain satisfaction and feed their ego in the conspicuous display of wealth through cars, homes, gifts, dining out, entertainment, clothing, and travel.

The self-concept of these businessmen dealers is highly positive and based largely on conventional values. They typically describe themselves in reference to work ethic values: ambitious, driven, successful, shrewd, hard working, and enterprising. Most think of themselves as successful businessmen and not as drug dealers. This view of self is reinforced by the fact that they are employed and/or have owned and/or continue to own legitimate businesses, and their everyday lifestyle resembles that of a businessperson. In addition, their associates in the drug world are also otherwise conventional, law-abiding people.

> When I got introduced to this [drug trafficking], I could see these were family men and good people, and you rationalize that it's okay to do this. I did it for many years and almost considered myself legit.

> I had two lives and one was secretive. I had three legitimate businesses in town and I purposely created this image. I kept the drug business away from my family and legitimate businesses.

> The people I dealt with were ordinary businessmen. I also had a wonderful group of friends, including some very prominent people.

A commitment to the conventional roles of husband and father also contributes to their sense of self as a normal, respectable, and moral person. A former fish exporter whose business went bankrupt before he moved into drug dealing describes his lifestyle:

> After our divorce, I moved into an apartment and let my wife keep the house so my kids had a home. I did all the things a parent does with his kids. Pretty law-abiding guy, except for the [drug] business. It's strange to think of it, but most of the guys in this business are law-abiding people.
> I know that I did wrong and I still have my values. I'm supposed to be this horrible drug dealer, but I am very law abiding in all other ways. It was just greed that motivated me. I don't see it as morally wrong. I was just making a living for me and my family.

Businessmen drug dealers also take pride in the shrewd and ethical manner in which they run their illegitimate enterprise. Many attribute admirable and conventional qualities to themselves such as honesty, integrity, generosity, and reliability. Helping others make money also contributes to their sense of pride and accomplishment. Suppliers are highly valued by dealers who rely on them for product, and their egos are buttressed by the way in which their clients treat them.

> I always had faith in my own ability and took a lot of pride in being honest and reliable and responsible. People knew my word was good. This is a business and there is no room for screw-ups.

> There is a sense of power that goes with it. People treat you like a god if you have the connections. You have this feeling of power and importance because you're the person who makes it happen and makes money for everyone.

> I considered myself to be an honest and generous drug trafficker. I didn't abuse the power and influence, and I made money for myself and for others. I'm proud of that.

Profits, Costs, and Losses

The profits and profit margins of higher-level drug traffickers vary considerably and typically depend on a dealer's position in the drug chain and volume of sales. It is not possible to determine an average income for dealers in this study since many subjects were cautious when discussing such matters. Others, however, were candid and gave a detailed accounting of their finances. The data provided by these subjects and police investigators make it clear that profits are enormous when compared to the incomes of the average wage earner or businessperson. Even lower-level wholesalers report incomes in the tens of thousands of dollars per month. A small-time importer who used couriers to smuggle cocaine into the country estimates his monthly earnings at $40,000 to $50,000.

> It's easy, though, ... it's like ... it's almost boring. I would get a kilo of cocaine in Guyana for two grand U.S, and let it off right here for like 30 grand. Subtract my costs and I'm still making a killing.

A mid-level dealer from Edmonton who received his drugs from suppliers in Montreal discusses his profit margins:

> I paid $36,000 to $40,000 a kilo and was moving 7 or 8 kilos a month. Prices fluctuated all the time and could vary around $5,000 a kilo. I would get it 90–94% pure and cut it to 80% pure. I had four to six distributors who would take 1 kilo each. One guy might take a little more and one guy a little less.
> My distributors made from $10,000 to $20,000 a month. That would be very conservative. They all did retail and they would have 10 to 15 clients each. I made $40,000 or $50,000 a month after expenses. None of my distributors were users. The people above me were strictly business. No room for that. They made it clear and I made it clear to my people. I made sure they weren't wired. They might use it on their time off, but not during business hours. I wanted to keep it controlled.

Dealers higher up the chain report greater sales volume and income. A 35-year-old importer connected to a seizure of 20 kilos of cocaine estimated his annual profit at over $2 million a year.

> My profit would be $40,000 to $70,000 a week. An average week is $40,000 and the best week was $80,000. December and January are good months because these are the festive months. There is less supply and more demand over Christmas.

A 40-year-old dealer who was apprehended in the RCMP "Eyespy" money-laundering sting (discussed in Chapter 7) exchanged $3 million Can. into U.S. funds in one month. He wholesaled the cocaine for $34,000 to $35,000 Can. per kilo and made approximately $5,000 on each kilo.

> I was laundering $1.2 million Can. into U.S. currency. That would be 35 kilos every 10 days. I was paying $28,000 a kilo and I would have to pay people $1,000 a kilo to bring it over the border. My profit would be 35 kilos × $5,000 = $175,000 Can. every 10 days—really big money.

An American citizen who smuggled cocaine into Canada over six years laundered $9 million Can. into U.S. currency in a six-month period in the RCMP "Eyespy" money exchange. He estimates his annual income at $2.5–$3 million Can. The RCMP seized 70 kilos of cocaine from an apartment he used as a safe house.

> A kilo of cocaine purchased in Los Angeles would cost me about $25,000 Can. and would fetch a price in the $30,000 range in Canada. The profit per kilo was about $5,000 Can. and I was bringing in 40 or 50 kilos minimum every month. I am not trying to exaggerate, but these are the kinds of

money I made with no taxes. I bought everything on a front and if I had paid cash for buying drugs, I could probably have doubled my profit because you're not operating on a front.

A 55-year-old high-level dealer who imported 200 kilos of cocaine per month into Canada and who owned his own currency-exchange business explains his costs and profit margins.

I made it in volume. I would buy at $23,000 Can. and if I sold 10 kilos, I would sell them for $30,000 Can. for each kilo and I could make as much as $7,000 on each. If I sold 50 kilos, I sell them for $27,000 Can. If 100 were sold, they would go for $26,000 apiece. There were times because of shortages that I could sell 20 and make as much as I did when I sold 50 kilos. I made so much money that I spread it around. A driver would make $100,000 a month.

The RCMP "Eyespy" storefront currency exchange in Vancouver provides valuable insights into the amounts of money generated by drug traffickers. Many dealers laundered tens of thousands of dollars per week, often dropping off hockey bags full of $20 bills to be exchanged for U.S. cash. Investigators report that several dealers could not be bothered counting the money, and trusted the exchange to provide an accurate count. Others used weigh scales to estimate the amounts of cash brought into the exchange. A number of subjects in this study report that the volume of cash generated through drug sales made money counting an expense and an ordeal.

You lose the value of money in this business. It's a disturbing thought to realize how much money you're

making. We would have five or six people counting money for days in hotel rooms. It sounds wild to say it, but it is really boring counting money day after day. We started using scales to weigh our money. You can get a fairly exact count by weighing the money.

Although the mark-up on illicit drugs is great, profits can be calculated only after all related costs are factored in. These include car rentals, cellphones and pagers, safe houses, lawyers, bankers, money-laundering fees, business fronts, and staff to count and exchange currency and move product. The transportation of narcotics across borders involves other costs: couriers, drivers, flights, accommodations, boats, airplanes, pilots, car and truck rentals, and/or purchases. Dealers report that bribes are needed on occasion to pay off officials or to move drugs through Customs in foreign countries. In the case of marihuana grow operations, expenses include such items and services as the purchase or rental of land and/or buildings, staff and electrician fees, hydroponic equipment, soil, gardening supplies, and fertilizer. Dealers who manufacture methamphetamines will have to invest in chemicals, an experienced chemist, a laboratory, and laboratory equipment.

Costs vary considerably with some dealers running relatively small and lean operations and others investing hundreds of thousands of dollars in their illegal enterprise. The costs of purchasing drugs depend on the quantity, quality, and where the purchase is made. Narcotics that are not produced or grown in Canada will be smuggled in, which is a major expense for dealers. High-quality cocaine, for example, can reportedly be purchased for as low as $1,000 to $2,000 U.S. a kilo in Colombia and neighbouring South American countries. Clearly there is a huge potential for profit if one sells it for $35,000 Can. at wholesale rates in Canada. The costs of bringing the product from South America to Canada, however, will drive the price up significantly. There is a very high risk in transporting illicit drugs across national boundaries, and each crossing adds to the price. A 39-year-old Canadian national, married to the daughter of a woman the RCMP described as a Colombian drug lord, explains the problems and costs in moving the cocaine from South America into Canada.

Transportation is the most difficult and expensive part. You always know where to get it and once you have it, it is very easy to sell, but getting it from A to B is the key to this business. That is what causes the big problems. Hence, transportation is extremely expensive and most of your costs are in transportation.

A unit [kilo] may not be very expensive depending on where you buy it, but you can sell it very expensively. A unit cost can vary in price depending on where I buy it and pick it up and where does my responsibility start. If I buy it down the line, it is cheap in unit cost, but the transportation cost is highest.

If I take responsibility for a unit in Southern California, then I would pay a lot higher than if I took it in South America. If they were so kind to deliver it to me in Canada, I pay a higher price. I would love to have it dropped off on my doorstep because it would reduce the risk. I've never had it delivered to Canada.

There are ways of purchasing cocaine. If I say to you, "Look, come to Colombia and I'll give you kilos for $1,000 or $2,000 U.S.," you know you can sell it for $35,000 to 40,000 Can. up here, but you have a problem. The purchase price is insignificant if you can't get it from one country to the next. There's an old economic adage that profit is directly proportional to risk. You take a lot more risk when you take it down the line.

If you are going to be a successful drug trafficker, the secret is having the means to move it to your destination. You have to get in on a pipeline. This is a proven route that brings the drugs across frontiers. Providing the line is different than owning the line. The guy who owns the line may only charge $4,000 U.S., but you have to go through a middleman and he sells it to you for $6,000 U.S. There are always cowboys who will smuggle in 20 or 30 kilos, but those are small operators. You need a line to operate in bulk.

So the guy might come to you and say, "I have a line and I can bring it into Southern California, but it's going to cost you $6,000 U.S. a unit." You've just had a big increase in your costs. You pay for movement in this business. You have to know a line is safe and not infiltrated or you can lose your load. There are a lot of lines and you have to jump in on one. There's other costs you have to pay for, including handling and storage and movement and he'll keep it in his store until you pick it up.

If you're in Canada, you now have to go to Southern California.

I would have a driver pick it up. I may have depots and storage places along the way and I certainly don't move it all at once. Some of it stays in the states and the rest comes up here. I may have someone who does the border crossing and he has a set fee. It comes into the city and another person gets a fee for sittting on it.

People get paid a certain amount for certain tasks—X dollars for Y units. There's a formula. No jobs are equal. Border crossings are the most important jobs. There is more work and more risk involved. There has to be a reason for a vehicle to cross the border. There has to be a commercial entry because you have to have a reason to put something through the border. You might run it through in chemical or hay trucks, or you might pay off a Mexican Customs man. Everybody gets paid. You have to make an investment to cover that 500 kilos.

We moved the cocaine from Colombia through Panama and up to Mexico through the U.S. and into Canada. This was a large operation with a lot of drivers—not a mom-and-pop operation.

Then you have other costs. You have money counters. You have your exchange people. Drivers get a lot. Money counters don't get much since all they do is weigh the money and box it up in cardboard boxes or army canvas bags so heavy you can't carry them. You pay money exchange on points or percentage.

Money exchange is a problem and the weakest link because you have to surface. That's how I was caught. You are susceptible for an attack and can get sunk. Everything else is with criminals and now you have to go to a bank and you need very specialized people for this, and there is just not enough U.S. money in Vancouver.

Even though this dealer worked closely with a Colombian cartel, his own crew operated in Canada and consisted of a partner—his best friend since childhood—his brother, and a handful of close associates. He was responsible for importing cocaine into Canada and his crew was responsible for sales within the country. His female cousin operated their money-laundering operation.

Other dealers report similar costs to smuggle drugs across the border. The 55-year-old dealer who smuggled 200 kilos of cocaine each month from Los Angeles into Canada spent thousands of dollars on transportation.

My monthly costs to operate the cars on the road and drivers were unbelievable. The product [cocaine] was moved from the U.S. to Canada partially overland and partially by water. I would buy a new vehicle every week for this purpose and never used it more than five times, which is approximately five weeks. Each would be fixed up in California with secret compartments in the gas tank and, depending on the car, the airbag system. Put in a little switch as fine as a hair and hit the switch and the defogging button, and the dash would pop up. You could put up to 40 kilos in hiding spots and unload really quick. In that business, time is of [the] essence.

It was very costly and detailed. If I used a van or a pickup truck, the body is lifted off and a subfloor put in. The steering wheel is extended and the brakes and pedals are extended so everything would be in proportion. These were Mexicans in L.A. who did it, and they were very good. It was ingenious. They would build a space between the floor and raise the floor an inch and elevate the box by an inch, so they had to lift the cab and steering arm and pedals noticeably out of place. Even the radiator is lifted.

Once they had dogs in the cars and they couldn't find the hiding spot. They knew there were drugs in the car, but couldn't find them. The driver panicked and divulged the compartment, so I lost that load.

It cost about $7,000 U.S. to outfit cars and $10,000 to $12,000 for vans and pickups. You could get one as low as $2,000, but it would only carry about 7 kilos. Purchasing the vehicle would cost on average about $25,000. You don't worry about spending money because you spend to make money.

After I was done with the vehicles, I had a deal with the supplier so he would take them back and sell it to someone else. I virtually gave the cars back and he made a great deal of money. I changed cars frequently so they didn't get known. Any auto that we thought was known would be put through shredders—chop them up and crush them.

Several subjects reported that corrupt officials in other countries added to their costs. Two men purchased their way out of prison through bribes. A 30-year-old smuggler who was apprehended with 5 kilos of cocaine in Guyana paid for his release.

I spent a lot of money in Guyana because I had a problem there and I had to buy my way out of it. I had this guy who made body packs for a courier, but she had some metal on her and the metal detector picked it up at the airport when they were dinging her with that wand. They did a body search and said, "What the hell is this?" She started to cry and told them my name. I never travel with couriers, but I was still in the country and they arrested me.

I spent a week in jail. I said to my lawyer, "What does it take to get out of here?"He goes, "Well the trial is going to be ... " I said, "I don't give a shit about the trial. I have money." He said, "Oh, okay." That was it. He said, "I'll get back to you." He came back and said that it was going to cost

$1 million Guyanese, which is like $10,000 Can. and then $1 million Guyanese for the girl and he goes, "Do you want the drugs back?" and I said, "Yeah, how much is that going to cost me?" I got everything back. I got the drugs, records, fingerprints, pictures, but it cost me a lot of money. It's a joke. Those guys are corrupt.

Many drug traffickers in this study report significant losses in the course of their illegitimate career. The most common losses come from police drug seizures and the inability to collect money owing from distributors. Others losses result from fronting dealers who fail to pay; being unable to collect money owing because of their own arrest and imprisonment; lending money to friends for ventures that do not work out; losing money or drugs through theft or robbery; investing in legitimate businesses that lose money. It is very common for traffickers to report losses from legitimate investments and businesses. A number of subjects retired from drug trafficking only to return after losing money they had invested. One dealer, who had been retired for two years, began importing cocaine again in order to recoup a $1 million loss.

I introduced a friend to my Mexican suppliers in the U.S. and and he ended up losing $1.7 million worth of goods [cocaine]. He gave it to some buyers and they ripped him off. They called me and they tell me that he's disappeared! I find him and he tells me what happened. I called them back and they say he has to pay. They told me the consequences if he doesn't pay. I made a deal with him to cover the debt. I had a side business of loaning out money at 10% a month. I called the Mexicans and asked them their cost on the deal, and it was $1 million and I covered his debt. Unknown to me, he had ripped other people off in California and they come out and shot him. I can't talk about the shooting. Anyway, I was out $1 million.

Now there is nobody to pay my money back. Goddam it, I'm broke. I had all these assets and I was worth millions, but I was low on cash, so I went back to work. I was two weeks away from closing down when I was arrested. I was so close to retirement, but it's all hindsight.

Another cocaine smuggler, who quit for several years, similarly lost millions of dollars on investments and came out of retirement to make more.

My partner and I had a lot of money for investments and lost most of it. We were going to use sugar cane for building products. I met this guy and he's invented a sugar cane separator and he had a machine that separated it. You can use it to make lumber and it is structurally sound and can make cane plywood. We were going to set up a sawmill in Puerto Rico to make lumber. I thought I would be the richest man in the world.

They had an idea, but couldn't finance it, so we poured our money into in. I could never get control of the lumber company and had to battle with the management and it was all my money and I wanted control. They would never give me control and the contracts were getting so complicated and insane. Our legal bills were up to $200,000 in contracts alone, and we had not even done a patent search. It's extremely expensive to do a patent search.

It just went on and on and we got beat out by a German company. We

sunk over $3 million and a lot of time, and we just said fuck it. I went on holidays for three weeks. It was like a nervous breakdown. My phones were running 24 hours a day from all over the world. It was too much and I couldn't handle it. We called it off and bailed out. Lost $3 million. Nothing came of it from that company.

We were so stupid, we bit the next hook from them. The "agro-magnet" lost us about a million and a half. The agro-magnet changes the mineral properties of water. We invested in a mango farm in Thailand and had other investments in Asia that lost money.

The Dealing Lifestyle

Spending the Money

There appears to be two distinct lifestyle and spending patterns among higher-level drug dealers. Dealers who are older, married, and with employment histories and conventional lifestyles spend time with families and spend money on houses, cars, jewellery, furniture, children's expenses, travel, entertainment, and investments. Younger dealers and those who are committed to a criminal lifestyle are more likely to party extensively and spend freely on clothing, dining out, and expensive toys such as cars, boats, and motorcycles. The latter describe their day-to-day living as a party lifestyle that involves frequenting bars and nightclubs and being surrounded by women, friends, and associates. Several describe a high-rolling celebrity lifestyle in which they pick up the tab for their friends and other hanger-ons.

That's where most of the money goes. I partied six days a week, six nights a week, night and day. Even when I was going to college, I went out with most of the girls in my class and then I expanded to the rest of the school. You're just a playboy. You take a different girl to lunch every day. After you buy her a big lunch, you take her to the hotel, and you move on and that's it. You move on to the next girl. Girls realize that you're a player, but they don't care. It's exciting for most girls. They love it. It's like a thrill to them.

We partied and partied and partied. When I went on vacation with a girlfriend, I went to Antigua, I spent two weeks and $35,000—35 grand just partying. I don't know what the hell I spent it on. First of all, anything that I do, I like to do it first class, so we went to a five-star hotel. Then I rented a Jeep and we were driving around partying and buying this and that. A lot of poor people there, so I buy them a lot of clothes, whatever. I didn't care. Who cares? It's just money and money comes like that.

The lifestyle would be clothes, cars, and partying. There is a Versace store in Yorkville that I used to shop at. Every time that I bought a pair of pants, it's never less than 400 bucks. I buy my shoes at Brown's and it's like 500 bucks. Everything is top of the line. Sometimes I would go out and, with the jewellery and everything included, I'm wearing like 40 grand.

A 38-year-old hairdresser addicted to cocaine describes his lifestyle.

I'm not married and my lifestyle was a partying lifestyle. I was a high-profile hairdresser involved in the fashion and music industry and that scene. I had the flashy girls, cars, drugs, and I liked being seen. Lots of parties—promotional parties for the movie industry. I was a kingpin and well connected with women and into the bar and dating scene. I don't regret a day of my life. My [drug-dealing] partner was involved in the restaurant and bar industry.

A 40-year-old married dealer owned a clothing import business that he used as a front for his lifestyle and as a means of importing cocaine into the country. He admitted having several girlfriends and enjoying the party life.

I got caught up in that lifestyle. I like experiencing toys, parties, and the girls. I was easily seduced into that lifestyle.

A dealer who worked the bars and nightclubs describes his high-profile partying lifestyle.

I was a shitty drug dealer because I wasn't much for sneaking around. I didn't mind reaping the profits and the party lifestyle.

You're a night owl or a vampire. There is always women around and parties. You have a celebrity drug-dealing status and you get caught in the lifestyle and you don't want to get out of it. You are always exchanging bills. We're talking about mountains of money. You drop bills all over the place. Dealing with large quantities and lots of cash around, you have a lot of friends, drugs and parties, and limousines—until you get busted.

Others similarly enjoyed the party scene. An ex-professional hockey player from Montreal, with a lengthy criminal record and biker connections, worked several nightclubs in the downtown area.

> I was flashing too much. I had the big cars and would change girls twice a night and party non-stop, and people see this and they become jealous. I would laugh at the undercover cops and tell them to go fuck themselves. I was too cocky with them. Dope and partying go together. Drugs and sex and fast life and money. I would wake up at home and make some phone calls and meet with my business associates in the morning. Then I would go and do some sports and work out, and then go to the beach, or I might play some golf in the afternoon. Business is night-time or very early in the morning. Most business took place in the bars, so I would go and check it out. At the end, I had people work for me and I didn't have to go.
>
> Living life in the fast lane, you always have people around and lots of chicks, of course. I was a high roller and paying the shot on everything. I began using cocaine through women. They'd say, "Come on, come on" and we started doing it together. They'd do a line on my dick and be more and more kinky, and you're out every night and you start sniffing every night. You know the girls like it and you offer it, and without you knowing it, you're hooked. After 10 years, I was doing an ounce to 2 ounces sniffing a week. I could easily afford it—I was making $10,000 to $20,000 a week. I was not the richest, but I was living pretty good. Women, gold, Harleys, Jaguars—cocaine brought me lots of fun and lots of sadness too. It's the worst right now.

Many dealers spurned the club and party lifestyle, but still lived the good life. A 33-year-old married dealer preferred sports and family over partying, and used legitimate businesses as a front for his wealth.

> I've grown up and I don't need to party anymore. I was a man of leisure, and loved to exercise and play competitive sports and water sports and biking and ski and snowboard. I spent a lot of time doing all of that—a lot of time with my family. I owned a $26,000 Harley Davidson. I drove the new BMW 328 and owned a Porsche, and I had other luxury cars like 'Vettes and two or three cars at any given time. I never went to nightclubs and did not socialize with people I worked with except behind closed doors. I was somewhat discreet and would do things like go fishing with my father and go to my niece's skating competitions.
>
> Sometimes I worked from 8 in the morning to 9 at night meeting, planning, and moving around a lot to see people. Other times I would go to the mountains, especially on weekends, but if something had to be done, it was three or four days of all-day work.
>
> In retrospect, I see that if you have a young person who has nice cars and homes, you bring attention to yourself. A nice car and boat and a Harley and nice clothes—I did enjoy the finer things in life. I should not have been that obvious even though I thought at the time these things can be accountable because I had a legitimate business. I should have been a little bit lower in my profile, but the persona you present is expected among your associates. I would do my buying in Montreal or Toronto to not bring attention to myself.

A 55-year-old marijuana importer who made millions of dollars in a 25-year smuggling career describes an extravagant lifestyle that required his coming out of retirement to maintain it. He was arrested in a major cocaine-importing conspiracy:

When I retired years earlier, we had made so much money that one of my partners went to Switzerland and bought himself a castle, and the other went off on his 116-foot pleasure yacht throughout the Caribbean with every toy available—jet skis, ski boat. Then he went into a gold mine operation in Africa and lost money and got back into smuggling. I moved my family to Vancouver and we travelled the world, and I spent a lot of time with my wife and girls [two daughters].

I was spending half a million or more per year in living expenses. We'd take a trip to London and take $50,000 cash in my briefcase. Spending money in the Alps and staying in the best hotels. I wondered how people went on holidays with five grand. It's impossible. I would see a watch for my wife for $14,000 and just buy it. A nice necklace and leather coats and the best cars—just buy it. Buy it. It's not hard—stay at the best hotels and entertain our friends, rent the best cars and travel.

A 33-year-old cocaine smuggler claims to have made over $2 million a year. He invested in legitimate businesses and owned some very expensive toys.

My lifestyle was extravagant. I own a twin-engine airplane. I have a pilot's licence and I own a Ferrari and a couple of small businesses—an auto-repair business and the land that it's on and a car wash. My family is taken care of and I have assets to go back to, but when you're making large amounts of money, you don't even treat it as money anymore. The way a normal person would spend $100 at the store, you would spent $10,000 and think of it less than he would. It's hard to describe—you tend to lose the value of money. The quantity is too much and you don't work hard for it. My values got screwed up because of the money—get to the point where you think that you can buy anything. I would go down to L.A. and they have a wholesale jewellery place, so why not bring some cash and pick up a Rolex?

A 55-year-old cocaine dealer, who regularly sold 200 kilos a month, describes his extravagant lifestyle.

I owned three homes in the city and I had purchased a home in Spain, and we were going to live there after I retired. We were going to have another home in Italy and be there during other periods. I bought my daughter a house at 19 so I could be on my own. I gave her the cash she needed to start her own business.

I had a collection of 11 antique automobiles and they seized that. They seized 17 cars in total. I owned two cars that I drove, and so did my wife and daughter. The police seized $12 million in dollars and assets. They put restraining orders against everything. I had Whistler properties and $812,000 in cash that they seized.

I have my pilot's licence and I owned two airplanes—a twin-engine 420 Cessna worth $480,000 Can. and a smaller 172 Cessna worth $145,000. I was able to sell one and the other one was never in Canada. I owned two boats, which I had at marinas, and I berthed one yacht right at my home in Vancouver. I had five apartment properties in Whistler.

I had eight hiding places that I used for distribution—homes and warehouses, and most of them rented. I looked for homes in well-established neighbourhoods and paid $2,000 per place on average. My costs were high. My own personal needs were in excess of $45,000 a month. Unbelievable.

I would travel for three months a year with my wife. From early February to late May it is hard to purchase cocaine or you can only get it in small amounts. There are no suppliers or supply is low. I would just shut down. The peak months are late August to December during the growing season. I would shut down and all debts were paid off, and we travelled. I was always in the States, but very secretly and always with false ID. I never allowed anyone to know where I was going or where I was going to be. We took trips to Mexico and South America and Africa and Europe and Australia. I would shut down for three months and travel and live my life.

The money provided other benefits. We saw the world's best entertainers. Jerry Seinfeld was performing in L.A. and I got tickets, and we went down there and spent $10,000 for that weekend. I saw this ad for a clipper ship that takes 12 couples on a two-month trip around South America and we decided to do that. I could lighten my life that way and did things spontaneously and very often.

Stresses Associated with a Life of Crime

Being a higher-level drug trafficker has many rewards, and most enjoyed the lifestyle while it lasted. Some report, however, that the fear of arrest and imprisonment took its toll on their mental health. The need to be secretive, suspicious, and distrustful of others creates stress, anxiety, and paranoia.

> I like working in my business [a painting company] because it's clean money and you can sleep good. If I work, I know I can sleep. With drug money, I couldn't sleep too well because you never know what will happen. You can be arrested any time.

> I was constantly on guard and thinking of it. It was on my mind 24 hours a day. There was a lot of stress wondering if the cops would come kick down my door in the middle of the night. I had other stress too. There were always people who owed me money and I had that on my mind at all times. I would often have $300,000 on the street.

> I may have had maybe 15 hours a week of hands-on business, but the stress and mental anxiety was constant. I couldn't go out for dinner with my girl without thinking, "What's so and so up to? Why is he late with my money? What if he's been picked up?"

> I was always worried about something. I was always owed money and I always owed someone money. "Am I going to get my money? Are the cops on to me?" If I see a car drive by my place, I start to worry that it may be the cops. It was always in the back of my mind and I could never relax. Always wondering. One of my guys wants 2 kilos a week. "What's going on? Who is he selling to? He usually only takes one."

Paranoia is amplified by drug addiction or heavy usage.

You travel in crowds and you are not a person to be messed with. When you start getting larger, you start getting more paranoid and careful. Lots of my friends expressed concern about my doing coke—my wife and friends and partners and people above me. I was told to smarten up and come back after. I had too much heat. It was my own fault. People liked me, but they didn't want me around for business.

I was becoming unreliable. I was nuts. I was fucked up. They didn't know if I would shoot somebody or not. You're paranoid. If you get like that, you know you're done. I pulled muscles in my legs just from stress. The last few years killed me. Fight with my wife. No patience with my kids.

A 44-year-old career criminal, who was involved in drug trafficking most of his adult life, describes the sense of alienation that comes from leading a secret life.

Secrecy becomes your main tool. I often equate the life to being a shadow because you really don't have an identity anymore. Your life is such an illusion. You take out women, you meet people, and everything that you're living is an illusion. They don't know what you do, who you are, or your background. You're constantly on guard and you're constantly presenting a false image to them, so you really become a non-identity. You remove yourself away from society and the only world you know is the world you're living in—the drug business.
You're so far away, alienated, and in a state of anomie that you don't read the newspapers. You don't care about anything political because you're not part of that world. You're living an untruth and it is such a strange feeling. You become so out of it, so out of synch with society, that you are not part of society anymore.

Five of the 70 interviews took place with offenders on parole and living in the community with their families. Four of these men emphasized how relaxed they had become since retiring from drug dealing. A 40-year-old cocaine importer who was interviewed in a McDonald's restaurant described the weight that had been taken off his shoulders now that he was working in a legitimate job.

Now I have a better life and family life. We do things together as a family and have more fun with no money. The money didn't make life better, but you don't see that when you're in it. I would go to sleep at 2:00 or 3:00 in the morning and be up at 7:00 a.m. I was checking all the doors and always paranoid that my neighbours were watching me. I would go out the end of the driveway to see if anyone was looking at me. I look back now and I can see how it affected me, but I was not conscious of it at the time.

A 30-year-old parolee similarly notes the absence of stress in his life now that he is no longer in the business of selling drugs.

Now that I'm out of it, I can say that it is a great relief to go home at night and watch the hockey game like any ordinary Joe and not worry that the cops could come crashing into my house at any minute. I have no stress and I don't miss it.

It is difficult to determine from this research whether or not significant levels of stress are common among higher-level drug traffickers.

The topic was not explored in depth, but the fact that several men raised the issue suggests that being involved in an illegal enterprise over a long period is indeed stressful. It is perhaps significant that four of the five parolees described the stress of being a drug dealer. They appear to recognize the anxiety retrospectively after they no longer live with the fear of arrest. It may be that many dealers experience a high degree of stress, but are unaware of and/or unwilling to acknowledge their fears and concerns.

Leading a Secret Life

Most subjects in this study attempted to protect their families by keeping their illegal activities separate. Several characterized themselves as leading two lives—a public life involving their families and a secret life that revolved around drug trafficking.

> I had two lives and one was secretive. I had a family and my own contracting company and I was almost as legitimate as I could be. I purposely created this image. I kept the drug business away from my family and other businesses to protect them.

> I kept my work and family life separate. I would stay in a hotel and get it done.

> I had two separate lives. I had a straight life on the one hand, and a criminal one on the side. I have never brought drugs home. My wife does not do drugs and had no idea what I was up to.

Some dealers described feelings of alienation over their secret lives. They complained that their deceptions prevented them from getting to know people, did not allow others to get to know them, and often made them feel alone

and disconnected with the world. A 28-year-old unmarried dealer describes the feelings he experienced:

> The worst part of this whole thing that I hated the most was that I had no friends. I met a couple in Antigua from Brooklyn and I really wanted to be close to them, but I couldn't because I knew that they were honest working people. I actually liked them. We had similar interests, but I couldn't. It wouldn't be fair to them for me to be their friend and never say, "Yo, I'm a drug dealer." I met a lot of people who have the potential to be friends, but I can't because I have to be honest. How is this guy going to feel later on when I wasn't honest with him, you know?
> The friends that I had are the friends that I don't want. There is a reason why they're your friends. Most people want something, and the friends that I want, I know that I can't have because I am a very open guy and I can't have a friend and have secrets. You have all of these people around you—lots of women—it's better than being a rock star, but you are very lonely.

Others similarly commented on the feelings engendered by having a secret life:

> There is another side to my life. I was involved in making money, but I couldn't brag about my successes. I was totally on my own. I became an introverted person by my wealth. I was frightened about people asking me because I didn't want to lie. I kept a low profile and wore jeans and t-shirts, even though I was a multimillionaire.

> I had that feeling I'm living in a different world all the time to the point

where you can't really express yourself like you want to. You meet all kinds of people and you have conversations and they want to get to know you and things about you, and you can't be truthful. It's almost living a lie to a certain extent.

Not all dealers found it difficult to straddle both worlds and several respondents moved back and forth with ease.

I have my friends from the club scene and I have another group of friends who are straight and play baseball and I spend 80% of my time with them. They are both exciting for me and I've known this group of friends since I was a baby. They all work and have careers and knew nothing about my illegal activities.

I kept my family first and would party hard once a month with my partner and a few other dealers. It was like a treat and something to look forward to. "Hey, next weekend is the one. We rent a hotel room and go to town." Once a month I would treat myself to the girls, an eight-ball of cocaine, and bottles of champagne. I never let any of my business come close to my kid or to my wife.

The Failure to Get Out of Drug Dealing

Men who rob banks continue their holdups until they are caught because they make very little money from each score. They are soon broke and in need of more. In addition, they lack attachments, commitments, and involvements in conventional activities, have few job or business skills, subjectively

define themselves as having nothing to lose, and live their lives in a criminal milieu with an accompanying deviant lifestyle and value systems. For many, crime is a way of life and they have few jobs or other legitimate opportunities as an alternative (Desroches, 2002 [1995]). Most traffickers in this study, on the other hand, made plenty of money, had much to lose if caught, and planned to retire from drug dealing once they had accumulated sufficient wealth. They have typically earned huge profits and can often afford to retire in style. In fact, many subjects in this study knew dealers who had retired from trafficking prior to being arrested and convicted. Since most are committed to conventional values and a legitimate lifestyle, why haven't they quit when the quitting was good? Why do they continue long after they have made their wealth? Why are they not deterred by the possibility of arrest and imprisonment?

From a methodological perspective, the sample used in this research is biased since all were arrested and imprisoned. There are good reasons to assume that many higher-level drug dealers do quit before it is too late. Most have conventional values and can easily resume a more law-abiding lifestyle; they have achieved the wealth that motivated them in the first place, and a rational assessment of their position should make them realize the risk of further involvement. There appear to be several factors and reasons why they continue in drug trafficking despite the risks.

1.   Greed: Expanding/Elastic Desires

The main reason dealers continue trafficking is because they are making huge amounts of money and are greedy for more. They do not wish to give up tens of thousands of dollars per month in income. Although they may set some initial financial goals, they raise their sights soon after reaching them. As Durkheim (1951) suggests, people's aspirations are elastic and expand after quick and easy success.

I wanted money for a house and you get a house, and now you want a house in the country and then in the Caribbean. It's a neverending process.

You have a certain quota and it changes. You have goals and you reach them, and it's going so smooth, it's hard to give it up. You get there and a million was easy and it came quick, and why not go for another one?

I thought that once I reached a million, I'd quit. But it started with a half-million, but your goals keep expanding. Once you get to a certain level, you set your sights higher and higher and want more and more. It's greed.

I was never close to quitting. No, but I know a few people who did. No amount of money is enough. You tell yourself this is what you need and you get it, and you need more and it never seems to stop.

Dealers become accustomed to an affluent lifestyle and family members, too, develop extravagant spending habits and expectations that dealers feel pressured to maintain.

My wife put pressure on me to quit, but she, too, was accustomed to the money—fly to Paris to buy a dress.

My own greed. The money from illicit dealing is very overwhelming and very addicting. Addiction is not just a substance-abuse problem, there is also a lifestyle addiction. Your family gets addicted too. Once you reach that, you want to maintain it and it escalates.

Retirement is likely to lower one's standard of living, and this makes the decision to retire difficult. Even though dealers have made a

great deal of money and invested some, most spend lavishly and have not put sufficient funds aside to retire without severely cutting back on their spending.

I never had enough money to retire. I never had more than a quarter of a million dollars at one time.

A number of dealers failed to retire because they couldn't bring themselves to give up so much money, particularly when it flows with little effort. Most of the work has been done, they have trusted and reliable sources, associates, and distributors, everything is in place, and the business almost runs itself.

The challenge was walking away from the money, which was coming fast and furious without much work or effort or danger.

It's tough to walk away from $40,000 a month.

If you decide to stop and become an ordinary Joe, there is no more $20,000 a week. You have decided to give yourself a huge pay decrease. You are now going to have to dip into your savings. You don't do it.

2. Ego and Self-Confidence

Perhaps the second most significant reason why dealers continue in their trade is because of their egos. Most see themselves as clever and cautious and believe in their ability to continue dealing without getting caught. They think they can outsmart the police and see no reason for quitting. They have been successful for so long that they begin to believe they can operate indefinitely. Related to this is a faith they have in the people who work for them and a security system that gives them ample protection. This self-confidence sometimes becomes arrogance and contributes to their downfall.

> I may have been too arrogant and smug and confident. I'm invincible. I'm smarter than them [the police].

> You think you're clever enough not to get caught. You think you're better than they [the police] are.

> I had planned to stop, but got caught up in the action and began to think I was smarter than the police.

> It's not explicit that you're smarter, but you think you have a system that cannot be beat and you've covered all the angles.

3.   Identity, Power, Status, Lifestyle

Some dealers become addicted to the role and lifestyle, which brings with it wealth, status, power, and excitement. They enjoy being dealers and develop a sense of self-worth and accomplishment from doing what they believe they are good at. Criminal traffickers in particular receive great respect within their milieu, and dealing becomes their identity and life. Being a drug dealer is a role they enjoy and they are reluctant to give up all the benefits.

> I enjoyed having the influence to control people in daily life because you have power and money and prestige.

> It's a feeling of success and accomplishment, and it's addicting and alluring. If you quit trafficking, you withdraw from that lifestyle.

> You can ask favours and people will do it. Making money for people and you are an employer, and you have power over employees and can dictate how their job goes, and you can call a lot of the shots.

> The women, the money, the fast cars, the status, the prestige, the power, and the control—being a drug dealer is very prestigious and attractive.

> Power is an intangible. I'm referring to power within the criminal element. The higher you are and the more successful you are, the more people under you look up to you.

Men who are heavily involved in a criminal milieu face an additional problem in leaving the drug trade since their work is their life, and retirement would require them to leave behind their friends and associates.

> It would have been difficult for me to start over. You don't want to get out of something that is making so much money. We were all friends and I probably would have had to change my associates. Most of the people I hung around with were into crime.

4.   Sense of Responsibility: Peer Pressure

An unusual reason for continuing to traffick relates to a sense of responsibility and obligation. Several dealers report that others depended on them for their livelihood and did not want them to retire.

> That was part of the motive. Once you are deeply entrenched in drug trafficking, there is a certain responsibility with your customers and your suppliers. And I had my family. I had responsibilities in different worlds.

I wanted to quit, but when you're making money for other people, you can't quit now! Even my younger brother was telling me, "You can't quit now" 'cause my suppliers liked dealing with me and they said that they didn't want to deal with anyone else.

You can walk away, but it's difficult because people depend on you to make business deals and I felt responsible.

I was caught up in it, and so many people were relying on me to make a living, and the ego and pride thing that it was going so well.

I've been doing this for a while, and these people are counting on me and I've gained their trust on both ends, and it's a business responsibility to get it from one place to the next and make sure it all runs smoothly. Obligation— that is what I felt.

5. Addiction

For a small number of dealers, drug addiction is a factor that requires them to stay in the game. Trafficking helps them to maintain an expensive habit that would be impossible without a huge source of income.

I couldn't quit dealing because I had a drug addiction. I went from not using to being an addict in a short time.

I started talking about getting out of the business and I wanted to start my own business. I wanted to stop many times and I always went back because I was addicted. I needed it for the drugs and the money.

6. Complacency

Several dealers became complacent after operating for a long period without problems. Many refused to consider the possibility of being caught, purposely ignored the risk, and underestimated police capabilities.

All the security makes you complacent. It's like having a guard dog and a fence. You think you're safe from a break-and-enter.

My complacency led to my downfall.

I was not concerned about getting caught, not really, no. I was dealing for two or three years. I started believing I was doing something right. You forget about it. It's routine.

When I was rolling out there, you are cognitively aware you are doing something wrong and there are consequences if you get caught, but until it happens, you are not aware of the impact on your life that comes if you do get caught. I would not have done it if I had known exactly what I would have to go through and the costs of getting caught—losing my wife and children, my business, hundreds of thousands of dollars, and my life in the community, and my freedom, and a lot of the little things I loved about life. And having to endure the things I have had to endure while in prison—it probably would have been a deterrent.

My wife said to me, "One day you will wake up and we will be gone and you will have nothing." I dismissed it. "You're talking silly." I never gave much thought to the consequences.

7.   Lack of Deterrence

Although some men gave little thought to arrest and imprisonment—believing they would not get caught—others considered this possibility, but were still undeterred. They viewed the risks of apprehension as low and realized that sentences in Canada are relatively lenient. In their minds, the risks were more than offset by the rewards.

> Lighter sentences was a consideration in coming to Canada.

> You know there are consequences, but I just thought: "I could go to jail, I'm a cool guy. I can go to prison. Big deal." But it *is* a big deal because your life comes crashing down around you. It really hurts, and I have had to endure a lot of pain for what I have done. I had a lot of thinking errors and irrational thoughts.

8.   Pushing One's Luck

Several dealers planned to retire, but pushed their luck and waited until it was too late.

> I can't tell you how close I was to quitting, but I knew it couldn't last forever. I thought about it frequently and thought when the time comes, I'll know it. At least I was hoping for that anyway.

> Most of us wouldn't admit it, but we're all gamblers and risk takers even though we're businessmen. Like somebody gambling at a casino—if you're on roll, it's hard to quit. The best gamblers in the world say that you have to quit when you're ahead. You try to put the odds in your favour, but things do go wrong.

> I got out the wrong way. There's a right way and a wrong way.

> It wasn't until my wife started putting pressure on me to stay home and not leave town all the time. I was thinking that I needed to get out. I would have given it another six months or year. My partner and I were discussing him just taking over, but I left it too late.

Summary

Becoming a higher-level drug trafficker takes conscious, deliberate effort and requires ambition, self-discipline, caution, entrepreneurial skills, and connections. Higher-level dealers demonstrate a great deal of planning and rational thought before embarking on a career in crime. Consistent with learning theories, all subjects in this study gained entry into higher-level trafficking through contacts with dealers above them in the drug chain who acted as suppliers, lenders, mentors, and/or partners. Although one-third (25/70, 35.7%) of the sample moved upwards from retail into wholesale, the majority (45/70, 64.3%) gain direct entry into higher-level drug sales through connections with suppliers up the chain.

The majority of subjects in this study had ample opportunity to earn a comfortable living through legitimate pursuits. Anomie theory does not apply particularly well since most were employed, owned businesses, were financially secure, and led middle-class lifestyles. Subjects confess that greed motivated and kept them in this business long after they had made huge amounts of money. Higher-level drug trafficking is a crime of temptation and opportunity. Opportunity theory clearly applies since entry is based on connections to other dealers. Ethnicity and friendship are variables that influence opportunity since many use contacts in their country of origin and local community to purchase and distribute narcotics. Opportunity for some offenders is tied into their connections and reputation in the criminal world. Approximately 30% (20/70, 28.5%) of subjects in this study were career offenders and entered drug trafficking through criminal associates who were already engaged in the drug trade. Opportunities also become available through employment and business ownership, and one-third of the sample (24/70, 34%) used work and/or business experience, knowledge, contacts, and entrepreneurship as a point of entry into higher-level dealing.

The majority of the sample have strong social bonds—contrary to what social control theory would predict—and risked reputation, family, property, and freedom by engaging in drug trafficking. Many were aware of the relatively light sentences handed out in Canada and the lenient provisions for parole—variables that diminished the deterrent threat of arrest and conviction. Subjects also perceived trafficking as low risk because they were cautious, viewed themselves as competent, and dealt with trusted associates. Most of the inmates' families are still intact and supportive despite the offenders' arrest, conviction, and incarceration.

The lifestyle of higher-level drug traffickers reflects the wealth accumulated through this activity. Younger dealers and those committed to crime as a way of life typically enjoy a partying lifestyle that involves the nightclub scene and spending on cars, clothes, women, friends, and other hedonistic pursuits. Dealers who are older, married, and who maintain otherwise conventional lifestyles also spend lavishly on families, homes, automobiles, and travel. The latter maintain public identities as businesspeople and often hide their illegal activities from their families and friends. Some dealers described their involvement in crime as stressful and are happy to be out of it. Many had planned to retire from dealing, but found it difficult to walk away from the profits, power, and status that goes with being a successful, higher-level drug trafficker.

Few offenders express guilt or remorse for their crimes and most used a variety of justifications that subjectively diminished the harm done to others. Subjects tended to view illicit drug use as no different than tobacco and alcohol, and saw themselves as businessmen rather than criminals. Greed and materialism are common values in the drug-dealing world, and traffickers are willing to be flexible with their morality in the pursuit of wealth.

CHAPTER 5

The Modus Operandi of Higher-Level Drug Traffickers
Marketing, Organization, and Security

Marketing Illicit Drugs

Legitimate businesses reach out to potential clients by advertising their goods and services in the open market. Drug traffickers, on the other hand, must operate covertly, yet still search for people who are willing to purchase and distribute their product. Higher-level dealers operate in a manner similar to wholesalers because they service a select number of clients. Time, money, and energy are spent primarily on networking, transportation, security, currency exchange, and money laundering. Even though they do very little marketing, wholesale drug traffickers frequently use terms such as "doing market research," "testing the market," "breaking into new markets," "capturing a share of the market," and "maintaining market share." Dealers report that a number of variables are significant in the marketing of illicit drugs: quality, quantity, price, service, reputation, and credit. The use of credit and debt collection are discussed in Chapter 6.

Quality, Quantity, Price, Service, and Reputation

Drug enterprises seek to acquire a reliable supply of quality products at low prices to give themselves an edge in competitive illicit drug markets. Most dealers contend that quality determines market share and sales. The bottom line, one dealer explains, is that people who are looking to "get stoned" place great value on the "high" they experience, which is determined by the quality of the drugs they purchase and consume.

113

Having good-quality dope is a prestige thing and an ego trip for the user. It allows him to sit around and party with others and brag about his dope. It makes him a somebody because it means that he's got good contacts. That means that he's important in the drug world if you have good contacts. On the other hand, nobody wants to say, "Let's get stoned. This shit isn't very good."

Quality not only dictates the price, but it strongly influences a dealer's reputation in the drug world and affects business. Selling high-quality drugs is clearly a source of pride among dealers, and most subjects boast about the quality of their narcotics.

I sold quality drugs. When hypes hang out and do junk, they could say, "Man, this is good shit. The best quality on the street."

The quality of your product is important in an industry in which there are so many people bringing in so much. The only thing that will give you business is quality and reliability.

One of the things my name was good for above all other drug dealers was my product. I always had the best cocaine, so when I came out of prison and started dealing, I immediately captured a large part of the market.

Drug importers or manufacturers typically receive or produce the purest quality narcotics and forward them uncut to their distributors. Cutting a drug means adding a substance similar in colour and texture in order to increase the quantity available for sale. Most distributors claim that they do not cut drugs, but make their profit by selling smaller quantities

at higher prices. From the dealer's perspective, purchasing high-quality drugs is essential since quality sells, clients will return, and one's reputation is enhanced. Traffickers report that on occasion, only lower-quality drugs are available, and they will inform clients that the drugs are not up to standard. The customer can decide to purchase them, look elsewhere, or wait for better product. A norm that operates throughout the drug distribution chain is that buyers have the right to refuse shipments if they are unhappy with the quality of the drugs available.

Adler notes that prices for certain drugs tend to remain relatively stable and refers to this phenomenon as the prevailing price market (1985:45). Most dealers in this study similarly report that the price of drugs at the wholesale level tends to remain fairly constant, although prices do fluctuate somewhat based on supply and demand. A shortage will drive up the price, and surpluses lead to price discounts. These fluctuations are sometimes seasonal, but they also result from the success or failure of smuggling operations.

The city [Vancouver] is often flooded in cocaine. Right now, the wholesale price for a kilo is $42,000 [Can.] if you're well connected and $44,000 if you're not. There is a shortage. By July, this price will fall and you'll be begging people to take it for $31,000.

The quantity of drugs that one can afford to purchase also influences the price. As in any wholesale business, discounts are available for large purchases.

So if you came to me and you already had a name and a reputation, but you had no money, I would front you. But you're going to be paying top price for my risk. I'd charge you more of a mark-up. If you come to me with money, it's less price. If you can come to me with larger quantities of money, it's even less price.

The competitive nature of drug dealing is such that dealers will discount their prices to maintain and attract customers. At the higher levels, suppliers will similarly lower prices to keep their own dealers from jumping ship. Drug wholesalers can gain an edge on their competition by reinvesting their profits with cash purchases of large quantities of quality drugs. This ensures lower prices and allows them to undercut other dealers and/or increase their profits.

Higher-level drug traffickers realize that it is more difficult and dangerous to break into new markets and attract clients than it is to service and maintain present customers. Repeat business is valued and good customers receive good service. Adler's research (1985:57, 70) on 65 higher-level dealers and smugglers in Southern California describes many enduring relationships and considerable loyalty between suppliers and their customers. One of the primary reasons for customer loyalty is the concern with security. As Morselli explains, criminal participants are motivated to maintain trusted relationships.

> In this sense, future commitments are not obligatory, but a good contact, marked by reliability, trustworthiness, and a capacity to offer consistent access to new or stable opportunities, is a contact which must be retained. Since one cannot realistically trust everyone, those who have established themselves as reliable and trustworthy are usually those with whom additional transactions will subsequently be made. (Morselli, 2001:209)

Certain practices employed by legitimate businesses are used by drug dealers to retain clients. Several traffickers in the present study offered a money-back guarantee or promised to exchange drugs for clients who were disatisfied with their purchase. Although not all crews will offer refunds or allow drugs to be returned, those who do develop customer loyalty and maintain market share.

> If for some reason the drugs were not up to quality, he [the supplier] would take them back and replace them. With some suppliers, once you take the drugs, they're yours, good or bad.

> He [the supplier] sent me the best. There was sometimes 1 or 2 [kilos of cocaine] that had been cut and I could return them or find some people who didn't care and I would sell it to them.

Other research similarly reports that success in drug wholesaling depends on one's reputation as a trustworthy supplier of quality drugs (Adler & Adler, 1992; Hafley & Tewksbury, 1995; Redlinger, 1975). Reputation also relates to personal qualities such as one's judgment and business acumen—variables that are adversely affected by drug usage. Higher-level traffickers avoid doing business with people who use narcotics, and those few dealers who use or abuse drugs will attempt to hide this problem from their suppliers.

Another important factor in securing and maintaining market share is the ability to deliver sufficient quantities of product on a regular basis. Heavy users and addicts desperately need drugs and will look elsewhere if their regular source dries up. Importers and distributors who can deliver on schedule will easily establish and maintain a customer base and client loyalty. Although many dealers are content to stay with a dependable supplier, other drug wholesalers purposely develop a network of suppliers to ensure deliveries and obtain the best prices in the marketplace. Adler and Adler spoke to dealers who used this strategy:

> Major dealers generally prefer to operate with a larger selection of supply sources .... The largest dealers tend to maintain two or three connections that they buy from, going to one or the other when product is needed. They can thus be consistently counted on to have the desired substance and offer it at a dependable level of quality. (Adler & Adler, 1992: 269)

Morselli and Tremblay (2004) argue that the key to success for market offenders is to network through a non-redundant strategy by spreading out their working contacts in a brokerage-like rather than a clique-like way. Non-redundant contacts lead to different suppliers and so provide security of supplies and enhanced opportunities in criminal settings. Beare and Naylor (1999:19) similarly argue that the most reliable flow of narcotics comes from a myriad of small-scale uncoordinated firms. By using a number of sources, dealers ensure that some deliveries will get through and the market continues uninterrupted even when the police are successful at intercepting other shipments.

Relationships among Dealers

Many higher-level drug traffickers develop co-operative business relationships with other dealers at the same level as themselves. Despite being competitors, relationships are typically described as friendly and helpful. Over time, dealers learn one another's identity and will meet to socialize, discuss security concerns, share information, buy or borrow product from one another, pool their money to purchase drugs, and occasionally enter into partnerships. One subject describes how he developed working relationships with other traffickers.

> Over time I would hear about other dealers at the same level as myself and would be curious. I would know people who bought from them and I would try to get to know them to make alliances and check out the competition. But if the person turns out to be a total jerk, I insulate myself and avoid them.

Subjects enjoy socializing with others who have the same interests, occupation, and lifestyle, and several routinely partied together, sometimes spending huge amounts of money on their hedonistic pursuits. A 22-year-old dealer, who specialized in selling Ecstasy through organized raves, describes his connections to other wholesalers.

> There were always four or five of us at this level and we were all traffickers, and the rounds would come out and we would drop money all over the place—never saved any money. We spent it the day we made it and went out and made more—distorted values regarding money—crazy. We would give a stripper at the Zanzibar $1,000 just to sit with us. "I have to work." "No, here—sit with us." We would rent nice cars for the day or weekend. It was all lifestyle—no investments—nothing.

An organized crime figure and biker associate from Montreal explains his connections to other dealers.

> Most of the time you have five or six guys who hang out and do the same business. We're all suppliers and we know each other and drink together

and do one another favours. They may control other bars, but we are all independent and we are all friends and we all make money. We may have an agreement that in some bars we only go drinking.

These gatherings also provide dealers with valuable intelligence on police activities, suspected informants, and what is happening in the drug trade. A marijuana wholesaler from southwestern Ontario describes a similar relationship among suppliers in his community.

There were six of us who worked at the same level and all of us got along. We would tell each other what we had heard and what to look over. There were organized parties, and we got together with our wives and rented cottages and had meetings and talked. We had a weekly meeting and would party on my boat.

It is common practice for dealers at the same level to borrow or purchase drugs from one another when supplies run out. These purchases—known as spot sales—occur frequently because deliveries are notoriously irregular, yet client demand is steady and predictable. A number of subjects describe this practice:

If they were out, you tide them over until they got their next batch— professional courtesy.

There were four to five of us who were kilo-level guys in [a city of 150,000 people]. We were the main guys and we worked as a co-operative and would help each other out if one didn't have any. We were all about the same age and started in our mid-twenties. We

would help each other out when we could and occasionally party together.

I would know and meet other dealers at the same level as me. I had a nice arrangement with one lady from the same area of the city as me. If I ran out, I could send my people over to her and get what I needed to supply my clients. It would work on an exchange, and I would pay her for it or give her back the same when my supply came in. But she would occasionally borrow from me. She wasn't greedy and it turned out to be a nice arrangement. I heard about her over a period of years, and we just struck up a good relationship and we knew each other's people.

I supplied other dealers when they ran out. Then you always know if you run out, you had a place to turn to. That happened all the time. I had clients who wanted it and I had to provide it. I would pick it up from other dealers and they often trusted me for it. I would pay them later.

Not all drug traffickers report amiable and professional relationships with others at the same level. Some have had conflicts and are very cautious, and most will avoid dealers known to be violent, untrustworthy, and flamboyant. Dealers who socialize and work with other traffickers choose their associates carefully and deal primarily with people who have solid reputations in the drug world.

Partnerships

Almost all subjects in this study operate as independent entrepreneurs, employ their own staff, and are free to purchase and sell to whomever they wish. Slightly over one-quarter of the sample (20/70, 28.6%) worked with a business partner. The advantage of partnerships include a reduced workload, a more reliable supply of drugs, and increased security. A career criminal who controlled several bars in Montreal explains why he formed a partnership after years of operating on his own.

> I have a friend who is my partner. We met because we were both dealers and we would have a few beers together and talk. We worked on our own for years and decided to be partners. I decided to have a partner because it became too much work, and if something happens, the business still goes on. And you can buy and sell more because he knows other people.
>
> If I go on holidays or if I do not want to go out for a week, somebody is there to check on the business. You have a partner to be more secure. You share the tasks. I may want to take a break or it may be time to not show your face. There may be some heat. The heat comes! Oh God, the heat comes. We both make decisions and we both may do the tour. It's a 50/50 split on everything.

In this case, each person had different connections, allowing them to shop around for the best deals possible. Having several sources ensures a reliable supply of drugs if one supplier should run dry or go out of business.

Partnerships also allow dealers to pool their resources, move to a higher level, increase profits, and expand the business. Four cocaine dealers in Toronto formed a partnership and moved from street sales into wholesaling and importing. One of these men describes the arrangement and his shock at having a partner turn informant.

> My business partners were also my friends. It was a business friendship. There were four of us at the same level. I didn't stray too far and I knew them for a long time, and we all went to school together. We had all been independent and selling on the street, and pulling ski masks on our faces and selling right in front of the police. We had been through a lot together.
>
> Then we had a meeting and decided to organize. Once you move off the street, you move out of the line of fire. You can avoid potential problems easier. You also make a lot more money. We pooled our resources and used each of our strengths.
>
> You can have a business and not be close to someone, but me and these guys were friends also. There were things I didn't expect from certain people. If you and I are friends and we deal on a daily basis, trust is a lot of that friendship. I would not have believed you if you had told me this guy would have done certain things. Let's just say that he had his own agenda. I don't want to get too deep into that.

Some partnerships involve limited co-operation as in instances in which dealers simply pool their resources in order to maximize their buying power. They nonetheless refer to themselves as partners because they are also friends, socialize together, discuss security issues, pass on relevant information, and assist one another in various ways. However, each has his own clientele, makes his own sales, and collects his own profits. In some instances, they may compete on a friendly basis for sales and guard their customers from one another. In other cases, they agree not sell to one another's clients without permission.

Although most partnering relationships are egalitarian, others involve an older established dealer taking on a junior partner in a mentoring capacity. The junior person typically takes more risks and does not receive an equal share of the profits. In most partnerships, however, dealers are close friends who socialize together and share tasks, risks, and profits equitably. The friendship is typically long lasting and precedes their involvement in drug trafficking. The partnership appears to fulfill expressive as well as instrumental needs, and dealers develop strong bonds with their partners.

> It's not just a business partnership. You have to be on the same page on virtually every aspect. You have to be close. Once you decide to put that kind of trust in someone, it can't be all about business.

A former street-level dealer who moved to wholesaling and later imported cocaine describes his partnership:

> I have a partner for life, and we grew up together and we're really close friends and we're tight, and I would never stab him and he wouldn't stab me. This trust is deep and we are like brothers and we are connected and think alike. We hit it off from about age 15 and have been through a lot together.

As discussed in Chapter 4, some dealers experience feelings of alienation and isolation and a high degree of stress because of their criminal lifestyle. This appears to be less of a problem for dealers who share the risks with partners. Partnerships provide traffickers with an opportunity to discuss problems and concerns, receive encouragement and support, share risks, endure setbacks, and celebrate successes together. Partnerships have expressive as well as instrumental functions and appear to diminish or make manageable the stresses involved in a life of crime.

Modus Operandi and Security

Criminal organizations exist in an environment in which law-enforcement agencies threaten to put them out of business, so this has clear implications for their structure and functioning. Illicit enterprises are required to engage in risk-management strategies in order to protect their assets from seizure and their personnel from arrest and conviction. Because the risks they confront are varied and pervasive, risk-management strategies developed by higher-level traffickers are multidimensional and multipurposed. Their modus operandi includes a number of security measures that protect them against theft or robbery, diminish losses through bad loans or police seizures, shield clients from competitors, offer protection from would-be informants, and insulate themselves from arrest and conviction. The division of labour compartmentalizes tasks in such a way that the arrest of one person does not necessarily implicate others. In addition, the movement and storage of drugs and money is organized so that a police bust will result in only a portion of the assets being seized. The following is a discussion of the strategies used by higher-level drug traffickers to protect themselves, associates, and their assets from the threats posed by other criminals and the police. Considerable energy, time, and resources are devoted to managing these risks.

Security through Violence and Intimidation

The vast majority of dealers in this study describe themselves as non-violent and rely on techniques other than violence or intimidation to protect themselves from theft, extortion, robbery, and/or would-be informants. A major concern is the risk posed by informants. Offenders realize, however, that by the time a person has co-operated with the police, it is too late to use violence effectively. Dealers also know that the police can offer security to informants through witness-protection programs and a variety of informal means. Criminal drug traffickers are far more likely than businessmen dealers to use the threat of violence to deter informants, but they, too, admit that coercion is often ineffective. Nonetheless, the fear of violent retribution does have some deterrent value. A few subjects in this study made it clear that one reason for not informing on associates is because they feared the consequences for themselves and/or their families. A higher-level cocaine importer who smuggled drugs from Mexico through the U.S. into Canada turned down a tempting police offer partly out of fear.

> The cops offered me all my assets back and all charges dropped, and no extradiction and a minimum sentence if I turned over my supplier and buyers. Americans wanted the suppliers and Canada wanted the buyers. They would also drop the charges against my wife and daughter. They make it tempting. I would be in protective custody, but it wasn't in my character to inform and besides, I would be dead. The [name withheld] brothers were my suppliers and they control the Tijuana cartel. Last year they lined 25 people up against a retaining wall and shot them all, even the little kids. You don't fuck with Mexicans or you're dead. They will travel worldwide to find you.

A small number of subjects describe implicit threats made against family members. In three cases, offenders report that suppliers asked to meet with them and their families before doing business. Two others routinely had an employee meet family members of lower-level dealers as a security precaution.

> Before we do business with someone, a member of our group has to have known him and goes to his family home.

> We have someone go to their home, meet the family, and the message that one can glean is the insinuation that we know your family now. There is a certain method of doing things for security, and people are less likely to be informants or *agent provocateurs*.

Another subject describes his attempt to conduct business with a South American connection.

> Later we started to bring in drugs from outside the country. We started with 5–10 kilos each week. We started small and worked up. We made a deal with some Peruvians, and our Peruvian friend had to translate all the conversations. The way they work is to front you the drugs, but for security, they invite your wife and kids to Peru for a fully paid holiday. They stay in luxury accommodations for a month or so until you pay them the money you owe them. I told them that nobody was going nowhere. I showed them around and showed them my gym and my home and told them that my family wasn't going anywhere. We eventually got them to trust us and made the deal.

Some criminal drug dealers occasionally use force—primarily to collect debts—but most emphasize that they prefer to do business without the use of violence. Although several businessmen dealers would occasionally portray themselves as violent people, they rarely used force. A common intimidation technique is for players to imply or suggest that they are part of a larger and violent organization.

If a dealer was too slow paying, I would never threaten them, but I'd let them think that there were people behind me that expected to be paid. There was no one behind me, just me, but it didn't hurt to let them think there would be consequences.

Whenever I had to talk to someone, it was always "We." "We want our money." "We're getting impatient." Let them think there will be consequences.

It is difficult to estimate from this research the extent to which implicit or direct threats against dealers or their families are used as a security measure by higher-level traffickers since the subject was not discussed at length in the interviews. Although some respondents refused to co-operate with the police because they were concerned for themselves and/or their families, none of these men had been explicitly threatened. RCMP investigators paint a somewhat different picture of violence among higher-level dealers. They suggest that the use of force is not infrequent, and that intimidation is used on a regular basis to collect debts and frighten would-be informants and witnesses. It is quite likely that respondents in this study downplayed and understated the use of violence for instrumental ends in their businesses.

In general, whenever acts or threats of violence are used by drug syndicates, they are directed against other participants in the criminal marketplace. There were no reports from inmates or police respondents in which law-enforcement officials or members of the general public were targeted. Drug traffickers realize that the use of violence can increase risks and threaten security, provoke a police response, and interrupt the flow of transactions. This is especially inconvenient to criminals engaged in a market enterprise. Because drug trafficking consists of ongoing exchanges that benefit all participants, everyone has a vested interest in preventing conflicts that threaten the network. Most of the dealers in this sample appear to rely on friendship and trust, secrecy, diplomacy, and information networks for their security rather than intimidation. The use of violence is discussed in greater detail in Chapter 6.

Security through Trust: Friendship, Kinship, and Ethnicity

Trust and kinship are much more important than violence in running an illegitimate enterprise and reducing risks. Higher-level traffickers are very selective in choosing partners, employees, clients, and associates. Crews typically consist of people who grew up together and have known one another for many years. Friendship, kinship, and ethnicity are variables affecting trust, and associates are typically chosen from those known to the dealer in his immediate social circle. As discussed earlier, ethnicity is a significant factor since friendship and kinship networks are often culturally based. Understandably, there is a tendency to define members of one's social circle, kinship network, and ethnic background as trustworthy and view other groups as outsiders. Information networks within ethnic communities and in source countries allow traffickers to assess a person's character. There is widespread mistrust of strangers because there is always a possibility that they may turn out to be police agents or undercover officers.

Kinship ties can be exploited to build small, but sometimes very successful criminal enterprises .... The most stable illegal enterprises are those relying on pre-existing, non-economic ties ... and able to embed their economic activities in non-economic relationships of solidary type .... Illegal transactions or any other illegal action that requires the co-operation of two or more men are tremendously facilitated when familiarity and interpersonal trust already exist among the parties. For these reasons, illegal exchanges tend to take place within pre-existing networks of information and exchange capable of guaranteeing the trustworthiness of the parties. (Paoli, 2002:83–85)

Among career criminals, trust is often based on the person's standing within the criminal milieu. New personnel can normally enter this select circle through associates who vouch for the person's trustworthiness and integrity. Higher-level traffickers recognize that the police use informants and undercover officers to infiltrate drug syndicates, and dealers will check the background of new clients through their information networks. A number of dealers explain the caution taken.

> In our group, a guy must vouch for a guy and if anything happens, that guy is responsible for him. You have to be very careful who you propose and he has to be an asset and a good worker and one who you can get along with. If he loses money, you are responsible to make up the losses.

> If I didn't know you, I didn't do business with you. If you and I were buddies and you had a friend who wanted to buy drugs, he would have to go through you. I would never meet with him directly. Another principle I followed was to keep to a minimum what people knew about my business.

> If you're bringing someone into the business, you look for the same attributes you would in a legitimate business. He has to be a good guy and good reputation and hard working. Someone has to vouch for him to prevent betrayals and deceptions.

> At our level, there has to be a lot of trust. I have to know that someone is solid. There has to be a chain of trustworthy people. I may not know you directly, but we both know other people who we both trust and they vouch for us. We looked for older people who had a reputation—people who were in the criminal world and were known to be trustworthy. The middle person also had to be trusted.

The police attempt to overcome this security measure by introducing undercover officers into a drug milieu through an agent/informant who will validate the operator's cover story. The agent is typically an offender who has been arrested and offered lenient treatment in exchange for his or her co-operation. The agent may also be paid large sums of money to make the introduction and vouch for the undercover officer. Police investigative techniques are discussed in Chapter 7.

Although trust relationships help to ensure security, relying on informal kinship and friendship networks clearly limits growth possibilities. Dealers will frequently neglect promising ventures and avoid potentially lucrative markets because they lack the trusted counterparts. Opportunity theory suggests that access to these types of networks provide would-be dealers with considerable advantages in the pursuit of illegal business.

Security through Redundancy

Legitimate businesses minimize costs by ensuring that personnel are used efficiently and activities are not replicated. Illegitimate businesses, on the other hand, value risk reduction ahead of cost efficiencies and will purposely duplicate activities to maximize safety. Thus, it is common for dealers to use multiple storage facilities, bank accounts, cellular phones, couriers, smurphs, etc., in order to minimize losses in the event that arrests and seizures are made. This built-in redundancy minimizes the damage that is inflicted by law enforcement and allows the syndicate to recover. Because of these security measures, the drug network is resilient to disruption and can quickly reconstitute itself and resume business as usual. Williams argues that redundancy is a necessity for organized-crime syndicates.

> For networks, which almost invariably face the problems of degradation and attack by law enforcement, redundancy is a virtue. It provides a range of options to move commodities to the market and to repatriate profits, allowing the network to exploit the path of least resistance. Even more important, it enables network members to take over tasks and responsibilities from those who have been arrested or killed. (Williams, 1998:158)

Security through Size and Structure

Higher-level drug syndicates protect themselves in part by developing and maintaining a small tight-knit organization. A small group offers considerable safety advantages since crew members can be chosen from trusted and known associates; associates and employees can be monitored more closely; and the organization is difficult to penetrate by law enforcement. The 62 crews in this study ranged in size from three to nine members, and most operated exclusively in one metropolitan area and made no attempt to expand beyond their city (see also Hafley & Tewksbury, 1995:216; Reuter & Haaga, 1989:50). Crews typically

consist of a few core members made up of the dealer, occasionally his partner(s), one or two trusted associates, and paid employees or lower-level operatives. Leaders make deals, oversee the flow of money and product, supervise employees, control information, and make decisions regarding security. These central figures protect themselves from the more dangerous activity of crossing national borders, moving drugs from storage areas to distributors/clients, and exchanging currencies by a process known as "layering"—i.e., by hiring others who follow orders and take most of the risks. These underlings will know little about the criminal enterprise other than their assigned tasks, and may not even know the identity of core members. Peripheral or fringe members will include couriers, money changers, drivers, and enforcers and are likely to be employed on a fee-for-service basis. These workers are more vulnerable to arrest and may be considered expendable by those above them. Fringe members may also include people in legitimate businesses who ship drugs across borders, as well as professionals such as lawyers, accountants, and bankers whose job is to launder money, conceal its source, and invest profits. Higher-level dealers rely upon a division of labour and layers of personnel to distance themselves from the most dangerous activities—the physical transfer of drugs and money.

One marijuana/hashish importer describes his crew as consisting of himself, a boat captain who smuggled his drugs into the U.S. from Jamaica; a pilot who flew them into Canada; and an associate who received and distributed the drugs in Canada. He also worked with three independent drug wholesalers who purchased his drugs and passed them on to their own distributors. In addition, he occasionally employed couriers who drove the product from Florida to northern U.S. states where it was picked up and flown into Canada. This dealer defines his crew as consisting of four people: himself, his boat captain, his pilot, and his "right-hand man." Although his three distributors had dealt exclusively with him for several years, each was fully independent and free to deal with whomever they chose. Even his captain and pilot occasionally moonlighted by transporting drugs for other importers.

In his latest indictment, 30 co-accused were arrested, including all members of his crew, his three distributors, a lawyer who helped him establish legitimate fronts for laundering money, several independent smugglers of American citizenship who shared the cost of importing drugs into the U.S., his boat captain's girlfriend and assistant, lower-level dealers, and some of their clients. His suppliers in Jamaica were not arrested or charged. The police investigation that led to his arrest took two years to complete and was coordinated by the RCMP and involved Canada Customs, two Canadian municipal police departments, the FBI, and the DEA in the United States.

Another drug-dealing crew was run by a career criminal who sold 1.5–2 kilos of methamphetamines per week through a network of lower-level dealers. His crew consisted of himself, an associate who received 25% of profits, and three people who transported drugs on a fee-for-service basis. Drugs were sold to a network of 15 distributors, all of whom were independent entrepreneurs who cut and resold the product to their own clients.

One high-level cocaine importer in this study cut back the size of his operation out of concern that it had grown too large and that too many people had learned about his business. He laid off people and took a six month sabbatical. Later he started again with fewer employees and clients.

> I had been in it for six or seven years and things were going well. I had good people working for me, but I heard they were flashing their money and I decided to take a break and get out of

it for awhile. The business had got too big and there were too many people who knew too much. The more people who are in the know, the more that is said, the more the danger.

> I started getting rid of people by telling them that I was getting out. I told them to go out on their own. I sort of meant that I was going to retire, but it was a plan to get rid of them in a nice manner. I had 15 to 20 people working for me, including eight distributors in Canada.

> I sat out for about six months, thinking about things and taking a break. When I came back into it, I cut it down to one main supplier, two drivers, one guy who moved the product, and two distributors. I dealt with six of my most trusted people. It was leaner and safer.

Several dealers passed up opportunities to expand their drug business or to partner with other syndicates because they wished to maintain both their independence and small size. Most believed that risks increase with the number of players involved and considered it too dangerous to expand beyond their circle of trusted associates. They also note that a large organization is not necessary to run a drug-trafficking business since costs are relatively low and small quantities of product can be easily handled by a few people and reap millions of dollars in rewards. A major marijuana importer turned down offers to become partners with an American drug-smuggling crew and an outlaw motorcycle gang because of safety concerns and because he preferred being his own boss.

> I always chose to be independent. I didn't want to be hooked in with a whole bunch of other people. I operated in a small cell. I didn't want to be a

part of anybody else. I wanted to make my own decisions and reap my own rewards and accept my own mistakes and downfall if it came.

A study conducted in Germany found that the majority (54%) of criminal enterprises targeted by organized crime bureaus between 1991–1999 involved fewer than 10 people and only 7% of the organized-crime proceedings involved more that 50 suspects at a time (Paoli, 1999). Research in other countries similarly describe higher-level drug dealing as consisting of small flexible organizations that compete with one another for market share. There is little evidence in these studies that drug traffickers enjoy a monopolistic power over supply or can significantly influence prices by varying the quantity or the output of drugs (Adler, 1985; Adler & Adler, 1992; Dorn, Murji, & South, 1992; Dorn & South, 1990; Hafley & Tewksbury, 1995; Reuter & Haaga, 1989).

Security through Secrecy

Higher-level traffickers are secretive about their activities and operate on a "need-to-know" basis (see Reuter & Haaga, 1989:46–47). This means that underlings are not informed about activities that do not affect them directly, nor are they allowed to know the identities of people above them in the drug chain. Knowledge and information are tightly controlled and norms prohibit crew members from asking too many questions. One dealer states:

If someone has no need to know something or someone, they are not allowed that privilege. Only me and my partner knew who our source was. Most of the people who worked for me did not know who my clients were. We always used nicknames when

discussing clients. Most people know not to ask questions. All you know is what I want you to see, and what you see is not enough to convict me. If you start to ask questions, then something is not right.

The division of labour in most drug syndicates is such that subjects know and interact with only a handful of people. A 44-year-old career criminal describes how he and his partner worked their drug laboratories.

When you become a laboratory man, everything is done to ensure the utmost secrecy. Here's me and my partner of 12 years. We've done multimillion-dollar deals together, yet he doesn't even know where the dope is kept or where the cash is kept. Only me. He doesn't need to know. He dealt with other customers that I never met. There was no need for me to meet them or to know who they were. You divide up the division of labour and everything is so segmented and secret. Everything is compartmentalized.

A dealer who moved from street-level sales to importing and distributing cocaine employed his brother as a buffer between himself and his clients. He kept part of his operation secret from his brother who, in turn, kept secrets from him.

I had a house that nobody knew about it, not even my brother. I used to keep the storage there. My brother was a go-between the people on the street and myself. Maybe my brother is selling stuff on the street, but that is a level that I don't need to know about. He would be letting off ounces here and there, but that has nothing to do with me. I get my cut and he would put it in my pile, and he'd give it to me in a month and I don't care. I don't need to know certain things.

A number of dealers emphasized the importance of keeping their drug business secret from the women in their lives.

You can't tell anybody anything. At that level, women must not know anything about the business. She knows nothing, nothing, not a thing. She doesn't know who you talk to, who you deal with, she doesn't know names, she legitimately doesn't know. She is kept totally in the dark.

In one cocaine syndicate, the "financial manager" was responsible for money laundering and setting up legitimate fronts. He knew nothing about the drug-distribution activities and was never allowed to meet anyone but the dealer and his closest associate. Most subjects report that clients will meet only one or two crew members and would not know the identities of others. For example, a police investigation into a cocaine-importing ring led to the arrest of 28 people. One of the kingpins behind this smuggling operation knew only six of his co-accused: his partner, two people who acted as runners and couriers, and three clients. The other co-accuseds were people he had never met, including several couriers employed by his partner and a number of independent, lower-level drug dealers. Individuals employed on a fee-for-service basis typically know even fewer of their co-accused and little about the structure and functioning of the business.

Higher-level dealers operate under the principle that security concerns require that as few people as possible know about their illegal activity. In some cases, suppliers and distributors conduct business through intermediaries and never even meet one another. One British Columbian cocaine importer, who lived in a relatively small town, sold most of his product to clients in Vancouver. He took over a drug-smuggling operation vacated by another dealer and dealt with his two main clients through their respective intermediaries. He never spoke to either client, did not know who they were, and assumed that his identity was unknown to them.

The big purchasers were from Vancouver and were purchasing any amount that was for sale. All I know is that the product would end up in Vancouver. They would each purchase 10 or 15 kilos a week and it was a cash on delivery. Where it ended up after that, I don't know. I never had the drugs in my possession at all and could unload them in one day. I never met either of them and we didn't even talk on the phone. My guy would talk to their man and I kept my distance. That's just the way I liked it.

Other dealers report that they were aware of the identity of their supplier, but had never been introduced. An offender who purchased his drugs in California and smuggled them into Canada had minimal information about his suppliers and clients. He, too, had taken over another dealer's operation and knew little about his contacts.

I knew who the suppliers were, but I never met them personally and I don't know much about them and I didn't want to know. I knew they were getting large amounts, so they had to be high on the chain. I met with my clients in the beginning, but after that, I had my right-hand man take care of the transactions for money and drugs. I knew little about my clients and I don't know what they were doing. I didn't want to know—like, for instance, I didn't know anyone's last name and no one knew my last name. I was just Bill.

This situation is rare, but it illustrates how drug traffickers prefer to operate on a need-to-know basis. In the vast majority of cases, traffickers interact with people immediately above and below them on the drug-distribution chain and keep a safe distance from those outside this inner circle. Several dealers comment on this principle.

Somebody below me doesn't get to know anybody above me. Moving up the ladder takes time. Having the connections is the main thing. I keep my people and nobody will take my spot and take my business. We all try to protect our back. If someone is busted, they can't talk about what they don't know.

The guy above me doesn't know where everything goes. The only time I talk to him is if somebody wants a big purchase, like 30 kilos or more, and then we discuss it.

I had somebody whose job it is to take care of the couriers and when it reaches that stage, I don't even know who the couriers are anymore. They don't know me and I am not going to get to know them. Their contact is with him and as far as they are concerned, he is the boss and running the whole thing.

There were no conflicts between us during the grow operation. Everything was discussed and done by consensus. All was going to be split evenly. I didn't know how it was going to be sold. That wasn't up to me. Two of my co-accused knew some people who would buy it. They said they could get $1,800 a pound. A plant can produce a half-pound. That's approximately $1,000 a plant and we had 3,758 plants. I didn't care where the money came from and I didn't feel I was being left out of the loop at all.

A number of dealers were introduced to higher-level suppliers as a courtesy. The meetings usually took place over dinner and drinks and business was not discussed. A dealer who had earlier served five years in a federal penitentiary for bank robbery later moved into drug trafficking in Southwestern Ontario through a prison connection. His source was a former inmate linked to organized criminals in Montreal. Although this syndicate operated on a need-to-know basis, he was eventually allowed to meet his sources.

My network consisted of contacts and linkages with people I grew up with and knew from prison. I didn't know much about the Montreal organization I was dealing with. I knew there were prominent crime connections in the Montreal underworld. I was invited down and my contact introduced me to some people and we had dinner at their clubs. These were bars they owned and they were well-known crime figures in the city. These were organized crime figures and we met over drinks, but we didn't talk business.

Security through Information Networks

One mechanism by which higher-level drug traffickers protect themselves is through the use of information networks. Dealers attempt to stay abreast of what is happening in the drug scene through their various contacts. Many traffickers seek out information on a daily basis and may even meet with other dealers to discuss and analyze everything they hear. Topics of interest include who has been arrested, who is considered an informant, who is making money, and who is connected to whom. Also discussed are police strategies and investigative techniques.

Information networks are informally structured and consist of people who are connected to one another in the drug chain. Typically, observations, hearsay, and other information are passed up the ladder to higher-level dealers from distributors and employees. Suppliers will also proactively seek specific information and will ask crew members and distributors to research the background of people and topics of interest. All dealers keep their eyes and ears open, but not all make reference to having an information network. Some offenders are highly secretive, insular, and deal within a very small circle of trusted friends. They usually have tight control of their operation and pay little attention to what is happening beyond their own level of involvement. The majority of higher-level traffickers, however, make use of information filtered up through the distribution chain.

> The purpose is to build a network. It doesn't happen overnight. When I started, it took me two years to build this network by watching and observing and finding information and seeing how people do things. You become good if you're aware of the information around you.

> As you move up, you move out of the line of fire, but you are still always in touch with what is going on. You don't totally detach because you go out every day and people know you, and you talk and they tell you what is going on.

> You become successful with what you know and the information you

have. You need information and good information. You're only smart if you have information.

Information networks develop over time and career criminals typically have a more sophisticated communication network than businessmen traffickers. Most career criminals receive information from other criminals, people in their neighbourhood, and from their illegal drug business. These dealers actively gather information and often meet regularly with other traffickers to share their knowledge.

Dealers who are closest to the street (retail) are able to tap into what is happening in their neighbourhood, the club scene, the courts, and throughout the city. Information flows up the chain from drug addicts, street-level dealers, petty criminals, prison inmates, prostitutes, strippers, bartenders, doormen, drug users, and other distributors. This information is discussed, analyzed, and attempts may be made to verify the data. A career criminal who operated in Montreal bars describes how he gathered information to protect himself from informants and the police.

> Your network helps you look for the rat. Every day you keep in touch, and at night at the bars you talk to people and you find out who got busted and you send a guy to court, and the undercovers testify and you see their faces. You try to get a photo and if there are rats, you do something about them. We had an information network that would give us as much information as possible as to what the police were up to and who they were investigating.

> Your network is the main way of keeping informed of what is going around. If you're around bars, the doorman tells you the new faces and everybody looks for people who are

suspicious, or a regular person who is no longer showing up anymore. If a bust happens and he disappears, you try to find out why. The doorman, the barman, and the waitress know when something suspicious is going down. The dancers will pass on information. If someone asks a waitress, "Did you see Charlie tonight?" I'll hear about it.

Dealers are primarily focused on their personal safety, and many assert that the information network is a vital component of their security. Networks allow dealers to trust certain people and avoid others.

I never did business with certain types of people. I would avoid anybody who was known to be sleazy or into crime. You get to know who these types are and I would avoid any criminal types.

I chose my people extremely carefully. In one case, I took two years before I allowed this one guy and checked him out. I was selective.

I wanted people who were trustworthy and intelligent. I would never allow any low life in my business.

I try to get information on the police or informants. If someone is arrested, and for some reason is in and out, if you know the situation of their arrest, that may tell you that he's giving up someone.

You have to have trust in selecting your people. You can do that by checking around and asking friends. I might ask the main guy above me. Who I run with is my business, but you ask advice from the big guys and they will be helpful.

I will ask other dealers on the same level about someone to see if they know anything. We try to protect each other's back.

Some dealers use their networks to discover whether or not they are under surveillance.

One time, someone was at the corner on a phone calling me, saying that there was someone in a car across from me in a Buick convertible. It looks like he's watching the place. Then I get another call from the guy in the car telling me about the guy in the phone booth, walking back and forth. The guy in the car was a security person and the other was a customer.

I had guys watching for cars that drive by or stay a little too long on my street. They take down the licence plate numbers and try to get a good look at the driver.

I heard about that guy [undercover agent] before it happened. I was even offered a chance to purchase from him and I told him I didn't even do that stuff. He said, "Oh, I just saw you with the nice clothes."

Information about police strategies and investigative techniques provides dealers with knowledge that can help them to avoid police traps and improve security. One smuggler used information learned from other dealers to help select drug couriers.

It's more like learning on the job. With smuggling, you need to find out what they're looking for so you can avoid being zeroed in on. Once I found out that they have profiles of mules carrying drugs into the country, I avoided hiring people like that.

Another supplier learned that the police had cleverly busted one of his distributors by tempting him into selling 40 kilos of cocaine to an undercover officer. The sting involved a newspaper plant announcing that the client—an undercover officer—had won a lottery. This information made the supplier appreciate how crafty the police can be and strengthened his resolve to be very careful in dealing with others.

In addition to providing security, information networks help drug traffickers develop and protect their business interests. Dealers actively monitor the availability of drugs, the quality and price, shipping routes, and what the competition is up to. Some will scrutinize the actions of their own distributors to ensure they operate according to sound business principles.

> I would use my information network to find out what was happening on the street. I might want to know how the market is going and prices and quality of cocaine. If I learn that there is a lot of very good quality, then I know that certain people have managed to get a delivery through. I might use that to adjust my prices or try to tap into the supply.

Information networks are used to seek out new suppliers, better-quality product at better prices, and help dealers locate reliable distributors to expand operations. Networks can help to gain introductions and verify the identity, reputation, and trustworthiness of all parties. A cocaine dealer describes how he used prison contacts to find potential distributors.

> My network consisted of contacts and linkages with others. These were mostly people I grew up with and knew from prison. Sales became a problem because we were importing so much

cocaine that our distribution network couldn't keep up. We were importing more than we could sell.

> We were scrambling to find buyers to handle the product. They don't just pop out of the woodwork. It is difficult to find reliable people. I had contacts with ex-cons and I learned who had been released from prison and where they were.

Other benefits gleaned from having connections include information about and/or access to weapons, passports, couriers, foreign suppliers, money laundering, corrupt officials, and other illicit goods and services.

> You can learn a lot about cellphones and pagers on the street. People talk about these things all the time.

> Networks mean that you might know people who can get you free stuff, cheap airline tickets, clean your money, make big purchases, and hide it for you. You may know people in different parts of the country who can sell for you.

Subjects report that there is a lot of unsubstantiated gossip and rumour that goes around drug circles. Information is not always reliable and must be used with caution or verified.

> Stories are so hard to believe and you have sift through it. I was not quick to pass judgment.

> If I heard something, I would check it out to make sure the information is reliable.

> Obviously you try to find out about potential informers. People's names get bantered about all the time. Most

people have their name mentioned at one time or another. It is very easy for somebody to tag you with that label. I'm not quick to jump to conclusions until I can check it out for myself.

Police report that biker gangs will occasionally have a representative sit in court during the trial, listen to the testimony, and gather information on informants and investigative tactics. In one case involving the arrest of a several Colombian-based dealers, their pilots, and the seizure of four aircraft and a huge quantity of drugs, the RCMP observed men transcribing the trial testimony of officers and witnesses. Further investigation revealed that the transcripts were faxed to a law firm in New York City and passed on to bosses in Colombia. The smugglers were interested in finding out how their associates were caught, who the informants might be, and to learn from their mistakes.

The information system that dealers rely upon is seldom supplemented with more formal research. With the exception of a few subjects who gleaned information from the Internet and marijuana growers who read magazines such as *High Times*, *Cannibis Culture*, *Heads*, and *Weed World*, most higher-level traffickers do not read books, legal documents, or police manuals in their attempt to develop security systems. Information is gathered informally through observations, gossip, hearsay, and word-of-mouth, and most dealers have little or no idea what the police are up to. The fact that so many are surprised at the way in which conspiracy laws work is testimony to the inadequacy of their intelligence and information. Although most respondents in this study believe that information networks assisted them in their business enterprise and were an integral part of their security, these networks did not protect them from arrest and conviction. As one dealer states:

You never know if information you get is true or false, and you don't know what the police are doing until it's too late.

It would be a mistake, however, to conclude that information networks provide little or no benefit to higher-level drug traffickers. These networks provide access to suppliers and distributors and contribute to the growth and financial success of their illegitimate businesses. Many subjects in this study have operated for years and their information networks no doubt contributed to this longevity. There are also traffickers outside this sample who operate untouched by the law or who have amassed their fortunes and retired. Information networks may have played a vital role in protecting them from detection and arrest. While it is clear that informal information networks do serve several purposes for most dealers, it is also clear that they are unlikely to protect drug traffickers from a sophisticated police investigation.

Security through Corruption

Many subjects in this study paid airline employees, truckers, and ordinary citizens to store, hide, transport, and courier drugs. Lawyers, bank employees, and accountants are also used to establish legitimate businesses, launder money, and facilitate foreign exchanges. Although this type of graft is common, few dealers corrupt public officials. Only one syndicate reported bribing a law-enforcement employee—a secretary who worked in a police department and provided information on car registrations. Three drug-dealing syndicates reported bribing officials in source countries to assist them in exporting illicit drugs and/or avoid criminal prosecution. Apart from the police secretary, subjects made no attempt to bribe or corrupt public officials in Canada. Most believed that police and

Customs officials were difficult and dangerous to bribe, and that their business could function without corrupt officials.

Despite the lack of corruption, four dealers reported that police contacts occasionally informed them about ongoing investigations, informants, and possible raids. This was apparently done without the exchange of money because of pre-existing friendships between the dealer and officer. A former professional hockey player maintained friendships with several police officers he knew from his childhood and through sports.

> I get word of the heat often because the cops tell me. In the sports world, there were lots of cops and they might tell me they hear my name. When you hear that from cops, you don't ignore it. You trust the word. If you hear it two or three times, you take off for a month and you let the others do the work.
>
> One time, a cop called me and I had him training my dogs. I had a couple of German shepherds that would attack on command. I received a call to come for training for my dogs and I knew something is up since I wasn't scheduled to show up. I go there and I got information that the RCMP was coming for me for a bust. He heard they were coming to my house and they would come with income tax people, and he advised me to get everything out of my name. And I changed all the cars and house into my sister's name.

A cocaine dealer from a small town was friends with several of the local police and claims that on occasion, certain officers would warn him to lie low because the police were interested in his activities.

> The network tells you who is doing what in the drug trade. That never

hurts to know. Police agendas. Any police sources. If you want to find out, you can find out. Sometimes police would out and out tell me who is not trustwrorthy or to watch friends, jealous people. If you are getting ratted, they are more likely jealous of the money and success.

A number of studies of higher-level drug traffickers in the U.S. and Britain also reveal little evidence of official corruption. Dorn, Murji, and South (1992) report a relative lack of corruption among public officials in their interview study of 25 drug dealers incarcerated in British prisons. Similarly, cocaine wholesalers in the U.S. tend to avoid contact with authorities, preferring instead to operate in the shadows without resorting to corruption or violence (Reuter & Haaga, 1989; VanDuyne, 1996–1997). Adler (1985) similarly found little official corruption.

> Because Southwest County drug traffickers were entrepreneurial and disorganized, their ability to corrupt drug agents was insignificant at best. (Adler, 1985:119)

These findings contrast starkly with the widespread and systemic corruption of politicians and public officials in developing source countries. In Colombia, for example, the loss or weakness of authority of the central state has helped give rise to the emergence of drug trafficking on a large scale (Garcia Marquez, 1990).

Several hypotheses may explain the relatively corruption-free status of public officials in Canada. In addition to the strength and moral authority that government institutions command, Canadian cultural values and traditions instill a pride in the civil service and help prevent criminal behaviour. In addition, the relatively high salaries and benefits paid to civil servants help to create job satisfaction and offer a measure of deterrence against corruption since public employees have much to lose.

The small size of drug syndicates also explains why they seldom corrupt public officials. Independent drug traffickers operate in a relatively small, secret network and are unlikely to have close contacts with civil servants or law-enforcement personnel. They also lack the resources that huge foreign cartels have to corrupt high-ranking public officials. Instead, they maintain a low profile, operate within a closed network, avoid contact with the police and public officials, and keep themselves off the law-enforcement radar screen.

Williams and Godson argue that countries with strong democratic traditions and institutions are less vulnerable to the scourge of corruption.

> Well-functioning democracies with a high level of political legitimacy, a strong and deeply entrenched culture of legality, rule of law, structures for accountability and oversight, and high levels of transparency inhibit the emergence of organized crime. If these characteristics are present, it is more difficult for organized crime to develop a symbiotic relationship with the political and adminstrative elites and come into the mainstream of political life in the country. (Williams & Godson, 2002:320–321)

Because Canada is a wealthy, democratic country legitimized by an open and responsible political system based on strong moral values, corruption among government official is relatively uncommon.

Security through Diplomacy

Higher-level dealers operate under the principle that it is wise to treat people with respect and avoid making enemies. This requires that dealers keep their word, pay their debts, sell quality drugs, be generous and understanding, and otherwise build goodwill with employees and associates. Drug traffickers are keenly aware that people with a grudge can easily jeopardize their operation, whereas friends and allies are unlikely to become informants. Having "people skills" is a major component of being a successful drug trafficker.

> You don't want any discontent because people can hurt you even if they are on a need-to-know basis. We never had any discontented people in the mix. They all get paid on time and make lots of money. You treat everyone well.

Problems inevitably arise with drug associates, and dealers frequently find it prudent to stop doing business with certain people. Reasons for ending business relationships include drug abuse, dishonesty, cutting the product, non-payment or late payment of debts, violence, laziness, unreliability, indiscretion, and attempting an "end run." One dealer provides his list.

> There were many reasons why I would end it: due to negligence, abuse of drugs, tampering, cutting, violence, cheating, disrespect to a customer. I hate dishonesty. The golden rule is you cannot lie to me. If you tell me anything, we can work it out, but if you lie to me, you cannot be trusted.

The process of eliminating someone from the business is referred to as "cutting them off." Some dealers disassociate themselves from others without any problems.

> When a dealer has problems and cuts someone off, there is usually a good reason. It's likely to be because he's

ripped him off or he owes him money. You don't even have to tell him he's cut off because he's not likely to come around. He knows he's screwed up and he avoids you. If he does come around, you just tell him straight out. You're not going to do business until he makes things right. People understand.

Not all clients take being cut off in stride, particularly if they are losing their main source of income. Employees and distributors may also feel betrayed because they have worked hard, earned a great deal of money for their supplier, and taken all the risks. One offender in this sample is serving a life sentence for murdering his former drug supplier.

I was working for this guy for a couple of years and we had a falling out. I was a heavy user and he confronted me about it. He said, "Pete, you're getting really wired. I don't think you realize how wired you're really getting. People are saying you're really messed up." I said to him, "What are you talking about? I'm fine. Everything is going well."

But you don't see it in yourself and you don't listen. He was right, and we eventually had a falling out and he cut me off. He told me he was really concerned giving me all this product, and I said, "You haven't been concerned up to this time. I've been the one putting the money in your pocket, so what's the problem?" He said that the problem is that I was heading for a pinch and could take him down with me, so he cut me off and I ended up killing him—shot him in the leg and bludgeoned him to death.

Because dealers wish to avoid making enemies, they typically attempt to end

relationships in a diplomatic and non-confrontational manner. A common strategy is to avoid clients by not returning phone calls and making themselves hard to find.

I had a client that I didn't like the way he did business, so I cut him off, but I would never confront him. All I did is I never called him back and I changed my phone number. Everybody has got my cell and my pager, and I just dumped them and got new ones. I changed cells every month anyways. Then I give people I want to know my new number. And then everybody that I didn't want to call never got my number. They never get it, [so] they can't get hold of me.

The most common strategy is for the supplier to tell a distributor that he has no product available. The client is likely to search for other sources and the supplier has solved his problem. A number of subjects describe their experience.

You don't ever fire anyone. I had people I disassociated with. I had people I cut off. I just never have the drugs when they want them.

I met one guy who I thought would be a real mover and I started grooming him for big things. I fronted him 30 to 40 grand a week in coke. I gave him the stuff on consignment and it was the highest quality and I gave him a good price. It was the key to making a lot of money, but he turned out to be a poor businessman. He had no drive or ambition and his payments were always weeks late. Then I found out that he was boasting to a guy who was cutting his hair that he was connected to one of the biggest coke dealers in the city. I cut him off and stopped doing business with him. I just kept telling him I had no product. I didn't confront him or anything.

I had one guy and I helped him so much. He had only been working with me for six months, but he was greedy and selfish and I think that he was trying to mess me up. He got jealous of my success, so I just cut him off right away. I don't have anything to do with him. I could be sitting on 20 kilos and he called me for a one or two, and I say "Sorry, I've got nothing. If you find anything, then tell me 'cause I'm looking too." After a while they get the message. I don't confront him. I'm just evasive. Even here in prison, that is one of the main things that I never do is confront a guy 'cause anything can happen. Why make enemies?

I would check up on how my dealers were behaving and if they were bringing any heat. It depends on what I'm hearing. I might shut someone down for a couple of months or for good. I wouldn't tell them the reason because you don't know how they will use that against you. I would give them a polite excuse. I would tell them that I'm having problems with suppliers and my supplier is having trouble meeting my needs. You don't want to burn your bridges.

Some dealers will speak to problem employees or clients and attempt to correct the situation. This is typically done in a respectful and non-confrontational way and often solves the problem. Both are motivated to maintain a relationship that is mutually beneficial. If an agreement cannot be reached, the dealer may decide to disassociate himself from the client. One dealer describes his attempt to work with a problem employee.

> Not anybody will fit the role and if they don't, you have to let them go. You have to let them know they have made mistakes and you can't have that. I had to do that to one guy who kept doing something I didn't like, and I warned him and warned him, and he gave me some reason why it wasn't a big deal. I tried to understand him, but his behaviour was not acceptable. He didn't listen, so I cut him off. I explained why and did it in a way that he understood. He didn't agree, but he wasn't angry at me. He was back within six months and working for me again. He knew I was serious and wouldn't let that go on.

Dealers who wish to get rid of a client but do not wish to lose the businesss will sometimes attempt an "end run" and deal directly with the client's customers. This is a dangerous manoeuvre in the drug game since distributors who are cut out of the action in this manner may seek retribution. A major cocaine trafficker describes such an incident:

> This guy Gord was a great connection, but way too flashy, and he had a big mouth—dropping names. You never do that! I just didn't like doing business with him and I wanted to cut him out, but he was my best customer and I didn't want to lose the income, so one day I followed him all the way to London from Toronto and he drove right to Chad's house. What an idiot!
>
> I found out who Chad was and had him checked out. Guys that I knew went to school with him and he was selling to the bikers in the London area. Gord had told Chad my name, so when I went back later on, he knew who I was. We talked and hooked up and cut

Gord right out of the picture. He never knew what happened. We had a good laugh and then we started working and it was an instant connection. It was a wicked connection. He even brought me a couple of buyers from different surrounding areas. It was the best thing that I ever did when I cut Gord off. Business just flew after that.

Dealers sometimes disapprove of their clients' customers and will attempt to exert some control. One cocaine wholesaler threatened to cut off one of his dealers if he continued supplying a dentist client. He was concerned about the following incident:

This one client came to me because he needed cocaine for one of his best customers. This doctor had called him in the afternoon—an urgent message— he wants something this afternoon. He was a good client. My dealer takes this package up to his office around 5:00 p.m. He's a dentist and is about to do gum surgery. When my person walked in, he left this woman under anesthetic, did a major hit, and went back and did the surgery.

I made my client cut him off when I heard that. When you get someone who is that reckless, you have to drop him. He's becoming stupid. If I should be tied into him as his supplier and he badly hurts someone, it comes back on me, and I didn't want that on my conscience. I told my dealer to cut him off. If he hadn't cut him off, that dealer would have never got supplies from me again.

Security through Technology

Williams and Godson (2002:339) predict that criminal organizations will increasingly exploit technological developments, including information technologies, to enhance and improve their risk-management efforts. Prepaid cellular telephones are the most common technological aid used by dealers in this study. These devices can be purchased anonymously and protect the identity of the user. E-mails also help to communicate with associates, but are considered higher risk and used significantly less than cellphones. Only two traffickers in this study encrypted their communications in an effort to circumvent the efforts of law enforcement. Three others also used scanning devices to look for wiretaps and hidden microphones. Overall, the dealers in this sample did not rely on technology for their security. Trust, secrecy, and caution characterized their modus operandi more than technological sophistication.

Summary

Higher-level drug traffickers function as importers, manufacturers, growers, or wholesalers supplying narcotics to dealers below them in the drug chain. The arrangement involves an ongoing series of transactions between buyers and sellers, most of whom operate as independent entrepreneurs. Drug trafficking is a competitive activity and dealers seek to attract and maintain clients by developing a reputation as honest, reliable, and astute businesspeople. The cornerstone of a successful enterprise is the ability to supply sufficient quantities of high-quality product at competitive prices.

Many higher-level traffickers develop co-operative relationships among themselves and discuss security issues, share information, and buy or borrow product from one another. Partnerships are common in the drug trade and provide both instrumental and expressive benefits. The main difference between drug trafficking and legitimate business is that dealers must operate under the fear of criminal violence, arrest and prosecution, forfeiture of the proceeds of crime, and imprisonment. The illicit nature of this activity requires secrecy, caution, and a sophisticated modus operandi. Dealers cannot use the law to protect themselves or to enforce business contracts. Instead, they devise other strategies to minimize and deal with potential problems. These include the avoidance of violent people and dangerous situations; working within a small network of associates who are known and trusted; operating on a need-to-know basis; delegating or contracting high-risk activities to lower-level operatives; maintaining information networks on the drug scene; being honest with suppliers and clients; using credit carefully; paying one's debts; and handling people in a non-confrontational manner. These strategies help dealers to maintain a low profile, avoid conflicts, insulate themselves from danger, minimize business disruptions, and avoid arrest and conviction.

Most higher-level drug traffickers describe themselves as non-violent and few respondents in this study advocate or admit using force to control others or settle business disputes. Law-enforcement officials, on the other hand, argue that violence does occur with regularity and that intimidation is common at all levels of the drug trade. Drug syndicates in this study rely on secrecy and caution rather than corruption to conduct their illicit business and protect themselves from arrest.

CHAPTER 6

The Modus Operandi of Higher-Level Drug Traffickers
Fronts, Debts, and Violence

Marketing and the Use of Credit: The Front

Drug trafficking operates on a system in which higher-level dealers supply narcotics to lower-level distributors, who in turn pass the product down the chain to the eventual consumer. Upper-level dealers typically recruit others to act as distributors by offering to provide them with a supply of illicit drugs at decent prices and often on credit or what is known as a "front." Fronts are also referred to as consignments and operate on an ongoing basis, much like a short-term revolving line of credit (see Reuter & Haaga, 1989:45). Lenders use fronts to recruit distributors, tap into new markets, and increase profits. Several subjects in this study were able to resume high-level drug dealing immediately following their release from prison because suppliers were willing to extend them credit. One cocaine importer describes how he expanded his business by fronting recently released inmates to market his product in a number of Ontario communities:

> I would find out who had been released from prison and where they were. It was a network. I would know someone who knows someone and I would use the network to make contact. I would offer to front him 2 or 3 kilos and tell him this is the purity and this is the price. See if he's interested in moving it. He's likely to say yes because he just got out of prison and doesn't have any money. I wouldn't meet with the person directly.

Fronts will also help suppliers to retain clients. An American citizen who smuggled large quantities of cocaine into Canada originally used different sources in the Los Angeles area, but eventually settled with one supplier, partly because he was able to purchase drugs on credit.

> Other suppliers had the same quality and sometimes their price was better, but the credit was always there with the main guy and he stood behind the product. I had complete trust and it was easier working with him and I didn't worry about paying a little more. It was worth it not having to deal with other people.

Importers or suppliers looking to establish a network in other countries, provinces, or cities will typically solicit clients by offering to front the new business. For existing dealers, the front provides them with an opportunity to expand, increase profits, and perhaps move to a higher level.

> Consignments have many benefits. It makes it more enticing. It's free credit and you can move more. For the supplier, he doesn't have to hold onto it.

> You have to work on fronts. Everybody has to front or be fronted. It's the whole essence of hustling. That is how your word becomes your bond. You get fronts because you have sales.

> Fronts. Yes, I had some from my supplier. I started on a front and as soon as I got enough money, I paid cash. It helps you starting out.

> My own supplier gave me the chance through the consignments. I didn't have $50,000 to drop on dope. I'd put some money down and get some on consignment. That is how he makes his money and I would do the same from my smaller people.

Fronts not only attract and retain business, they also pay higher dividends to the supplier, and many dealers are willing to provide fronts because profit margins are higher than cash deals. There is a premium charged for drugs sold on credit partly as insurance against the inherent risks in making such loans. The difference between the credit and cash price varies, but the wholesale cost for a kilo of cocaine, for example, is typically $2,000 less for cash purchases.

> I would take a higher price if I fronted it [and] a risk of possibly losing if they got busted. If they paid cash, I gave it to them for less.

Market forces affect the availability and premiums attached to fronts. When drugs are scarce, suppliers will have less trouble finding buyers who are willing and able to purchase them outright. When the market is saturated, dealers are more willing to offer fronts.

> Supply may affect the fronting too. If there is a lot around, it's easier to get it on the cuff [a front].

> If the market was dry, there was no consignment. It was always cash— never a consignment.

Besides the higher profit margin, fronts also allow distributors to quickly dispose of their drugs. Dealers consider it dangerous to maintain possession of the product and attempt to move it as fast as possible—recall Morselli's (2001:219) "hot potato" analogy.

> I can make extra money on consignment and I don't want to have possession of drugs for any longer than I have to. Even if they only pay me for half, I'll front them the extra just to get rid of the product as quickly as I

can. It's dangerous to keep drugs around. Ideally the sales are lined up in advance, but things don't always work that way.

Principles and Precautions in Fronting

Fronting is governed by several business practices and by a system of subcultural norms and values that are meant to protect the supplier. Suppliers are careful about who they deal with and will usually front only those clients who have a reputation as reliable, competent, and trustworthy. This normally excludes dealers who are known to be heavy drug users or addicts.

I had no problems with people not paying me back because I dealt with people I knew and trusted. I showed respect and expected respect. The type of people I dealt with were well chosen.

If someone comes to me for 100 pounds of hash. I can get it, but the people I get it from want to know who it's for. It's partly fronted and they want to protect their investment. They would find out about the person and may meet them in a roundabout way. They meet them and the buyer would not be aware who this person was.

I just knew the guys and trusted them. That was my security. If I don't trust the person, I don't cuff [front].

I would give drugs out on fronts. You can't ask for all the money from all of them. Some you give fronts and others you don't because you don't trust them. Usually people don't ask you for fronts unless they feel they are deserving of it or the relationship is that good.

I may just give you some and you get what you want and I get what I want. You have no debts and I don't have to lose a friend or client.

To reduce the risk of loss, distributors will offer partial fronts and demand that clients put some money down. It is a common business practice to request half of the purchase price as a down payment.

You get it on credit and pay them a premium or percentage of the profits. The front would be partial because it is best to put as much money down as you can because you save the premium. They would usually want a deposit on what they gave you.

There were many occasions that suppliers would give me double what I purchased. If I had the money for 5 kilos, they would give me 10. Naturally, you try to put together as much cash as you can to increase your profit margins.

The difference between credit and cash—it would be from $1,000 to $2,000 extra on a kilo. I would have more risk, but I would also make more profit.

The partner that I had in 1994, he preferred to use zero amount of his money. That was his personal preference even though he had his money, but he would not take care of his debt right away and he got a bad reputation. He would take care of it over time and force the supplier to keep working with him to get his money back. It's a way of having a lever over the supplier. It's living on a fine line because if you take it too far, you're in danger. He was going out buying brand new cars and they knew it. They would talk to him, but he would cover it one way or another with some excuse. They didn't mind me taking over the business because I would be less problems for them. I had more business sense and reliability than he had. That's a big plus in this business.

Another precaution taken by many dealers is to front relatively small quantities and only what they can afford to lose.

I was not fronting anyone huge amounts. The amounts would be $1,500 at the highest. I would never front any more than I could afford to lose.

If someone comes by and asks for an outrageous amount of drugs, you know they can't do it so you give them a small amount.

I had trouble collecting debts, sure. People not paying people I had fronted to. They come to me and they say this guy hasn't paid me. That would never be a big deal because the amounts were small. For any large-scale sales, they would have to have the money up front.

Many dealers require that borrowers have collateral in the event they fail to pay their drug debts.

Repossessing stuff is common in the drug business. If somebody screws up, you take their truck or car or home or business. They would sign it over and the implied threat is that the alternative is worse. You give people 48 hours to come up with the money or they lose everything. Sell the truck and give up the money.

I've had several people who had to give up their house. A lot of times they were wannabe dealers who were nothing more than users. They come and get a pound and sell maybe an ounce and do the rest.

I have had guys tell me they can't pay and I see them with $2,000 worth of leather and I take the clothes and give it to whoever in my family they fit. Other guys, you take their clothes and they still have to pay you.

If I cuff to you, when are you paying it back? What is your collateral? If I am not paid, you may lose your vehicle or house.

It depends what they have to back it up. If a guy wants to go with a bigger amount, you look for collateral. You have to protect your back. If it's a small amount, it's not a big deal. If you go bigger than that, it's collateral.

A lot of people own so much, it's like collateral for a front. If you own two houses and one big boat, your net worth almost determines your loan or front. The modern-day drug dealer is more like a banker than the old strereotype street hustler. In fronting someone, there would be a definite collateral given.

Norms Regulating Fronts

Drug debts resulting from fronts are potential sources of conflict between suppliers and clients, and some dealers are clear about the client's obligations and the ramifications of non-payment.

You make it clear. Everything is on the table. Nothing is left unstated. No maybes. I'm clear and you are clear. I give you this and you pay me this on that day and that time. If something happens, it depends how much you have.

Surprisingly, most dealers do not explicitly discuss the "what if" contingencies: What happens if the client is robbed or arrested and loses the drugs through no fault of his or her own; or what happens if the drugs are lost because the client is at fault or partly to blame for the loss? Suppliers normally assume that once the customer takes possession of the drugs, the money is owed. Because clients do not always share the same assumptions, this creates a potentially dangerous conflict. In one case, the RCMP arrested a courier travelling from Montreal to Toronto by train and listened in on the communications between the suppliers and the client.

> Salbello placed an order for 5 kilos of cocaine from Riga and Ramone in Montreal. Salbello sent his favourite courier, Ricardo—who is now serving three years—to Montreal to pick up the coke. We learned all of this through our informant and through wiretaps and we determined where it was happening.
>
> Ricardo flew to Montreal and took a train back with two undercovers in the seats behind him. When he got off in Scarborough, we arrested him. We were ready in Union Station to follow him, but he got off unexpectedly, so the officers made the arrest. We didn't oppose bail for Ricardo, so there was no disclosure. He had to pay $10,000 bail.
>
> Salbello blamed Riga and Ramone for the loss and refused to pay for the 5 kilos. Salbello claimed that it was a mistake from the Montreal end and Montreal blamed him, but in the

drug world, Salbello owed the money since his courier takes responsibility for delivery once he has them in his possession. It is now his loss.

The dispute over the 5 kilos resulted in Salbello receiving threats on his life. The RCMP were concerned that he might be killed since they were monitoring the Montreal dealers and knew they were serious criminals. In order to prevent this from happening, the police intervened and arranged for the informant to travel to Montreal and work out a reduced payment to resolve the conflict.

Another Montreal criminal who imported drugs from Colombians in Miami was arrested and convicted but, nonetheless, he owed money on the front.

> The police were after me for 27 kilos, but the drugs had already been distributed and I had been paid $200,000. That is what they seized. The drugs were not lost, but just the money. The people in Miami still expect payment. What we lost is our profit. Not only are we arrested, but we lost our profit.

Although it is a norm in the drug business that money owing must be paid on time, these debts are often extended, reduced, or excused under various circumstances. Dealers will examine the reasons distributors have for being late or for not paying and often extend the due date, reduce the amount owing, or write off the loan as a cost of doing business. Suppliers are more tolerant and understanding if the problem is not the dealer's fault, and he or she is truthful about what has happened.

It is common for dealers to be late in paying the money owing on drug fronts. In most cases, the delay is of little concern because the amount is relatively small and/or the dealer is a trusted person who will make good on the debt. Suppliers typically seek an explanation for delays and are usually willing to wait if there is an acceptable reason because they wish to maintain good working relationships with customers and make money.

> I'll give some leeway and time for problems beyond clients' control, of course. I don't want to alienate my clients. You have to be understanding.

> Delays in getting paid are common. I don't lose any sleep over it. You have to treat your people properly and you get more in return.

A common problem arises when clients are arrested before the debt has been settled. In these circumstances, the debt is often forgiven or significantly reduced, providing the client does not inform on others.

> I lost a lot of money after my arrest because I had made a large down payment. The part that was on consignment, my supplier had to eat that. I don't owe the money because I am not pinning it on anybody, I have my lawyer's fees, and I'm going to jail. The coke is lost, it's gone, and my supplier would have to eat it. If you still owe the money after your arrest, then you're dealing with the wrong guys.

Another dealer, apprehended with 70 kilos of cocaine, was required to make partial restitution, and his partner who escaped was also expected to help cover the loss.

> I still owe the money after being caught. The debt is cut in half so everybody absorbs some of the loss. I have had some conversations and I gave up some property and a car (a Maserati) to take care of my end of it and satisfy my creditors. My partner was a little more reluctant and I'm

sure by now that they have reached an agreement of some sort. I'm assuming my partner is continuing to work with them, in which case some of the profit is used to pay for it.

It is common practice for suppliers to give clients additional fronts to pay money owing, particularly when the problem is beyond their control. Although they risk greater losses, the front allows them to keep a good customer and collect on the debt. Dealers also emphasize that honesty is a precondition to fronting clients more drugs.

> I'll talk to them to see what the problem is. If it's something beyond their control, I may lend them more. They have to be truthful and don't bullshit me. I will lend them more to get paid.

> Even on a large debt, it can be paid off fast within a year and still make your own profit as you do that. You can pass it onto the client at $4,000 a kilo and give the supplier $2,000 and still make a good living. You continue making money while you pay off the debt at the same time.

> If it's honestly lost—say you sent it in a container and it's lost—if you can prove it, then there's no violence. It's a misfortune—a loss—and we'll work it out. If they think I stole it, there could be violence.

> If the drugs are also seized, the guys in the U.S. may expect payment. It depends on the deal you make. If we get caught or the goods are lost in transit, we continue doing business and maybe pay a percentage. If I lose 40 kilos, I'll be charged for some of it, but not at the full price and I'll pay the bill when I get the money.

If you have trouble collecting, it will depend on the situation and the reason why. Many times you write it off as a cost of doing business.

Sometimes you have to understand what happened. If someone can't pay and it's not their fault, then you try to work it out.

Financial and Security Risks

Fronts involve financial risks on the lender's part since borrowers may abscond with the product, consume the drugs, fail to collect from their own clients, refuse to pay, are arrested and jailed, or find themselves unable to meet their obligations for a variety of reasons. Clients may also become violent and/or turn to the police for protection when suppliers try to collect. A number of dealers refuse to front drugs to their customers in order to avoid the problems associated with this practice. They operate on a cash payment basis and have no trouble finding clients with the ability to pay.

Nowadays in the drug business, you need the money up front. That avoids a lot of problems. The exchange is done at the same time.

One of the more serious risks in drug trafficking is to accept drugs on a front and then use the product to front lower-level dealers.

It's tricky and dangerous to get a front and then to front others. That's a good reason for not giving someone a front, "Hey, man, I can't front you because I've been fronted myself. You gotta come up with three-quarters of the money up front."

If you get it on a front, you have to sell it quickly and pay the money back. You have to have the sales all lined up

ahead of time to make sure it's sold before you even get it. It's not smart to front it yourself if you're on a front. You don't want to get into trouble, but people do it. Not me.

It was always a cycle of me owing my supplier money and my distributors owing me money. Say I purchase 10 kilos and I only collect $280,000. I owe him $20,000 and I'm owed $70,000. I tell my supplier he'll get it next week, but in the meantime, I need another 10 kilos. I take another consignment and I consign it out. Now my distributors owe me more. That makes it hard to disengage because they need more drugs to pay me off. I'm always owed money and when you're arrested, forget about getting paid.

A number of respondents were unable to collect on debts because they had been arrested and incarcerated. Dealers report that it is common for clients to take advantage of this situation and to renege on paying.

When I was arrested, there was a lot of money owing and I had to forgive them because I'm down and not in a position to go to collect. I had about $70,000 to $100,000 outstanding when I came in. Not a whole lot of money, but still ....

Another downside to fronts is the need to keep records of monies owed. Dealers who operate ongoing fronts with a number of clients cannot rely on their memory to keep track of all transactions. Written records, however, make compelling evidence should the police come across them.

I would write it down and it's for only two weeks and in totally different places like an encyclopedia and have a couple of numbers and pencil it in—nothing that they would ever find.

The police found my records of transactions. It gets complicated enough that I have to write some of the stuff down. Sometimes I would be saying, "Do you owe me some money?" I was smoking too much weed.

It appears, however, that the police seldom discover the written or computer records of higher-level dealers because those who keep such records conceal them well. In addition, most operate with a small number of distributors and have no need to record transactions since they can easily remember details about money owed. Street-level dealers, on the other hand, are more likely to keep records because they often operate on fronts and sell small quantities to a large number of clients. These records become incriminating evidence when seized by the police.

When I sold in bars, I had maybe 50 clients and I had to write down all the money that I was owed and all the payments. Then when I started dealing in weight, I had only five clients. I still fronted, but I didn't have to keep records. I could easily remember what everyone owed.

For dealers who purchase drugs on a front, perhaps the most significant downside is the loss of autonomy and independence. By accepting a front, dealers give their suppliers a legitimate claim over their activities, particularly if they have difficulty paying on time. Accepting a front can also force dealers to take unnecessary risks to make sales and/or collect money owing because they are under pressure to repay their debts on time. This is another reason why many distributors prefer not to compromise their independence.

I pay in cash and will not take fronts. I like to work at my own pace. There are guys if you owe them money, they are always hounding you. There could be a lot of heat, so it's smart to lay low for a while. But what are you supposed to do—jeopardize yourself to pay this guy?

Some dealers front you the drugs and call you hours later for the money. Your time ideas may not correspond to his schedule. I like to take my time and do things safely. I can control my own schedule and safety. You have to save the money to invest in this.

Personally, I never wanted to owe any money. I always paid straight up cash. I did not take fronts except at the beginning and I was getting into it. It goes back to not owing people because if you owe someone, they have a right to be upset because it's theirs and not yours. They have a right to get what is theirs and they may feel that they have a right to get it whatever way it takes. I don't like to be treated disrespectfully and I try to avoid it.

I was an independent. I paid cash for what I was doing—cheaper and I reduced my responsibilities and obligations. There is a risk if I get busted and I lose it. If I front off of a person, then I'm obligated to that person and I have to answer to him. If I pay cash, I can go and do what I want. If I want to front it, I can. No consequences if I lose it. It's my product. I think if you have been in the game long enough, you have the money, so you just pay for it. If I take drugs on a front, they have some control over me and I'm not comfortable with that.

In general, fronts tend to be used when dealers are starting up their business and have not yet accumulated the capital to make purchases outright. Once they are established, however, most prefer to pay for their drugs up front or will accept only small quantities on credit. By paying cash, dealers can purchase their product cheaper, maintain their independence, and there is no fear of retribution over unpaid debts.

Violence among Higher-Level Traffickers

Many theorists see violence as intrinsic to organized crime and characterize it as systemic (Goldstein, 1985, 1989). A few dealers in this study believe that intimidation is required in the drug business to enforce normative codes. Violence is typically aimed at other criminals and is used to exact revenge for thefts and other rip-offs, to facilitate robberies, to collect debts; in conflicts over territory and/or customers; as revenge for poor-quality drugs or for having one's supply cut off; and to silence or punish informants. Criminal dealers report that a reputation for violence in the underworld will prevent problems and diminish the need for coercion. A career criminal and methamphetamine manufacturer argued that a dealer cannot rise up the ladder unless his reputation is one that guarantees him respect. He states:

> It is not a game for wimps. You cannot expand your business and keep your connections unless you are willing to use violence. A dealer who cannot protect himself is a joke and nobody wants to deal with a joke.

A serious risk to accepting a front is the possibility of violent retribution should one be unable to pay one's debts.

When it comes to large amounts of money and drugs, an error can be fatal. Trust is only skin deep. For big money, it's amazing what people will do and how people will change—even people you thought you knew.

When you're getting large quantities on a front, you're putting your head on the chopping block. It means that you are not doing it as a second source of income or to support a lifestyle. You're a drug dealer. You have the reputation of a dealer in quantities. You're into it up to your neck and people at that level play for keeps. You better be able to pay your debts.

By far the most common strategy for dealers who have not been paid is to write off the debt and refuse to deal with the client again. This typically occurs because the amount is relatively small and not worth the trouble of pursuing; the dealer would rather focus time and energy on making new money; and he or she is unwilling to use threats or violence. Many view unpaid debts as a cost of doing business and blame themselves for their own bad judgment. Consequently, most traffickers will simply write off bad debts and move on.

> If it was clear that this guy had messed up and I wasn't getting my money, I'd just write it off. I never used violence because money is only money and I made it so easily. I wouldn't sell to them anymore and that would be their punishment.

> There are certain situations where you want your money and have to get out of hand to get it. It depends. On a small debt, it's often better to write off a certain person than to give them harm.

That depends on the person. There are different ways of dealing with it. For some, it's good riddance and you don't have to worry anymore and he can get nothing from me again and that's the end of it. In a lot of cases, it is a very cutthroat business. People have this perception that it is that and only that, and that it is not the way it is. Good business principles means minimizing violence. There are drug dealers and there are businessmen. It may not sound right, but it's true.

If somebody stiffs me, what I do is cut them off. I don't act stupidly. If I get stiffed, it's going to be for an amount I can afford to lose, but you can no longer deal with me—not you or any of your friends. I cut them off and tell others that you're bogus.

Write it off. If someone is busted and in jail, you might write it off as a cost of doing business.

I can spend money trying to collect money I may not get or I can spend money trying to make new money. That's the way I prefer.

It all depends how much they owe. If it's a lot, it's your own stupidity. I gave them too much or took a big risk.

The fronts would be smaller and nothing too much to get upset about. I could take the loss. The guy would know not to come back to me for more. I would just brush him off and and I write off the debt. I'm not a heavy and would not go collecting.

For me, it's also the acceptability of charges. I don't want to have any record of violence or extortion. I would never want to be arrested for that and be labelled for that. It's all morals, too, and I would not want to do anything to anybody that I wouldn't want done to me.

Although some criminal drug dealers occasionally use force—primarily to collect debts—most emphasize that threats alone will usually convince clients to pay. Businessmen dealers sometimes portray themselves as violent people, but rarely used force in their drug dealings. Violence is considered harmful to business since it gains significant media play; draws unwanted attention from the police; leads to retaliation; damages reputations and business relationships; and a violent conflict between criminal syndicates requires time and resources that are more profitably invested in dealing drugs. The almost unanimous consensus among higher-level dealers is that violence is largely unnecessary and that market forces, not coercion, govern business relationships in the drug trade.

There were never any guns involved. The deals took place in nice restaurants and ended with a handshake. The guys I dealt with have millions of dollars pass through their hands and I bet they have never held a gun in their lives.

There are not many thugs at the higher levels. It takes too much business sense.

I've been in front of a lot of money and I've never seen a weapon put in front of a deal. There was no violence with any of the people that I dealt with.

Violence does not make for good business. I would like to avoid that as much as possible because you also put yourself at risk.

A smart businessman doesn't need the problems, but things happen.

You don't give anyone a reason to be violent. We were honest just like any other business. We were interested in doing repeat business.

We never used guns and would not deal with anyone who used guns. It's much easier to have a meal at the Park Plaza Hotel and discuss business. It was totally non-violent.

There were no weapons charges laid against anyone. That was a norm for us—don't play with them. If you have to pack guns, you're dealing with the wrong people.

As previously discussed, higher-level drug traffickers emphasize the importance of paying people well and treating them with respect. In this way, they gain the loyalty of employees and associates, which prevents problems from developing. In addition, most traffickers are selective with whom they deal, avoid people and situations they perceive as dangerous, and choose distributors with similar attitudes and values.

These five dealers were all in their late thirties to mid-forties. They had professional and business backgrounds. They were not career criminals and I did not consider any of them dangerous. That was my conscious choice.

There were times I crossed the paths of career criminals, but I would back right off. I chose to deal with non-violent people. It's simple. If I had a kilo and two guys want to buy it and one carries a gun and the other doesn't, I sell to the guy without the gun. I establish some

of the rules of doing business. One of the rules is no guns and no violence.

The relative absence of violence in higher-level drug dealing is reported in studies done within the United States by Adler (1985:119) and Reuter and Haaga (1989:25). Morselli's analysis of the career of a high-level British drug broker also provides evidence that it is possible to persist and actually succeed in illegal enterprise without having to rely on instrumental violence (2001:228). *The Economist* similarly comments upon the low levels of violence among higher-level drug syndicates in the United Kingdom and attributes this to effective law enforcement.

Gone is the violence. Increased enforcement has taken out the most "disorganized" and most violent organizations. The ones that are left are more careful and less violent. They run it like a business and avoid violence and try not to attract attention to themselves through violence. (*The Economist*, July–August 2001:12)

The marijuana and hashish market in particular appears to attract a variety of middle-class dealers who are not part of the criminal world and who are typically non-violent. Other researchers have similarly noted that marijuana-dealing subcultures are characterized by ideologies that frown on the use of violence (Adler, 1985; Hafley & Tewksbury, 1995; Langer 1977; Sorfleet, 1976; Weisheit, 1990). Several respondents in this study report that "hippie" types still operate in the marijuana market and differ significantly from career criminals. Police also confirm that violence is uncommon in the marijuana and hashish trade. One major marijuana importer was proud of the fact that he had never used violence in his 22 years of dealing drugs.

The pot business has no guns and there is no intimidation. I never had a gun and my friends never had guns. The drug business lures all sorts of people of less character, but they're not in it long if they rely on muscle. I've never had a gun stuck in my face and been ripped off.

A cocaine importer with no past criminal involvement also repudiated the use of force.

We had no guns. That was a total no. We would never do any business with anyone who used a gun. Why should I? If you have to use a gun, then you don't trust me. And I don't want to deal with anyone who's into guns and violence. There is no trust when guns are involved.

Not all dealers abhor the use of force or are willing to forgive drug debts. Criminal drug syndicates are more prone to violence, and several men in this study routinely used force to collect money that was owed to them. A career criminal who operated in Montreal dealt primarily with other criminals and demanded that all debts be paid.

I would know they partied and sniffed it because you heard about it from the girls that they were up all night for a few days. They say to me that it's all out on fronts, but I know they're lying. They also rat each other. One wants to be in good with you, so he'll rat out the others, but I never write off the debt. I was always paid. Every time you see him, you give him a beating. He's fucked because he can't go anywhere because his reputation is shot. All the bars are closed to him. They can do what they want, like a robbery, to get the money. I don't tell them what they have to do. I just want to be paid.

Debt collection can be dangerous for suppliers, particularly if it requires the use of force, which may lead to violent retaliation and/or police involvement. The same Montreal criminal discusses the danger involved in collecting money owed.

There is some danger involved. You always live with danger in that business. You never know if a guy is going to have a gun or rip you off. My buddy was killed because he was a supplier and one guy shot him instead of paying him. Sometimes you never know. For him it was a guy who owed him money and came to talk to him and he was shot.

Sometimes you go to collect and you have to be ready because a person who is scared is very dangerous. The first time I went to collect, I was shot at by a shotgun. I went with another guy and we were told to give a guy a beating and we knocked at the door and he shot at us. The guy was dead the day after and I never knew who did it.

A dangerous life with lots of fun and lots of worries. The cops are a worry, but so are other cliques. You never know when you go into a deal if you may get shot. Dealing with new people is a risk. It's high pay with high risk. A lot of stress and I have friends who are 25 years old and they are all grey.

Lots of time it's not good to scare people too much because they go to the cops. That's a risk you take if you frighten him too much. These days, it's worse because there are more rats than before. More honour back then, but none now.

Although most dealers do not use violence, physical harm or death is always a possibility. Many subjects describe incidents in the drug trade they've heard about, witnessed, or narrowly avoided.

Case Example: Murder and Revenge

This 55-year-old dealer imported huge amounts of cocaine into Canada over a 12-year period. He had few serious problems for most of his career in the drug trade until he was suddenly swept up in a series of murders.

A few years ago, I decided to retire. I had been in the drug business for 12 years and my partner Gene and I were both quitting and building a hotel in Mexico. He was handling the construction in Mexico and he did things poorly. He messed it all up. We needed a water-purification plant and our own electrical system, and he was unprepared for that. Costs kept rising and we needed a sewage system or the stench would be horrible. I had already invested my half million and now he was broke. I was retired and well off, but he had sunk all of his money into this and it wasn't finished.

So he's broke and he calls me up in Vancouver and he says, "Look, I have some packages I'm sending up." I said "No way, I'm retired." I had promised myself I was going to quit. He called me up and he tells me he has a Mexican friend coming up and has 4 [kilos of cocaine] for me. He gives me a sob story and I wasn't going to get involved, but I feel guilty so I said okay.

A few days later, I get a call from this young Mexican, Alvero, and he needs help getting across the border into Canada. I told him to wait at a certain spot for instructions and he would get picked up in an airplane. I am supposed to help him move these 4 kilos. I had a guy, Dale, who always wanted small amounts and I set it up. They agreed on the price and set up the deal. Everything went wrong and Alvero got shot. These three guys were setting up Dale without him knowing about it. Alvero jumps one guy and is killed by these guys. Three times shot. I'm two blocks away, but I wasn't seen at the scene.

I had this Chinese friend who is a major heroin dealer and he knew Dale. I wanted to know what happened, so I met with him and he told me what he had heard. In a few hours, I found out who had done it. The guy who did the shooting was East Indian and not very intelligent.

I put the word out that I was going after them. I called the Mexicans and they said they would be up the next day and they just wanted me to supply the weapons.

Then this East Indian's brother called and they come by to see me at my mother's house. They were very infamous people. I was upset and I tell them the Mexicans are coming. I was not being rational. I was pissed because I had been questioned by the authorities and mad at Gene from Mexico for getting me involved in this mess.

Then I find out that the East Indians are coming for me because I had made the threat. This made it a battle between me and them and they threatened my family too. I sent my wife and daughter away. Family members too. Then saner heads prevailed. The brother phoned me back. I didn't know who I was dealing with. These people were part of a movement toward a Sikh private country in India and had connections to a terrorist group. Holy fuck! What am I doing? He phoned and said we cannot let things get any further. He told me the names of the bikers who did this.

I made a truce with the East Indians and told the Mexicans I had to wash my hands of it. The Mexicans would not drop it and they came up and they took care of the bikers. I did not want to have anything to do with it. I put out the word to the East Indians that the Mexicans were coming and that I was not involved. I told them that I had been wronged. The bikers were expendable and they set them up to be captured and from that point on, I don't want to know. I don't know the methods. I just know it was taken care of.

Two years later, the East Indian who did the shooting is killed. Then Dale is talked into this alley and shot. The brother thinks that I did it at an opportune time and I am a suspect. I was in California and my wife told me about Dale being killed. I told her to get out of town with our daughter. I was serious and it scared her. This is where my problems with her came. I gave her a feeble excuse that was not very believable.

I came back in my own airplane and made some calls. I get hold of the brother and I explain to him that I had no involvement. He said he would take my word, but that if I was lying, he would kill me. Luckily the police were able to determine that it was his own people. There were two factions of East Indians who had gone to war. There were lots of killings in the news for two years.

The brother was eventually shot and killed in a nightclub about five months ago. I know all the details of the war because my Chinese friend kept me filled in. He dealt with the East Indians.

The biggest thing I took pride in and worked hard at was to keep my business as non-violent as possible. I pushed myself away from conflicts or solved them immediately. It was going to be a business and dealing in the dollars I did, it had to be business. There was no room for violence, for weak people, for alcohol, or for drug use.

Several subjects had suppliers who offered to settle conflicts and/or use threats or violence on their behalf. A major cocaine dealer describes the violent nature of his source.

> The suppliers always confirmed that if I had problems, they would take care of it. If I heard that someone was taking business, I would mention it and they would have a talk with that person. I never saw it done. They provided security so I didn't have to worry about an informant or showing any muscle if something should go wrong. That's part of an illegal business. Dealing with suppliers, you let them into your profit margin so they supply that service.

An American offender who dealt with Mexican-American suppliers reports that his decision to operate in Canada was based on market conditions and the relatively non-violent climate in this country.

> About three years ago, there was a friend of mine who was actively selling drugs in Los Angeles. I lost

contact with him for one-and-a-half years, and he was killed right in front of the courthouse as he got out of a car. An arrest has never been made. Three armed men walked up and shot him in the driver's seat the day he was supposed to testify.

I have had guns pulled on me on a couple of occasions. The one time, the person was waiting to rob me and a buddy of mine. I was getting out of the car and we both ran because we saw this guy with a gun. I came back to the car and he was still there and he came up and said, "I want the drugs." He fired a shot through the back window of the car and the bullet hit the seat, and I drove away very fast. I assumed it was a set-up because he knew I had drugs.

In the other incident, somebody was arrested and one of my suppliers thought that I had something to do with their people getting into trouble. They had me get into a car and held a gun at me and insisted that I tell them what had happened. After a few hours, they let me go and I was phoned the next day and they apologized because it was a mistake and they know what happened.

I didn't get out of the drug trade because I figured that that was an isolated situation and that it wouldn't happen again. I can't say how else I can explain it. After that, we did take a little while off—a few months to think about it. This was happening in L.A. and it confirmed that we should stay out of the marketplace in that area. The U.S. was becoming very dangerous and saturated in the drug trade.

There was a huge growing lucrative market in Canada that was apparent to me. Very lax drug laws in Canada and very violent in the U.S. with a lot of people being shot or robbed for drugs. There was no violence and no worries of being robbed here in Canada. I was not having any problems here, so I figured there was no reason to get out of the business.

Outlaw Motorcycle Gangs and Violence

Outlaw motorcycle gangs in Canada and the United States are highly structured organizations that are known to systematically engage in a variety of illegal activities, including the narcotics trade. The sample contains only three biker associates, but information from the police and other traffickers indicates that motorcycle gangs are heavily involved in the drug trade, are highly secretive, and are known to use violence in their illicit dealings. Most dealers in this study avoid bikers because they are dangerous and attract police attention.

Bikers have their own gig, but they would come to us on occasion when they ran out of supplies. I severed myself from bikers because I believed that those organizations were targeted by police. We tried to be a secret society.

A biker associate describes his involvement with motorcycle gangs and his awareness of their violent tendencies.

I had a lot of friends who were bikers and I partied and drank with all of them and the different bike clubs back east from Satan's Choice to Paradise Riders and Hells Angels. I have been biking with the Angels for the past 20 years and I owned a bike and partied with them and went on rides and lived their lifestyle for a while. I got in enough trouble on my own. I didn't need to wear clothes.

They were always there with money if I needed it—a couple hundred grand if I needed it. I became more cautious with them because they are not into the second chances. The money would be a loan at 20 points a month, and they expected to be paid on time. I always paid a couple of days before. I had them owing me money and the trust worked both ways. I was fortunate that my best friend was the president of Hells Angels.

Bikers control strip bars and the drug trade. Vancouver is open apart from all of the bars. I don't know about the street level, but wholesale level is not controlled. The market works on quality, which is a big factor. If your stuff is good, they will always come back and if you are a drug addict, you know when something is good or not.

This subject also claimed that outlaw motorcycle gangs provide useful information for smuggling purposes.

I would make use of their counter-intelligence. A lot of my knowledge came through the bikers and when I became trusted, it was shared—who not to trust, which border crossing to do. There was someone who would wave you through.

A career criminal and biker associate also describes the instrumental use of violence to collect debts and keep dealers in line.

Violence wasn't a problem in 95% of our business dealings. We were a crew that worked together, that would

pitch in and take care of it. If one guy was ripped off, he would come to me and we would go to the other groups and try to work it out. This guy who did the rip-off might be associated to some other group and before you do what you do to him, you have to clear it. I'm not a shooter and it gets jobbed (contracted) out. Somebody would be brought in.

I sometimes worked as a collector and if I showed up, these people would know that I was their last hope. I weigh 300 pounds and I know how to get the message across. If it went past me, they were in mortal danger. Most of the time, people find a way to come up with the money. Most of the time it never went further than a beating that we had to give them.

If they had a good reason—if they were ripped off and if it was legit—we only charged them cost price. We helped them get their money back by fronting them or give them a job taking a run to Montreal. If they come to me and say I have a problem, that's one thing, but if they just disappear and we have to find them, we interpret it differently.

Violence is a concern, but it is something that has to be done. I put the fear of God into them and they would never take it further because this was made clear that they wouldn't live any longer. There is somebody more violent behind me. We even reached people who were in jail if we had to.

Another career criminal biker associate describes the routine manner in which violence was used in the Montreal drug world.

Some bar owners tried to give me a hassle and you have a talk with them.

I tell the owners that we attract people in here and if I sit in the other bar, the customers will come there. Or we will start causing shit. Sometimes you beat the owner. Sometimes a new owner comes into town and he thinks he's going to run the bar the way he wants it.

Territoriality definitely exists in the Montreal bar scene. If I was going into another person's area, you take a chance for a beef. You never give your bar away. You make a contact and to go bigger and expand your business, you keep the bar. After a while, you control 10 bars.

I was all over the city and into friends' bars. I would have people move into my territory and I would have to shoot them—shoot them in the legs—or they lose a few fingers.

I remember being in a bar and my buddy was shanked, and we had to run out with him holding his intestines. They just came out of the knife wound and we held it and ran to the car and rushed to the hospital. It was a big joke a year or two later. We used to talk about it and have a big laugh, but it was pretty serious at the time.

We fixed the other guys after that. The fight was over territory. They came into our area from another town and we had a fight. We control everything. The doorman is working for us. The bar was called the Vanini, but it's closed now—a disco bar in East Montreal.

I always carried a gun. My buddy was killed because he was a supplier and one guy shot him instead of paying him—a drug deal gone wrong.

Several dealers report a higher degree of territoriality in the province of Quebec—particularly Montreal—and among outlaw motorcycle gangs. A biker associate from Montreal serving 16 years for attempted murder explains how disputes over territory can lead to violence.

> In Montreal, in the drug world, bikers are very serious and very violent. They have wars in Montreal. Bikers are not as serious in Ontario.
>
> I was convicted of attempted murder in Montreal. It was about a turf war—territory related. I was managing a bar and he was trying to sell in my bar and around the area to people who used to buy from us. I warned him and then he went shooting off his mouth at other places. He was in the bar one night and I waited until he came out and that's how it happened. I had an argument and it was him or me. I shot him six times and he lived. I got 16 years. I served my first two years in a violent-offender program.

Businessmen dealers in this study condemn the strong-arm tactics used by bikers, view their strategies as unprofessional and dangerous, and refuse to do business with them. Most of the criticisms of outlaw motorcycle gangs focus on their willingness to use violence and the fact that they cannot be trusted. Typical comments include:

> Bikers never import the stuff. They buy it here and repackage it and have their foot soldiers do the selling. I sold to bikers, but it was always on a cash basis. I hate them, but there was one guy I would deal with. A lot of them are idiots. They have two brain cells and they fight with one another. Many are drug users. I wouldn't be seen with them in public—only meet with them at the back of some strip joint. There are not many thugs at the higher levels. It takes too much business sense.

I loathe and hate bikers and they are scum and prostitutes. I have a Harley, but I rode with doctors and lawyers. No one in our organization lived off of the avails of prostitutes. I hate what bikers stood for, but I realize that it's hypocritical for me to say that and for me to exploit addiction.

I never deal with bikers. I don't trust them even though I have no experience personally. I know people who have and it's not worked out. Problem is they are shady and their group is first. They like to muscle people to do what they want. If you want to do business by yourself, then you don't want to be in business with people who try to muscle you. It's not worth the money. I'd rather be independent than report to them scumbags. It goes beyond drug dealing and has to do with treating people like humans. People want to deal with nice people and not with brutal arrogant people who slap you out—with civilized guys. Would you rather be feared or loved? That's a tough question that Machiavelli asked. Tough in the drug trade. A lot of people do run their empire with fear. The Russian Mafia today run it that way. I would rather be loved. You can expect that people will love you and you give them an option. They follow you and fewer will go against you and you have a lot of allies to back you up. If you run your crew on fear, they end up failing.

I didn't have too much to do with bikers. They are violent people and they love notoriety and you can't trust them. They are not very bright people. They have been on the fringe of the criminal world. A lot of fucked up people who can't make it. They

do business through control and violence—not good businessmen—and [are] considered to be stupid people. They try to recruit people through strong-arm tactics.

Bikers are also criticized for cutting their drugs and selling poor-quality product.

They sell bad drugs and tend to cut the drugs very heavily.

They would cut it [cocaine] and make 3 kilos out of two. Occasionally, some of their clients came to me because they were getting such poor quality. They make the money through cutting it. They bring in 50 or 60 a month that I know of. They add a vitamin that you cannot tell is a mix—can be ejected or cooked to a rock or snort it with no headaches, but it's not full strength and they force their buyers to take it.

Both RCMP and dealer interviews indicate that outlaw motorcycle gangs in Canada operate at both retail and wholesale levels. A biker associate describes the retail side of biker drug sales.

They are major suppliers of marijuana across the border. They control the strip clubs in Vancouver and own five of the major strip bars and it makes sense for them to be suppliers in these bars. A lot of these bars have prostitutes and cocaine. A lot of cab drivers provide prostitutes and cocaine through the bikers. The bikers are low-level dealers. They can control that. I could never control that low level. If you deal with low-level people, they are the users. Bikers will deal with users.

Small independent groups who import narcotics into the country sometimes lack a sufficient distribution network and will do business with bikers—despite their unsavoury reputation—because the latter can afford to purchase large quantities of drugs on a regular basis. This arrangement also benefits biker gangs who may lack contacts in source countries. A major cocaine importer in Vancouver dealt with an outlaw motorcycle gang for several years without problems and describes top bikers as reliable and steady clients.

> I never associated with any bikers who wore colours, only ones who wore suits. They were very high level and they were extremely good businessmen. They would take so much every week and pay for it in one lump sum and go away.

A Montreal businessman who worked with an Italian syndicate importing cocaine through the United States also had biker clients.

> There were bikers involved. This partner from Montreal knew some people from Hells Angels and introduced him to me and he was one of the buyers and got arrested along with me and got seven years himself. There was never any violence, no, because I am a very straight person and there is no worry about getting hurt unless you double-cross them.

Outlaw motorcycle gangs represent large criminal syndicates with chapters in various provinces and contacts in most major cities and towns across Canada. These chapters provide a national distribution network that allows bikers to move drugs from the lab or from source countries down the chain to consumers. Their organization and structure comes closest to resembling the traditional image of organized crime as a large, bureaucratic structure that uses violence, aims to be monopolistic, and exists as a secret society.

Organized Drug Syndicates and Territoriality

Previous scholars have suggested that organized criminal syndicates grow so large that they are able to gain monopolistic control of illicit goods and services within certain geographic areas (Cressey, 1969; Maas, 1968). The present study indicates that drug traffickers in Canada are organized into small, independent crews that compete, but sometimes co-operate with other syndicates to maximize profits and minimize risks. These groups seek to acquire quality products at low prices to give themselves an edge in competitive, illicit drug markets. Narcotics are supplied to Canadian-based groups, which then sell the product to other organized crime syndicates, which subsequently distribute the drugs within certain geographic areas. These groups may operate in one city or defined area, but typically do not control the territory. Although trafficking within certain areas of the country and particular cities often reflects the race and ethnic composition of the population, various independent crews are likely to compete with one another. A 60-year-old career criminal describes how times have changed in the drug world.

> Somebody trying to muscle has never been a concern of mine at that time or even now. Like I would move in myself, but I wouldn't come in like with guns and all that. I'd come in with a proposition. Using muscle is thinking along the French mentality, Quebec thinks like that. I'd find out what they want. "Give me a wholesale price and forget about marketing. It's done." I take complete distribution.

In the early days, in the sixties and the early seventies, dope wasn't as sophisticated. There was a lot of violence and sometimes you had to protect your territory with violence or the threat of violence. "You're an East End boy, stay in the East End. West End is mine. Go put out where you purchased it from. You want to deal in this area, you purchase mine. Simple, because you're competing against my people." I got beyond that in very much of a hurry. I ended up controlling what I wanted to control by my product—by the quality and the price.

Criminal dealers are particularly resistant to the idea that someone would attempt to muscle them out of a city or geographical area and are willing to use violence to defend their business.

The bikers tried to muscle me in the early days, but nobody ever tried to use muscle when I moved up the ladder. I've never heard of it happening. The only people I've seen try to muscle are the bikers and they don't have the etiquette.

Both the police and dealers report that outlaw motorcycle gangs attempt to control territory by the use of force. In particular, bikers own or control various bars and strip clubs and use these as locales to sell illicit drugs. The limited data available indicate that outlaw motorcycle gangs represent an exception to this territorial norm. Certain outlaw gangs have established territories and although they may tolerate independent drug wholesalers, they will use violence on other biker gangs who infringe on their territory. To the extent that it exists, territoriality in Canada appears to be characteristic of retail rather than of wholesale drug trafficking.

Retail Sales, Violence, and Territoriality

Several respondents who began their career in retail drug sales described their local neighbourhoods as territorial.

Street level is very territorial and people get seriously hurt. That's another reason why I moved out of the street.

It depends on what level you're dealing. In the projects [public housing], outsiders were told to move on. Yes, that did happen on the street.

I was still independent on my own. It means not getting in each other's faces in the same area. We had our own bars and we sent our guys to these bars and not other bars.

Street level is territorial. At the higher level, it is like a price war.

I knew all the people I worked with for years and didn't have to worry about outsiders coming into our neighbourhood. In most cases, a conversation would convince them to leave. There were more of us than them. Everybody knew everybody and the neighbourhood was closed to outsiders.

Not all dealers who had sold drugs at the retail level observed territorial behaviour.

Not many people came into the area. It just didn't happen. When I went out each day, it was always the same people. We were all young. I wouldn't call it territorial in the sense that people protected their turf. We mostly did business in our own neighbourhood because we felt safer dealing with people we knew. Dealers in other neighbourhoods would probably feel the same.

I saw a little evidence of it [territoriality] from street level, but not a lot. It thins out at the higher level.

If people had tried to move in, then it may have been defined as territorial—hard to say. I have nothing to base that on because it was always the same dealers on the street.

A number of subjects report that liquor establishments are often used for retail drug sales and that many are territorial. Although there are limited data on this topic, it appears that bar owners may tolerate or encourage this practice for several reasons: (1) they engage in drug trafficking themselves often through their staff; (2) they profit from drug dealing through kickbacks from dealers; (3) they profit through the increased sales brought in by dealers and their customers; (4) they tolerate the practice because they are fearful of drug traffickers.

Case Example: The Mob

A few criminal dealers in this study report using violence to force dealers in their territory to purchase drugs from their crew. An Italian-Canadian who served time in the U.S. for manslaughter used violence to maintain clients and protect territory. He organized his crew along a Mafia structure, attempted to give people the impression that he had ties to the "mob," and even used Mafia terms to describe his organization.

We had very intricate rules. One crew was known as the working crew. They would enact enforcement against rule breakers. They did no trafficking at all, so police knew little about them. These were not the smartest guys and they were thugs and muscle. They slept in and worked out in the gym every day. They were big, intimidating individuals and they got a salary of $5,000 a week each. They were kept busy.

They would deal with problems. Some of the distributors were too passive and could not resolve conflicts through violence. There are people in the underworld who rip off and kidnap people for ransom.

The violence makes business difficult and we used the working crew to keep the sharks out of the waters so the rest of the fish can do their thing.

An example of how we would use the working crew—say the first crew is buying steadily 1 to 2 kilos a week off a capo and selling in ounces to customers underneath them. We keep records of our sales and we know how much everyone is selling. The week passes and their customers are not calling them. We find out that one guy has hooked up with another supplier and convinced a few others to pool their money and buy from another dealer. It may be someone they used to deal with and they figure they can buy for less and make a better profit, so some of our customers are going elsewhere outside of the organization.

The person that supplies them might have heat and that brings it to the clients and then back to us. Their connection runs dry and these guys come back and purchase from us again and now we're under surveillance. Unfortunately, we have to resort to force to protect ourselves. They're sleeping around, so somebody has to go wake them up.

The working crew shows up and grabs them at their home or in a parking lot and takes them to the ocean or holds them over a bridge and gives them the fear of God. Should we do it? Hang them upside down by their heels over a bridge. They are stripped of their product and money and told that if they get back in business, the crew will put them in a hole, but they aren't really put out of business. After this, these guys would be visited by our guys. The capo will show up and say we heard you got ripped off and this is awful and act sympathetic and tell them we can take care of this. The capo tells them how the organization works and if they are willing to play by our rules, he'll work it out.

Then the capo will bring the working crew to meet with these guys and they will give back the product. The capo will say, "These people have decided to give you back your drugs and your money because they don't want any problems from us." The working crew make it clear they won't fuck with the capo and act respectful and act like they pray that nothing will happen to them. We used the working crew to give people the idea that they were dealing with an organization.

Some higher-level drug syndicates are protective of their own customers and regard any effort by another dealer to steal their clients as an infringement on their "territory" and are willing to use violence to protect sales.

I would not take another dealer's customers. It's different if someone approaches me, but even then you have to be careful. I told my buyers not to sell to certain people in the Chinese community. I did not want this Chinese dealer coming after my buyers or threatening them because I would be involved.

You don't infringe on other dealers' customers—very important. If it did happen, you were warned. If it happened a second time and you've sold him 20 kilos, you owe us $1,000 a kilo and you had better pay up.

Although retailers may attempt to prevent others from selling drugs in their neighbourhood and/or bars, it appears that territoriality is uncommon at the wholesale level. The vast majority of respondents in this study were never threatened by other crews over territorial disputes, nor did they regard their city or neighbourhood to be personal property.

There isn't such a thing as territory that prevents you from going from one area to another. Those are the old days. I don't even know where a guy lives. I sell four keys to a guy and he could live in Scarborough. I don't know.

People don't care where you live. Your money is good. If they know that you have the money, then they'll sell it to you.

There is no such thing as territory—maybe on crack level, but not with what we do.

You meet somewhere public like a mall and I'm not going to let him come where I live. And he's going to do the same. We meet somewhere mutual, like out in the mall, and you do an exchange. It doesn't matter where you live.

At the higher levels, there have never been any restrictions on territories. The people I deal with live all over and I'm free to go wherever I want.

That's a lot of baloney. No one controls any territory and you can also get out when you want.

A number of factors help to account for the open and competitive nature of drug trafficking at the wholesale level: customers are free to shop around and will purchase drugs from whoever provides reliable supplies of quality product at competitive prices; the use of violence may lead to reprisals and/or police attention; crews are relatively small and do not have the resources to attempt to control an area by the use of force; and the anonymity and secrecy behind drug trafficking makes it difficult to know who is in the game and prevent dealers from selling in certain areas.

Summary

Fronts are common in the drug trade and are used by dealers to attract and retain clients, expand sales, and enter new territories. Fronts refer to the provision of drugs by suppliers to distributor/clients on credit. This practice often operates on an ongoing basis and is akin to a short-term revolving line of credit. Fronts are more expensive than cash deals for borrowers because there is a risk premium attached to the loan. Several business principles and a system of subcultural norms and values govern the use of fronts and protect the lender's investment. Suppliers typically front only people they know and trust; often require money down or collateral to back up the loan; and keep the value of fronts relatively small and limited to what they can reasonably afford to lose. Dealers who accept a front from their supplier are expected to repay the debt as soon as the drugs are sold to their own clients. Although norms require that all money owing must be paid on time, drug debts are often extended, reduced, or excused if clients have had problems through no fault of their own.

Many dealers avoid taking drugs on a front because the debt makes them accountable to the supplier, thus reducing their independence and autonomy. In addition, there is the implicit fear of violence if one is unable to repay the money owing. The use of violence and the threat of force in the collection of debts do occur on occasion, but most men in this study simply write off the debt and refuse to do business with clients who owe them money. Most higher-level traffickers repudiate the use of force because it is harmful to business and increases the risk of violent retaliation and/or a police investigation. Although they may portray themselves as violent, the majority of subjects did not use coercion in their business dealings. The limited data available indicate that outlaw motorcycle gangs have a reputation for using strong-arm tactics and attempt to control the distribution of drugs in certain territories. It appears that there are no territorial boundaries among drug wholesalers in Canada, and that higher-level trafficking is an open market in which anyone with connections can participate.

Police Investigations of Higher-Level Drug Traffickers

Introduction

Police interventions in most crimes begin when victims, complainants, or witnesses initiate a request for assistance. By waiting to be called, the police have a clear reason to investigate and their intervention is supported by at least one citizen—the person who requested assistance. This reactive nature of criminal investigations helps to ensure that the police do not intrude too deeply into the everyday lives of the community. In this respect, a reactive strategy of policing protects privacy and civil liberties and economizes on the use of formal authority by keeping the state's agents at a distance.

It is obvious that the reactive nature of criminal investigations has limited value since it prevents the police from systematically dealing with crimes that do not produce victims and witnesses. Drug trafficking is a consensual crime involving financial transactions between willing buyers and sellers, and usually there is no victim, witness, or complainant. Drug offences are rarely reported and the police cannot successfully investigate drug trafficking in the same reactive manner they respond to other crimes. These investigations are by necessity proactive and the RCMP actively and aggressively pursue offenders involved in large-scale, organized drug syndicates. Drug investigations typically involve undercover work, the use of agent/informants, physical and electronic surveillance, and sting operations.

Undercover Work and Drug Investigations: The RCMP

Illicit drug usage and lower-level trafficking are primarily the responsibility of municipal and city police services.

The mandate for combatting national and international drug syndicates belongs to the Royal Canadian Mounted Police (RCMP). As a federal police service, the RCMP have the resources and contacts with drug-enforcement agencies in other countries needed to undertake and coordinate the time-consuming and expensive investigations required at the higher echelons of organized crime.

The RCMP work under contract with most provinces in Canada (Ontario and Quebec are the exceptions) as provincial and/or municipal police forces. Most RCMP officers begin their careers in these eight provinces performing the typical duties of uniform police. Officers who show some interest and initiative in drug cases can apply for a transfer to the Drug Branch where they will take a drug investigation course at the Canadian Police College in Ottawa. The course includes lectures and classroom studies as well as a more hands-on interactive approach with simulated scenarios, wiretaps, surveillance, room entries, and affidavit writing.

An officer wishing to do undercover work must first have experience in drug investigations before applying to become an undercover officer. The RCMP are highly selective and applicants will go through three stages of interviews aimed at screening appropriate candidates: applicants are interviewed by their immediate supervisors, the division supervisor, and by course instructors in Ottawa. The applicant will undergo a psychological examination and he or she will be required to pass several written and oral examinations. Staff who run the course make the final decision on whether or not an officer is accepted as a candidate. Applicants who are turned down cannot reapply, nor are they informed of the reasons for their rejection.

The Operations Undercover Techniques Course

The Operations Undercover Techniques course (OUT) trains officers in the Drug Branch to operate as undercover drug investigators (operators) and prepares experienced officers to act as supervisors (cover people) for these kinds of investigations. A cover person is selected by field supervisors and is taught how to plan high-level drug investigations and supervise undercover officers in the field. The supervisor's role is described as similar to that of a big brother or sister and requires him or her to control and protect operators, ensure their needs are met, and ensure that their psychological and emotional health remains sound. Part of the supervisor's responsibility is to ensure that the operator follows the script prepared by the cover team and that he or she makes accurate and detailed notes on a daily basis. A typical cover team includes surveillance officers and wiretap operators.

One RCMP supervisor who trained and operated as both an undercover officer and as a cover person compares operators to professional athletes and actors and cover officers to coaches and directors. Operators are on stage and must play a role that is convincing to their audiences—targeted drug traffickers.

> Operators have to perform and they are like prima donnas. We don't allow them to act like prima donnas, but we treat them that way.

The role of the supervisor is to organize the support unit (cover team), prepare all legal documents, present the budget and obtain funding, and develop investigative strategies. Like a director, the supervisor remains in the background preparing, organizing, script writing, training, coaching, and directing. The supervisor plans and directs the investigation and has primary responsibility for safety. He or she is ultimately held responsible if anything goes wrong and the operator is injured. The RCMP are highly regimented and the operator does not go out the door unless he or she has a full support team, is psychologically ready, legal documents are in order, and safety issues have been addressed. Everything is discussed at length and the team attempts to anticipate and prepare for all possible contingencies. An experienced supervisor explains:

> It is planned and the cover man calls the shots. The undercover operator does not run the show. We'll discuss everything. What if this happens? What if that happens? What if he asks you this? What if ...? What if ...? What if ...? And we'll discuss what the operator should say or what he should do. We try to anticipate most things and generally we can because we have experienced people acting as covermen.

Stress is a major concern for operators and cover people. Officers experienced in both roles contend that supervisors' responsibility makes this a far more demanding and stressful job than that of the undercover officer. One senior investigator describes how stressful his work had become:

> My wife and I holidayed in the Cayman Islands last year and I went scuba diving on the reef. I was 60 feet down and settled on the bottom and just sat there to watch the fish. I was totally relaxed and realized that this was the first time in six or seven years that I felt completely relaxed. The stress of the job is so great that I never stop thinking about work. For the first time in years, I wasn't thinking about my projects and responsibilities.

The Training of Undercover Officers

Drug investigations within the RCMP are strictly controlled and operators must be willing to take directions and follow the scripts designed by the cover team. One objective of the training is to test their ability to follow orders and, to that end, candidates are made to do silly and embarrassing tasks throughout the course. One of the main concerns is that students learn to follow the law in gathering evidence against drug dealers. In particular, instructors wish to ensure that undercover officers are not overly aggressive in attempting to make purchases and in pursuing their targets. Students learn that there are many rules that must be observed. One officer explains:

> I had a judge sit through my course for the full three weeks. He wanted to see first-hand what type of formal training we were doing. He was impressed that we don't have cowboys in there and that there are a lot of restrictions on the operators.

The policy of the RCMP is for undercover operators to make notes on a daily basis and shortly after each drug purchase. Case laws also require this and defence lawyers will typically ask the operator when the notes were recorded in order to determine whether memory or intervening events could have tainted the evidence. Once a drug purchase is made, operators attempt to leave the scene as quickly as possible without bringing suspicion upon themselves. This requires constructing a legitimate reason for doing so, such as having tickets for a concert or some other event. Street-level dealers often expect clients to take the drugs in their presence. In the event that officers are placed in situations in which drug use is expected, they are taught techniques for making it appear that they have consumed drugs without in fact taking them. The RCMP generally do not face this problem with drug wholesalers because drug usage is frowned upon among higher-level dealers. Since operators play the role of dealers and not users, it is unlikely that they would bring suspicion upon themselves by declining to use drugs.

Many officers view the investigation as a game in which they try to outthink, outsmart, and outmanoeuvre the opponent. The RCMP make every effort to control situations in which they have undercover officers involved, but at the same time attempt to make targets feel that they are calling the shots. Undercover officers and agents are taught how to influence the actions of suspects in order to facilitate the gathering of evidence. For instance, operators will steer a dealer away from certain areas to other locales so that the cover team can better monitor their movements. They will also attempt to schedule meetings and transactions at times and locations that are advantageous to the surveillance team. Undercover officers must work within pre-established parameters and are restricted in what they can and cannot do. If suspects were to suggest a new course of action, for instance, operators would decline to participate by explaining that they would have to clear this with their boss. This strategy allows the police to better control the situation, protect the officer, and it gives them time to plan and implement their strategy.

Operators must possess the characteristics that deflect suspicion and be able to fit into their surroundings in order to be effective. Since dealers are often businessmen or play this role, undercover officers will similarly use the cover of a businessperson to infiltrate drug syndicates. Age is a variable as well and because higher-level dealers tend to be older, undercover officers will be selected to fit appropriate age parameters.

> We use older undercover officers in the big centres. A beard and grey hair will work because the bad guys are older. A

lot of them are businesspeople and this is a good cover for an operator.

The police have learned that traffickers are always on the lookout for undercover officers and are suspicious of anyone who will pay high prices for drugs, has an unending supply of money to purchase drugs, or whose buying patterns increase significantly in a short period. As one officer comments:

> Cops are known to pay top dollar for drugs because it is not their money and their goal is to make the buy! Dealers will suspect people who appear to have an endless supply of money and are always buying beers to make friends.

In order to deflect suspicion, police will sometimes walk away from a buy, telling the dealer that they are unhappy with the price. Another strategy is to postpone purchases, explaining that they are temporarily short of funds. Most dealers are cost conscious and undercover officers build credibility by attempting to negotiate the best deal possible.

The Operational Plan

Prior to launching an investigation, drug officers within the RCMP must develop an operational plan that describes the target, addresses legal issues, and includes a budget, a threat assessment, and an investigative strategy. The RCMP are results oriented, and in order to ensure that the project has a high probability of success, officers will gather as much information on the target as possible. Because investigations of higher-level drug syndicates are time consuming and expensive, the RCMP assess and approve projects and allocate resources based on the best intelligence available.

Operational plans are submitted to supervisors, who will evaluate them in competition with other proposals and rank them in priority before making decisions regarding funding. Budgets include items such as an agent's fees, witness-relocation expenses, and the costs of translation, meals, travel, and accommodation. The operations officer of a drug branch of the RCMP typically holds an inspector rank, has years of experience as a drug investigator, and is responsible for approving and overseeing operational plans. One inspector who was interviewed in this study, supervised 145 drug officers that worked approximately 20 drug investigations at any given time. The operational officer, along with senior investigators, review new proposals on a regular basis and decide which projects go forward and which do not. Frequently, they are unable to commit to a new file without diminishing the drug squad's ability to complete ongoing investigations. Often a proposal must wait until another is completed and personnel and funding are available. There is an almost daily discussion and debate concerning the relative merits of operational plans and an ongoing attempt to balance priorities. Not all files that have been open on traffickers can be funded, and supervisors continuously evaluate each project proposal and move them forward if warranted. Frequently, events will require the RCMP to act quickly in order to intercept a drug shipment and priorities will be shifted at a moment's notice. In other cases, the promise of a relatively inexpensive investigation and quick arrests may allow resources to be temporarily redistributed.

Cases are prioritized on a number of criteria, including the relative danger posed by the target. A threat assessment is part of any operational plan and threats are judged by whether or not the group represents an organized crime syndicate (as defined by the federal government), engages in violent acts, imports/distributes high quantities of narcotics, or poses a threat to national security (e.g., has links to terrorist organizations, which is rare).

Different ministries of the federal government provide funding for different political goals and priorities.

Whenever agents/informants are employed, the RCMP will conduct a threat assessment on the possible dangers the agent is likely to face both during and after the investigation. This requires an evaluation of the agent, the agent's family, and how well the police can protect them. If the witness-protection program is to be used, will all members co-operate and agree to be relocated? Will they follow the rules and/or advice meant to ensure their own safety? In one particularly tragic case, the agent, his wife, and seven children were relocated out of province following the father's testimony and the trial and conviction of several of his associates. Shortly afterwards, the eldest son moved back to his home community against the advice of his father and the RCMP and was murdered by members of the drug syndicate.

The RCMP must also consider the danger to families in other countries when agents are foreign nationals. If family members face retribution and the police cannot protect them, the RCMP will not use the agent and may be unable to take on a specific project at this time. The RCMP operate under moral and legal guidelines that prohibit them from putting agents and their families at undue risk of harm. As one officer states: "We know we're not going to stop the drug flow into Canada, so we're not prepared to sacrifice anyone's life to make a bust. We'll walk away from a case if it is too much of a threat to an agent or his family."

An operational plan must also consider legal issues and logistics, including the laws of other countries. Certain countries, such as Jamaica, for example, do not allow wiretaps, whereas other countries prohibit the use of agents and/ or undercover officers. Evidentiary issues are discussed at length since it is essential that the investigation is conducted in a lawful manner both inside Canada and outside the country to ensure that evidence is admissible in Canadian courts.

Even though the police attempt to follow an operational plan as closely as possible, they must remain flexible in order to react and respond to the ever-changing plans of drug traffickers. Dealers will often have to postpone, modify, or cancel drug deliveries and sales because of contingencies beyond their control. A drug-importation scheme that is supposed to take place next week may not occur for several months because dealers require additional time and money to complete the transaction. The amount of time needed to put large-scale smuggling and wholesale operations together provides the RCMP with the opportunity to plan their investigation, but it also works against them when it extends the duration of the project and requires more funding than was allocated.

A significant variable in assessing an operational plan is the likelihood of success. This is judged on the basis of the intelligence available, the reliability of the information, the proximity of the target (some dealers may live outside the country), the use of an agent and his or her credibility and competence, language barriers and the availability of qualified undercover officers, and the likelihood of drug seizures. The police always prefer to intercept narcotics since this will add weight to the evidence against the accused in subsequent trials. It is possible to convict offenders in a "dry conspiracy" case—one without drug seizures—but these are considered more difficult and less certain of success.

The Cover Story

RCMP officers are assigned undercover work in jurisdictions away from their home base and are frequently parachuted into communities and other provinces hundreds or thousands of kilometres from their families. The RCMP begin the operation by building a cover story

for the operator, which includes a new name, false identification and public records, and a fictional life history. Undercover officers must learn their new identity, including details of their "home town" in the event they meet someone from the same town, city, or neighbourhood. Officers study road maps, learn the restaurants and bars, and memorize the names of schools, teachers, and people who are well known in the community. This identity and cover story has to be soundly constructed since high-level dealers have sufficient resources to conduct a thorough investigation of an operator's background.

An officer's point of entry in a drug conspiracy is typically through an introduction by an agent/informant. The agent will also assist in maintaining the cover story and will vouch for the officer, often on a continuous basis. One supervisor explains:

> You have to keep bringing your agent back for cameo appearances. You can't cut an agent out completely because you need to give your operator credibility. I've covered five major projects in the past five years and as much as you would like to cut the agent out, you cannot do it. You give the guy some extra bucks and he'll come back. These dealers didn't get to be upper level without being cautious. The introduction is important, but it's often not enough. The targets are trying to pull the agent back in. Both sides superanalyze it. The bad guys analyze it as much as we do.

Although officers operate within certain scripts, they are inevitably asked questions outside the parameters of their cover story. Undercover work leads to spontaneous involvements with drug dealers, and operators must be clever and composed enough to handle situations as they arise. Undercover work involves acting, but dealers are unlike other audiences because they are cautious, suspicious, and they can feel, touch, and interact with the officer. To be successful, an officer must develop an alter ego that he or she takes into the field. This is an alternate self that is not only learned, but lived for months at a time. Experienced officers report that the work is so emotionally demanding that they temporarily "became" that other person.

> The cover story is essentially a book of lies that you must know and be able to use consistently. The operator must know it, feel it, and believe it.

A cover story is easiest to present and remember if it is as close to the truth as possible. One officer reports that he used personal life experiences as the basis for his cover story. His history included all the jobs he had worked, except for his most recent employment with the RCMP. As part of his cover story, he was allegedly divorced with three children and he used the names of his niece and two nephews when asked his children's names. These techniques help operators remember their answers if asked the same question at different times. Wherever he could not tell the truth, the officer was as vague or noncommittal as possible. This way, if someone caught him in an inconsistency, he could use the ambiguity of his answer to suggest that he had been misunderstood. On occasion, he would tell someone who asked too many questions to mind their own business. Undercover officers are taught to turn the tables on dealers, challenge them, and direct conversations onto subjects of their choosing.

The Reverse Sting

A common ploy for undercover officers is to engage in illicit activities such as fencing stolen goods or smuggling cigarettes and alcohol. The cloak of criminality often helps to give the undercover officer credibility with offenders. The "Eyespy" operation in Vancouver involved RCMP officers acting as crooked businessmen willing to illegally convert cash for a premium at their downtown money exchange. On other occasions, officers may play the role of dishonest government employees, Customs officers, or embassy personnel and offer dealers the means of transporting drugs across the border, false passports, work visas, and other useful goods and services.

It is very common in undercover investigations for officers to deal in drugs or engage in other illegal activities to gain evidence on criminals. Although the practice of undercover officers purchasing drugs from dealers has been accepted as legal by the courts, the use of reverse stings in which the police offer to sell drugs to criminals has been controversial. Although this is a strategy that has been used for decades, defence attorneys in recent years have challenged the legality of the police breaking the law. To settle the issue, the federal government recently amended the *Controlled Drugs and Substances Act* to legitimize certain police violations of the law. The law states that a member of a police force is exempt from criminal culpability when he or she engages or attempts to engage in a variety of illegal activities, including trafficking, importing/exporting, and conspiracy to traffic in an illicit drug if: (a) he or she is an active member of the police force; (b) is acting in the course of his or her responsibilities for the purposes of the particular investigation; and (c) acts under the direction and control of a member of the police. In addition, certain actions such as importing and exporting drugs require that the officer has been issued a certificate for a period not exceeding six months by the acting commander (RCMP) of the Drug Enforcement Section (sec. 10–12).

The Threat of Violence in Undercover Work

Drug retailers tend to make their profits through a large number of sales to a variety of clients. Higher-level wholesalers make fewer sales to a relatively small number of distributors and transactions typically take a significant amount of time to organize, finance, and accomplish. The time factor provides the RCMP with the opportunity to plan their actions in advance and minimize risks. Robbery is always a concern and the team solicits innovative ideas to prevent this from happening. Operators are trained to avoid situations that appear dangerous and/or cannot be controlled or monitored. Undercover officers will tell suspects that they do not feel comfortable in certain locales and prefer to do business elsewhere. For example, they may point to something suspicious as an excuse for avoiding a situation perceived to be dangerous.

> I noticed a car with U.S. plates and told them I thought it was a cop and that I was backing off.

Dealers are cautious, too, and they are often willing to accommodate clients who express reservations and concerns.

There is consensus among the RCMP that the most dangerous operations are street-level deals involving substance abusers and other desperate people. The street is a difficult environment to control and users are unpredictable. An experienced RCMP undercover officer offers the following assessment:

> The most dangerous undercover operations are not the high-level ones, but the ones that occur on the street where you deal with substance abusers and desperate people dealing for money for their habit. The street is a foreign environment and you're on their turf. They are more desperate and are out for a quick fix and could pull a gun in a second .... At the higher levels, the guy wants longevity for doing business tomorrow and next month. They don't want to harm anyone because that will only bring heat to themselves. You make your deals in a hotel restaurant and not some back alley. There is some physical danger in all of it, but it's less likely at the higher level.

Robbery is a short-term gain and higher-level dealers seek to establish long-term business relationships. They will take the time to investigate people to see if they might be police officers or informant/agents and avoid those they don't trust. They know that by using violence against an undercover officer, they would face serious legal problems. Dealers at this level are more likely to attempt to escape, especially if they are foreign nationals. The RCMP have many cases on file where suspects have disappeared and/or are known to be living out of the country. Although there is some physical danger in any police undercover operation, it is less likely at the higher level.

> We talk to these guys all the time and they are professional. Many are businessmen and non-violent. Often when we arrest the high-level guys, there is professional courtesy and no animosity. We will chit-chat and their attitude is that my job is to get away and yours is to catch me. I joked with one trafficker that if it wasn't for me, the price of cocaine would drop and so would his profits.

Although there is less danger investigating higher-level drug traffickers, the RCMP take every precaution to protect the life of undercover operators. Only one officer has died in a drug investigation and this occurred when he fell out of the back of a pickup truck in Thailand. The target realized that the police were moving in to make an arrest and attempted to drive off. The officer's death was unintentional.

Role Playing and Undercover Work: The Dangers of Going Native

The RCMP organize their investigation so that the operator returns to a safe house each day where he or she meets with the cover team to discuss all developments. Because the officer takes on a new identity and begins to live that role for months at a time, there is a danger that he or she can take on some of the characteristics of the criminal identity and "go native," to use an anthropological term. Going native suggests the possibility that the operator may be influenced by criminal values, develop friendships with criminals, and jeopardize the investigation. Consequently, the cover team monitors his or her psychological and mental state and looks for signs that the operator is overly immersed in the role. A former student who became an RCMP officer and worked undercover reports that he genuinely liked the people he investigated and felt somewhat guilty for having betrayed their trust.

> These are people that under other circumstances I could have been friends with. That was the hardest part for me—making their trust for the sole purpose of breaking that trust. I didn't enjoy that.

To help prevent operators from being overwhelmed by their fictional identity, it is RCMP policy that every three weeks the operator is allowed a trip home to his or her family. In addition, the supervisor is encouraged to make his or her home life available to the operator on an ongoing basis

throughout the investigation so as to engage the operator with people who are not part of a criminal milieu. One former undercover officer explains the problem of staying undercover too long and the importance of family contact.

> When I was out East, three cover men were not available to make their family life available. I was living like a shitbag. I didn't go back to visit my family every three weeks for three days. I did it every seven weeks for a week, which was a mistake. I was in Fredericton and I couldn't go anywhere. If I went to the gym, the targets would be there and I'd have to be an asshole. You're not associating with nice people when you're undercover. You're taken away from your family and you better have a good cover team and cover man.
>
> The cover man has to control the operator and make sure he's treated well. If you can't step out of that role, you become that role. Wives can spot guys who do too much undercover. I couldn't spot it in myself. I was taking on too much of the role and playing it too long. Others didn't recognize it in me because I was out of province. A good friend told me that I had to get out. The role playing makes you become the shithead. You have to realize that is not who you are and remember who you really are. You are not the person you're playing. I am not Steve Thompson. The signs are there: shortness of temper, foul language, twisting what other people are saying.

Informants and Agents

The RCMP rely heavily on the assistance of agents to place undercover officers into the criminal milieu. Agents are typically criminals who have been caught and offered the following deal: "Introduce our man to your supplier and vouch for him and we'll drop the charges." Once accepted within the drug milieu, operators will attempt to purchase drugs and gather evidence against dealers. The information and introduction provided by the agent speeds up the investigative process, saves money, and results in drug busts of higher-level dealers. An RCMP inspector explains the usefulness of informants:

> The agent/informant reduces the work involved in setting up the case. Somebody has to tell you that a guy is a drug dealer so you don't embark on an aimless strategy. The informant gives you a target. The informant also gives you an introduction and can provide the grounds for a wiretap. The informant is a starting point. He's an in and he can give you the inside story. With an informant, you can develop intelligence, create a strategy, and infiltrate the organization with an undercover officer.

Informants/agents increase police efficiency because by allowing them to zero in on active drug traffickers. Although agents are often paid fees in the range of $100,000, the police view the money as well spent. Many investigations cost millions of dollars and agents represent a fraction of the overall expenditure. RCMP investigators who have worked with agents argue persuasively that they are cost effective.

> If we undertook an investigation without a clear target, or if we put undercover cops in cold, we could end up spending millions with little result.

An RCMP officer describes a case in which an agent played a key role in the arrest of several high-level cocaine dealers.

> The informant was paid $100,000 plus expenses for the project called "Once," and he got another $150,000 for "Once More." My partner wanted to use him for another project we called "Once and for All," but he upped the ante and wanted $150,000 and expenses, which would result in another $100,000. It was too expensive to get approved. Our management would rather pay someone less and start over. The informant priced himself out of the market and we never did do the third sting.

Having criminals in the employ of the police is viewed by some citizens as morally questionable despite the efficacy of such a strategy. One reason for concern is the fact that agents may regard their contract as a licence to offend while they maintain their role as drug dealers. Of particular concern to the police is the possibility that the agent is engaged in drug dealing for his or her own benefit. The police caution agents against such conduct and monitor their behaviour. Investigators admit, however, that some agents take advantage of their relationship to traffick in drugs and commit other crimes. One officer describes how difficult it was to monitor an agent who frequently travelled to Colombia to set up deals:

> Billy is the son of a reputed crime boss and is one of the highest-level informants in the country. He is fascinating and highly co-operative. He is also on the cutting edge of what we're doing because he is so well placed and so accurate, but we know that he is possibly playing both sides. That's the reality of doing business

with criminals and there is nothing we can do. The allegation of whether or not they are clean or not will be made in court by defence attorneys. We try to cover ourselves by telling them that they can't do it.

This officer suggested that I attempt to interview Billy since he would likely provide a wealth of information. He offered to provide my name and phone number to Billy the next time they met. He also indicated that Billy would probably expect to be paid for his co-operation.

> Agents want to make money and get paid. That's what they're in it for. Billy wants to get paid and if he isn't paid, he would probably say no to your request to an interview. We've paid him a phenomenal amount of money to do the cases he did. It's a business and he has to treat it as a business.

A month later, Billy telephoned me at home on a collect call from Colombia. We discussed my project and he invited me to Colombia to further my research. He also asked how much I was willing to pay for his information. When I indicated that I had few resources with which to pay my subjects, he seemed disappointed and did not call back. The RCMP officer gave several examples of how Billy had helped them in their investigations. In one case, a high-level dealer was leaving for Los Angeles to set up a deal. He mentioned that his cellular phone wasn't working and Billy gave his phone to the dealer and told him it was clean. The dealer used it for the next three weeks, allowing the police to identify other players and make a large seizure of cocaine.

Police complain that their ability to develop informants has been severely eroded by case law that requires the names of agents be disclosed to the defence (*R. v. Stinchcombe*).

It is understandably difficult to convince dealers to act as agents when they know that the disclosure of their identities and roles in the investigation may endanger their lives. In the past, the police had the right to protect the identities of agents and would go to great lengths to ensure that they did not have to testify. A common practice was to arrest the informant in the initial roundup and later find an excuse to release him or her without charges.

The Source Witness-Protection Program

Other criminals hate agents/informants since they are typically trusted members of the group who sell out their associates for personal gain. Drug dealers rarely express animosity toward the police or undercover officers since they are simply doing their jobs. The actions of agents/informants, however, are seen as a violation of the criminal code and a betrayal and are taken personally. Given this animosity, the police are morally and legally obligated to protect the agent/informant during and after trial. One mechanism for doing this is through the Source Witness-Protection Program. This program provides funds and services to suitable agents/informants to establish a new identity in a different location in Canada. The person, in effect, goes undercover and incognito on a long-term or permanent basis. The police use the Source Witness-Protection Program to gain an offender's co-operation. One officer discussed the role of a particular agent and his experience with the program.

> Bill has since been relocated with a new name, city, and he is now on his own. I'd never do it. The Canadian program is abysmal and it stinks. There is possibly new legislation coming. He's still required for court for weeks at a time and he has to leave his work to do so. I am not a big fan of the

Source Witness-Protection Program, but I guess I could sell it to someone if I had to. I could also probably sell someone a Lada, but I wouldn't want one for myself.

Surveillance

Physical Surveillance

Physical surveillance refers to the process by which police officers surreptitiously follow and observe a suspect with the intent of learning about his or her criminal activities and associates. The police commonly use evidence gathered through physical surveillance in their affidavit requesting authorizations for search warrants and electronic surveillance. Although there are many legal restrictions on the use of electronic surveillance, physical surveillance of suspects can be initiated and maintained at the discretion of the police without judicial approval. The reasons for the difference has to do with a citizen's right to privacy and expectation of privacy. The *Charter of Rights and Freedoms* has entrenched the right to privacy and the police cannot infringe on a citizen's rights without proper authorization from judicial authorities. These authorizations are given only when the police have reasonable and probable grounds to believe that a crime has been or is about to be committed. The right to privacy and the expectation of privacy does not hold in public places, and citizens can be placed under surveillance while they go about their daily business. For example, a suspected drug dealer who drives to the airport to meet a courier can be followed, photographed, and observed. The police cannot place an electronic listening device in his or her car, however, without proper authorization. The dealer has an expectation of privacy while conversing in his or her car, but there is no violation of the dealer's rights through physical surveillance.

Physical surveillance is a highly proactive investigative tool since it is used to help the police to catch the offender in the act and/or to learn about and prevent future criminal activities. Because drug trafficking involves networking and interactions between offenders, one of the objectives of police surveillance is to identify the main players in drug conspiracies. Physical surveillance is an expensive investigative tool and personnel and budget considerations require that the RCMP use their resources as economically as possible. Financial constraints severely hamper the ability of the RCMP to follow every lead with an expensive investigation. This means, in effect, that the police must be selective in choosing targets. To this end, the RCMP typically rely on intelligence and/or information from informants to identify and target higher-level drug dealers. The RCMP prioritize cases and one major criterium in deciding whether or not to launch an investigation is the likelihood of success. An investigator explains:

> If a member of the public walked into our office and told us that he had heard that one of his neighbours was heavily into drug dealing, we would listen and write up a report, but if he had nothing more to give us, we'd thank him for his assistance and file it. The information could prove useful at some future date, but we would not actively pursue it. Without an agent or informant who could pass on detailed information that would allow us to get wiretap authorizations, we wouldn't act on it. We get a lot of leads like that, but we don't have the resources to follow up. We have to have a reasonable expectation of success before we'll spend the time and money.

Drug dealers are cautious and keeping them under surveillance is difficult and challenging.

A surveillance team consists of five or six operatives who are in constant radio contact with one another. Different officers will move in and off the target from time to time to ensure that the person does not become aware that he or she is being followed. Police will change their appearance, clothing, and switch cars from day to day in order to diminish the chance of being recognized.

If suspects are extremely cautious and aware of their surroundings, the police will fall back completely so as not to jeopardize the coverage. Surveillance will resume later or wait for another day. The fact that people follow certain routines allows the team to keep a safe distance if they can predict a person's habits, direction of travel, and eventual destination. Knowing a suspect's meeting place allows the police to "set up" on that location—i.e., to arrive beforehand and position themselves to observe, photograph, and videotape and/or electronically record the suspect's actions and conversations. A Vancouver drug squad officer describes the cautiousness of one high-level dealer:

> He was a challenging target from a surveillance point of view—a nightmare—very careful how he went off to do meetings on foot and use different people's vehicles. He lived in an apartment building and it was hard to know when he would leave. He was very careful on the phone. He watched who he talked to and arranged personal meetings. They are hard to listen in on. Depends on the circumstances. We figured out his meeting places after a while. We would set up on it and the advantage is that we don't have to follow him anymore. We can set up and let him come to us.

Although surveillance mainly depends on the skills of the officers, police will occasionally use helicoptors, airplanes, and tracking devices placed in cars to follow suspects who are surveillance conscious. Most drug investigators admit that even the best training and technology will not allow them to survey all suspects. A senior investigator states:

> There are some guys who are extremely difficult to surveil [sic]. They may have been caught before or been briefed by their lawyers—very surveillance cautious, always aware of their surroundings, never talk on the phone or in their car. They isolate themselves and the only way to catch them is to follow them for a year or more and be there when they make a mistake.

Electronic Surveillance

One of the primary strategies used by law enforcement to apprehend and convict drug dealers is the use of electronic surveillance. This includes video surveillance, but most often refers to the use of wiretaps on telephones and electronic listening devices in cars, residences, and other places used by offenders. An authorization for electronic surveillance is governed by Part VI of the *Criminal Code*. Sec. 185 sets out the procedures and criteria for granting the police authorization to intercept private communications and permits extensions for specified periods not to exceed three years. Police must make the application in person and in writing to judges in the superior court of criminal jurisdiction. The written application must be accompanied by an affidavit sworn on information and belief regarding the particulars of the offence; the identity of the people whose private communications are to be intercepted; a description of the nature and location of the place if known; a description of the proposed manner of interception; and information on the history of any prior applications.

The affidavit must also state whether or not other investigative procedures have been tried and failed, why they appear unlikely to succeed, or why the matter is so urgent that it is impractical to pursue other means of investigation. This requirement does not apply in relation to an offence under sec. 467.1 or an offence committed for the benefit of a criminal organization. Electronic surveillance also includes warrants to conduct video surveillance of suspects [sec. 487.01(5)]. Sec. 186 sets out the criteria that a judge is to apply when considering whether to grant a request for an authorization to intercept private communications and imposes strict limits on the use of electronic surveillance in the home or offices of a solicitor.

Sec. 196(1) requires that people whose private communications have been intercepted be notified in writing that they have been the object of such an interception within 90 days after the authorization expires. Sec. 185(2) allows the police to apply to have this time period extended to no more than three years. One offender expressed his surprise when he learned about the extent of RCMP wiretaps used to apprehend him and his associates.

> They followed me, they tapped my phones, they even tapped the pay phone by my house. They tapped everything. They tapped every phone of everyone that I contacted. When I got arrested, everybody got letters in the mail that their phone had been tapped.

Police experience indicates that drug dealers make extensive use of telephones in order to communicate with suppliers, distributors, partners, and crew members. Given the fact that associates are often on the move and widely dispersed, the telephone is essential for dealers conducting business. Wiretaps not only allow the police to monitor telephone conversations, they also help to identify people on the other end of the line, including sources outside Canada. Even everyday mundane use of the telephone can provide valuable leads and information. One offender in this study called an airline asking for the arrival time of a particular flight. The call was used by the police to determine that a high-level Colombian cocaine smuggler was arriving in the city, allowing them time to arrange for a surveillance team to target the suspect.

Drug traffickers are acutely aware that the police make extensive use of wiretaps and avoid doing business over the phone, but telephones are necessary and dealers are careful when calling their associates: "You watch what you say on the phone. It's a rule. You always assume that they're listening." Despite this awareness and caution, dealers and/or their associates make mistakes that allow the police to gather intelligence and information essential to making a case. The use of cellular phones is a favourite device that dealers use because they are thought to be safer, but these, too, can be monitored.

Police will also gain authorization to tap a person's car, home, office, parents' home, a favourite restaurant, and other locations that suspects use to conduct business. Investigators take advantage of the fact that people are creatures of habit and meet in a limited number of places to discuss business. A common strategy of offenders to thwart the police use of wiretaps is to move about the city and use several pay telephones. With sufficient evidence of criminal conduct, the police can apply for authorization to tap any pay phone that has been used by the suspect. Police must first observe a suspect use a particular phone and apply for authorization to intercept calls made on that phone. Case law requires that the police listen in on public telephones only during the time period offenders are observed making or receiving calls. The police are prohibited from taping all conversations that take place in the hope of recording the offender making use of a pay telephone. These constraints act as safeguards to protect civil liberties and privacy for the general public, but the police complain that they make investigations exceedingly expensive and time consuming. So many personnel are required to keep one person under surveillance that other cases are not worked and many dealers operate with impunity. Fortunately for the police, offenders will often return to a limited number of pay phones time and time again, thus requiring fewer officers to conduct surveillance.

Speaking in code is another strategy used by drug traffickers when discussing business. Police report, however, that the codes used are often primitive and easy to interpret. Certain street jargon is recognized and accepted in court as referring to specific drugs: e.g., "weed" or "grass" for marijuana, "junk" for heroin, "E" for Ecstasy, and "snow" or "blow" for cocaine. Most offenders refrain from using the common names associated with the drug and substitute prearranged codes in its place. A kilo of cocaine, for instance, might be called a "milkshake" or a "girl."

A relatively new development with drug traffickers is the use of cryptography to disguise telephone calls and e-mail communications. The conversation or e-mail will sound or appear as gibberish to anyone monitoring the message, but can be understood by the recipient who has the technology and codes required to decipher messages. Only two offenders in this study used cryptic messages and the police were able to decipher one of them. They did not attempt to decode the second case since they had sufficient evidence to make seizures and secure a conviction.

The use of foreign languages is a problem the police must overcome by using translators to monitor and translate conversations. This cost is factored into the budgets of proposed investigations, but finding trustworthy, willing, and competent translators is often difficult. Vancouver, for example, has many criminally active Asian drug syndicates (Vietnamese and Chinese) and because they rarely speak English, the police make extensive use of translators. Some translators are police officers, but the majority are civilian employees. Although the RCMP in Vancouver have successfully recruited a significant number of Chinese officers, they have far fewer Vietnamese recruits.

Even if suspects do not incriminate themselves on the telephone, associates may be less careful and provide police with valuable information and/or evidence to convict all or most of the conspirators. Police surveillance requires time, funding, skill, and patience. By being thoroughly prepared and alert, the police can position themselves to take advantage of security lapses on the part of suspects. It takes a great deal of caution and energy for dealers to be constantly aware of their surroundings, changing their routines, and watching what they say and do. Suspects often become complacent, drop their guard, and make mistakes that lead to their demise. Many will assume that their phones or locales are safe and that they have outwitted the police. In time, the police will catch them openly negotiating drug transactions, naming co-conspirators, and discussing drug movements.

The police do not sit back and wait for suspects to act. Instead, they often take the initiative to move things along and gain control of the situation. A favourite strategy is to proactively use agents/informants and undercover officers to direct offenders to locales that can be easily bugged. For instance, agents or informants may be told to arrive at a restaurant first and select the table that has been equipped with a listening device. Alternatively, waiters, hotel clerks, car rental agencies, etc., may be asked to co-operate and direct subjects to a particular table, motel room, or rental vehicle that has been prepared by the police for electronic surveillance. A dealer describes what he learned about police surveillance in his preliminary hearing:

The conspiracy was to traffick cocaine. It was eight months surveillance and they wiretapped a table in a restaurant the main guy frequented and threw a cop in there as a waiter. Unfortunately, I had several meetings with him there.

The police will often use innovative strategies to facilitate surveillance and stimulate subjects into providing evidence. A common ploy is for undercover police or their agents to provide "illicit" goods or services such as cellular telephones that are alleged to be safe (cool phones) but which allow the police to monitor their calls. In one FBI sting, undercover officers set up a room with alleged cool phones and sold targets time at the rate of $100 for a 10-minute call. The FBI provided the RCMP with information on calls made to Canada, which helped identify previously unknown members of a drug conspiracy.

The Surveillance Team

Surveillance typically requires five or six officers following a person over a 16-hour period. The shifts cover the waking hours since most suspects sleep at regular intervals. Surveillance officers rely on their training and experience to be effective and work together as a team.

Surveillance is something we're trained for. It's an art form and not everyone is good at it. It's a team effort and everybody works together. You get good at it as you do more of it.

Surveillance officers enjoy the work particularly when targets present a challenge.

On many files, we'll say these guys are good and very clever and our guys like working these types. Duncan was very good at counter-surveillance and

a worthy opponent. There are criminals out there who are not able to be placed under surveillance.

A high-level cocaine importer who became addicted to heroin was an easy target for the surveillance team and one officer expressed his disdain.

He was not the most challenging target. I never saw him do anything clever. He started to conduct counter-surveillance and we thought he burnt us, but in 10 minutes he made another dirty phone call.

We followed him everywhere and tapped the pay phones. He found a few phones that received calls and started to use them over and over. He had two or three pay phones that he used all the time. Here's an example. At one point, he fell in love with a specific pay phone and he went to it every time and made all these incredibly guilty calls. There was no challenge for us. This is not the pattern that most offenders follow.

He was a pathetic drug user and this is very uncommon at that level. We were shaking our heads at him. His is one of the most pathetic files I have worked on—a loser. Other than the amount of drugs he imported, he was not an impressive figure.

Even dealers who are extremely cautious can often be followed. When police learned from a wiretap that "the main man" would be in town the next day to meet with a supplier, they prepared a surveillance team. The supplier was exceptionally cautious and took evasive actions that made it difficult for the police to follow. The officers pulled back, but covered all the main exits from the neighbourhood the man had entered. He did not emerge, however, and the police could not locate his vehicle.

The following day, they interviewed landlords in several townhouse complexes and apartment buildings. Eventually, a landlord recognized the offender from a surveillance photograph and the police located his rented but vacant condominium. They secured a search warrant, but found no incriminating evidence. The offender reappeared two months later when he was observed meeting with the same distributor. The police followed him back to the condo, obtained a search warrant, and arrested him with 70 kilos of cocaine in his residence. The man was an American citizen who stayed in a local hotel whenever he visited Vancouver and used the apartment only as a safe place to store his product. In this case, police patience in their use of surveillance overcame the security and caution used by a higher-level drug importer.

Corroborating Evidence

A case that is based primarily or exclusively on wiretap is vulnerable to constitutional challenges. There is always the possibility that a judge may rule the evidence inadmissible because of some infringement on the accused person's civil liberties. Consequently, the police are reluctant to proceed on a conspiracy charge unless they can corroborate wiretap and surveillance evidence. This is commonly done through drug purchases or drug seizures.

> The evidence was mainly wiretaps and they would have had trouble convicting us on that alone, but the police had a drug seizure that they could link to our conversations.

Corroborating evidence is also obtained by offering one offender a deal in exchange for a statement and testimony against his or her co-accused.

> The wiretaps made us look guilty, but a lot of it was so circumstantial that

we decided to fight it. We were in court over a four-month period, then the police convinced the fellow in the U.S. to write an affidavit. This was my Mexican connection from the U.S. and he stated that he sold me a total of 100 kilos over these months and that it came over the border in amounts of 25 or 35 kilos. We had a good chance to beat it, but when our connection turned on us, that's when they had the corroborating evidence.

Any evidence of drug lists and amounts of money owing is also presented as evidence supporting the conspiracy charge.

> The police got some information from my computer. It wasn't much, but it backed up what they said. You keep files on everything, but not in your house. You can't keep it in your head. You keep it with somebody who is legitimate and you don't go over there often.

Surveillance outside Canada

An expensive component of drug investigations involves surveillance outside Canada. The RCMP will follow high-level dealers to other countries to observe their movements and identify the people with whom they meet. This provides intelligence that can be shared with police in other countries. Information and intelligence gathered in this way is used to learn about the network systems among dealers, the location of drugs, the method of transport, and the identity of foreign nationals who visit Canada to set up illicit drug deals. One dealer recalls a surveillance officer commenting about his travels.

The police followed me out of the country on vacations and business trips—California, Mexico, the Caribbean. I remember one cop asking me why we stopped visiting some of the places we were going to because he was getting used to the weather.

The RCMP are sometimes reluctant to use police in certain countries for surveillance since they may not be competent or trustworthy. It is common to ask for the assistance of U.S. drug-enforcement agencies, however, since they have both the resources and expertise to track drug dealers operating in their country. One officer describes a case that involved several foreign nationals and the problems involved in following Canadian suspects into other countries.

He went to Colombia on two occasions and we attempted to confirm who he was meeting with. We are always hesitant to ask for assistance from foreign police departments because a *faux pas* could throw our case down the toilet. It is dangerous to the investigation to jeopardize the outcome. I've gone and worked in Mexico and seen them do surveillance and it's very poor. We generally don't ask for surveillance from other countries, but the U.S. is good.

Case Example: The *Salmon Run*

In a particularly complex investigation arising out of the Vancouver "Eyespy" currency exchange, the RCMP followed several people conducting money exchanges (smurfs) to a formerly unknown crew of cocaine smugglers. The crew was run by two partners who were under surveillance. One suspect was seen meeting with an offender who had served time

for a large drug-importation conspiracy. This man was later observed meeting with another well-known smuggler who was on parole from a drug conviction in the United States. As the case developed, it was clear that several overlapping and interconnecting conspiracies were transpiring. Soon members of these various crews were observed meeting with representatives of the Hells Angels. The RCMP obtained authorizations to wiretap several of the suspects' phones and placed listening devices in their homes. The police discovered a plan to import a huge quantity of cocaine by ship from Colombia through Mexico into Canada. The vessels were decommissioned Canadian Coast Guard cutters and had been purchased at auction by another well-known smuggler. During the two-year investigation, several suspects left the country to meet with contacts in Miami, Colombia, and Mexico as surveillance officers followed and observed their meetings. The complexity of the investigation is revealed by one officer's summary of the case.

The following is an abbreviated summary of a complex criminal investigation involving electronic and physical surveillance of a high-level conspiracy to import cocaine into Canada. The investigation is described by an officer from the RCMP Vancouver Mother Ship Unit.

As a result of the Proceeds of Crime Unit's "Eyespy" investigation, Pierre Vanier came to our attention. He is a well-known drug trafficker in his early fifties and Caucasian. Vanier is well connected to other smugglers and was organizing conduits for cocaine smuggling into Vancouver. He was in the higher echelons of drug importers.

Some dealers network with one another and may cross over at different times on different conspiracies because they have different expertise and connections. I see them as contractors building a house and sometimes they work on the same house and other times they're off doing other things with other builders. They find out who is available and work with them.

Vanier could bring in cocaine by air, water, or land and would deal with anyone who used these conduits who was a similar ranking to himself. Surveillance led us to John Easter, who we identified as being on parole from a drug conspiracy conviction in the United States. John served time in the U.S. before he was extradited and sent to Canada where he was paroled immediately.

When we started out a Part IV (wiretap) of the *Criminal Code* on Easter, his only means of income was a T-shirt business. In the two years we had him under surveillance, we never saw him sell a single T-shirt. John Easter is a facilitator. His role in the drug subculture is to facilitate and to bring together certain parties for the purpose of importing and trafficking. He has contacts in different areas of the world, particularly in source countries. He would go to certain organizations and say "I can do this for you." He is his own boss. They all seem to be independents and work with different people. It's like pulling out people's business cards and giving people a call to see if they're available and interested.

I find there are crossovers among the different dealers and they may have nothing to do with one another for three or four years, and then they'll put together a deal and work with one another.

Easter was multifaceted in that he had three ventures he was looking at: bringing in cocaine via a mother ship; cocaine by air cargo with a Vanier associate; and also had another contact for smaller amounts of cocaine via trucking routes. The latter would finance the mother ship. Easter had several meetings with Peter Simpson, who was a medium-level wholesaler, and Simpson was able to act on behalf of Easter and line up purchasers for the drugs when they arrived in Canada. Simpson had a particular job and it was to disperse the drugs.

Easter then began to make contact with some of the people he had been in custody with in Miami who were now out and with a guy in Toronto. The guy in Toronto is now under investigation and has not been charged or convicted. Easter was in contact with two Miami residents who were well connected with the Colombian cartels. From our surveillance, we learned that Easter was associating with another person in Vancouver connected to a well-known marine importer. This particular importer made us sit up and take notice. He introduced Easter to Jeremy Rich, who had come to our attention in a previous investigation in which we gathered a lot of intelligence on two vessels he had purchased—the *Salmon Run* and the *My Fair Lady*.

Both ships were decommissioned Coast Guard cutters gone up for auction and about 100 feet in length. They cost roughly about half a million apiece and he had $300,000 mortgages on each. We had intelligence on Rich and we knew he was a nominee for an even larger known criminal figure in Vancouver who has to remain unnamed since no charges have been laid against him. This guy is Canadian and Caucasian and in his late fifties. He was convicted in the mid-1980s of conspiracy to import and appealed to the Supreme Court of Canada and had it overturned. He's an ex-lawyer and is well connected. This individual is known to associate and believed to have substantial ties to Hells Angels, although he is not a member himself.

Within the Hells Angels, the patch carriers are a small number and are made up of 12 to 20 members. Our experience tells us that in the organized crime world, there are many associates, meaning they are trusted and connected and employed to carry out various tasks. They are associates as opposed to being members, but this is primarily from a publicity standpoint. If they are ever arrested, the club can say he is not a member. In some respects, they are really driving the train. These are Bay Street individuals and well connected in the financial politics of the large cities and they rub shoulders with many prominent people. We often see these people rub up with some very prominent figures.

Through our wiretaps, we learned that they intended a marine importation and that's when my unit, the Mother Ship Unit, was called upon. Our mandate is to target organizations who import narcotics through a boat used for the explicit purpose of smuggling on a large scale. This would be in the quantities of tonnage. We also have a Water Front Unit

and their mandate is to target and identify particular vessels that come from source vessels such as Thailand and Colombia and they look at their vessels and the consigned freight for concealed narcotics. The Mother Ship Unit targets groups and organizations who purchase vessels that are loaded with narcotics and nothing else.

Easter was introduced to Jeremy Rich and we knew the ties Rich had. We knew this was going to be something large. As a result of his meeting with Rich, we had Easter's house bugged and overheard them discuss the amount of cocaine they could conceal in the boat. We learned that this was the *Salmon Run* and that the boat was in the Yucatan Peninsula. They figured about 5,000 kilos could be concealed in the boat. We learned that they planned to use the vessel to import narcotics through the West Coast of Canada. After the meeting, Easter contacted his Miami contacts and, using encrypted language, said that he knew a Canadian film crew in the Yucatan Peninsula who could assist in the enterprise.

During this time, the ex-lawyer made arrangements for Rich to meet some people who were Hells Angels associates. The lawyer introduces Rich to Harry Lyons and then sits back and ultimately he will get his piece of the pie. Harry Lyons is a member of Hells Angels and he ends up dead in all of this. Rich meets with Harry Lyons to discuss whether the Angels are willing to provide the front money for the initial purchase of the cocaine. A figure of $400,000 U.S. was discussed and thought to be sufficient to get the ball rolling. No importer is going to deal it on the cuff. They have to see some greenbacks.

Rich comes back and reports to Easter that he wasn't too happy with the meeting and the guy was too flamboyant and a loose cannon, and that he was careless. Rich's perceptions were accurate because Lyons had become a user of cocaine and heroin. The use of heroin in the Hells Angels is a no-no. He is also fighting with his common-law and she was unravelling as a result of his personal and narcotic problems.

The ex-lawyer then steps in and facilitates a meeting with Easter, Rich, and a different group of associates to a different Hells Angels' clubhouse. Both Rich and Easter express that they are completely satisfied that this group is stable and professional and has the financial and other capabilities to use the boat to import the cocaine.

There were conversations now between Easter and this group regarding the concern of friction between two different clubhouses. There was a discussion with Rich and Easter that they would hold off on using the *Salmon Run* because Harry Lyons might be angry. They had smaller vessels they could use in the interim.

The bikers wanted to meet the Colombians to show that they had the capability, and one of their associates who acts as a representative of their clubhouse travelled to Colombia and met with the main Colombian.

In the meantime, there are side ventures and Easter is looking for other avenues to bring in cocaine to provide some money for the *Salmon Run*. The Angels will take some of the cocaine, but Easter wants some for himself. The Angels will provide seed capital and take more of the pie.

Meanwhile, we followed Jeremy Rich to Mexico where he met with a member of the Colombia cartel. They travelled to the Yucatan Peninsula and they examined the boat at great length, and we watched them for 10 days as they conducted various meetings. Jeremy Rich is the captain of this vessel and spends time in Mexico over Christmas and oversees the outfitting of the boat. Their cover story is that they are fishing for octopus.

The meeting with the Colombians had been facilitated by the two guys in Miami that Easter had contacted. During this time, Easter was organizing other conduits and, subsequent to that, arranged for this same Colombian to meet another member of Easter's group to organize another deal to get the cocaine flowing into Canada. Easter was observed going to Colombia to meet the main Colombian cartel member. The Colombian then visits Easter in Canada and returns to Colombia via the U.S. In May 1995, Colombian B, whose name is Giraldo, arrived in Canada and stayed with John Easter and immediately begins to make all types of calls to get cocaine moving to get some seed capital.

Meanwhile, another associate of Easter (called Blower) and Colombian B travel to Toronto with the intent of meeting a contact of the Colombian in New York to arrange to conceal a quantity of cocaine into Canada. Through various mishaps, this never took place. On one occasion, one of their guys catches our surveillance in Toronto and they call everything off, but they continued to press forward to get an avenue to smuggle their cocaine into Canada from New York. They then gave it up and came back to Vancouver. We were able to maintain a wiretap on the various parties by tying into another investigation.

In July 1995, Giraldo orchestrates 24 kilos into Canada through Los Angeles on a tractor trailer unit driven by a person called Sergio Martinovic, who was a friend of John Easter. He was an owner-operated trucker and had agreed with Easter and Rich to drive it across the Canadian border. We followed him down there and we seized the drugs through the U.S. authorities on the I-5. He was bringing back sound and light equipment being used in a concert for Sarah McLachlan. He just put a box of cocaine in the truck and was busted on the highway.

Meanwhile, Jeremy Rich returns to Canada with an engineer who had been with him in Mexico and we have Canada Customs stop and question them at the airport. Rich is cold and defiant and refuses to answer questions. The engineer is very nervous and lies and says that the vessel is his. The engineer is carrying diagrams of the *Salmon Run* and they show work being done in the lower vessel. Through consultation with people in the marine industry, we were able to confirm that the work was to construct a concealed compartment. They are released from Customs.

Then the engineer is contacted by an associate of the Hells Angels and they are concerned because they had not received the documents outlining the compartments on the *Salmon Run*. In addition, they have not heard from Jeremy Rich and

they are beginning to think that he had gone back to Harry Lyons for backing.

It became evident that the conspiracy was unravelling and they were having difficulty getting their ducks in line. In January 1996 when it became time to rewrite our affidavit, we couldn't get the wiretaps extended. Within a week or two of our wiretap termination, Jeremy Rich was murdered. It was a hit and the car was still running in a residential district and he was dead at the wheel. The investigation into his death is still open. It is not unusual to come across murders in drug investigations. The following summer, Harry Lyons and his girlfriend are found executed in his residence in West Vancouver. There have been no charges laid in those murders.

Ultimately we conducted roundups of John Easter, Peter Simpson, Serge Blower, and the U.S. arrested Giraldo in Miami. What gave us the biggest hammer is that we had Sergio Martinovic in jail in the U.S. and he was facing the potential of 24 years for 24 kilos of coke based on California sentencing parameters. When we interviewed him in this godforsaken hole, he would have given up anybody if he could avoid doing 24 years. This was an excellent bargaining chip for us.

Part IV evidence (wiretaps) makes for trials that are very long and arduous for any number of reasons. If the Part IV authorization falls during a trial, we lose all the evidence garnered from our wiretaps. Bearing that in mind, we went to California to interview Martinovic and found that he would be more than happy to testify on our behalf against the three conspirators. In exchange for his co-operation and with the agreement of U.S. authorities, we struck a deal where he would serve only 14 years, of which seven would have to be served in the U.S. Given the U.S. drug-enforcement initiative, he would serve all seven years before being transferred back to Canada.

He provided us with a full statement implicating the other three conspirators. Again relying on the U.S. hammer, we travelled to Miami where Mr. Giraldo was imprisoned. He was in the U.S. illegally and was *persona non grata* because he had been arrested and convicted for drug trafficking once before. He had been sentenced to 14 years, of which he served seven years, and was deported to Colombia. His presence in the U.S. at the time of the conspiracy was a violation of immigration laws and he received four years for that and was advised that he had to serve his remaining seven years from his previous conviction. We struck a deal with him and he supplied us with a statement in exchange for five years, after which time he would be deported back to Colombia.

Armed with these two statements, and with the Justice Department lawyer, we got plea agreements with the defence lawyers. John Easter was on parole and was yanked back in. Ten years for Easter, six years for Peter Simpson, and 18 months for Serge Blower. If you compare Canadian and U.S. sentences, Mr. Martinovic, who was a lesser player, will have to serve seven years before being deported to Canada and he is serving very hard time in a state

institution. All of his co-conspirators will serve less time in Canada.

Before all of this, Peter Simpson and Sergio Martinovic had both been professional hockey players, and Martinovic had fought in Vietnam. They were known to be mid-level dealers. Martinovic's wife was a vice-principal of an elementary school in Whistler and he was a dealer there.

The Hells Angels associate who went to Colombia is the most dangerous of all the players and he is suspected in the murders of Jeremy Rich and Harry Lyons. The possible motive in the murders with Rich in that it was believed erroneously that he was playing both ends against the middle and getting financial backing from both clubhouses and this was against the code and he was deemed to be untrustworthy. You're playing high-stakes poker with the Angels and that's the ultimate outcome.

Prior to Jeremy Rich's death, he was ex-communicated from the Hells Angels, which is unusual for someone who is so highly placed. He had been considered as an heir apparent for the B.C. chapter. It is my belief that Harry Lyons and his girlfriend were killed because he was a liability to the organization because of his addiction.

Easter was still going full bore to the end. Easter is very self-serving and well spoken and a real shiny shoe salesman to the point of being a pathological liar. I spoke to him in detention and told him we had his phones and vehicle bugged, and he still denied that he even knew Jeremy Rich or that any of this was transpiring. He maintained that he was in the T-shirt business.

A lot of other criminal opportunities come up and these guys get into it. We tend to get tunnel vision in our divisions when in fact at this level, it really doesn't matter whether it's narcotics or anything that will make a buck. Stolen goods, passports, stolen vehicles, mother ships filled with illegal immigrants is just an extension of drug dealing and there are less risks. Ultimately, as a result of the arrests, there were several unindicted co-conspirators and they are unnamed because they were never charged. The main Colombian cartel member is still at large.

Taking Risks: Trafficking While under Police Surveillance

A number of dealers who suspected or knew they were being followed or under electronic surveillance nonetheless continued to engage in drug trafficking. Offenders typically give several reasons for doing so: (a) a failure to understand conspiracy laws; (b) ambiguity, uncertainty, and complacency; (c) ego and overconfidence; (d) underestimating the police; and (e) greed.

(a) A Failure to Understand Conspiracy Laws

Many dealers who knew or suspected they were under surveillance believed that their modus operandi made it too difficult for the police to gather the evidence necessary to arrest and convict.

I was under surveillance for a long time and one reason I didn't care is because I had nothing on me. What are they going to see or do? It didn't matter that they were there. There was nothing incriminating they could

observe. There were times you would know they were there, but you still didn't care. It goes back to what I said. It is one thing to suspect, but different to know or prove. You can follow me all you want, but it's irrelevant if you can't prove it.

I knew I was under surveillance, but I figured that I could still operate. The only thing that they could ever get me for is what they got me for and that was conspiracy. They had nothing but bits and pieces, but they still convicted me.

Many operators make assumptions about the law and law enforcement that are incorrect. Dealers believe that they are relatively safe if they keep their distance from the drugs and select partners and others who can be trusted. They assume that the police must gather hard evidence such as drug seizures and statements made by close associates in order to gain a conviction. Most fail to appreciate how enabling conspiracy laws can be and the difficulty in defending oneself against this weapon in the police arsenal. Their surprise is evident in the following comments:

I was convicted on a dry conspiracy [no drug seizures]!

They don't really need anything solid to get you for conspiracy laws. Exactly. I didn't know that they could arrest me with the garbage that they had.

I got four years because I picked up the phone and said, "Yeah, you got it. Okay. Leave it there. Don't touch it till tomorrow." Wow! Four years for that. The judge hands out years like they're Christmas cards. They had no hard evidence—no drugs on me, no evidence of me making sales.

They practically built a case. They took circumstantial evidence and made it lead up to this. They told the jury "This is the picture that we want to paint" and they just put pieces and pieces together. I didn't know that they could do that.

I thought that they gotta catch me with drugs or have evidence of me giving them to this guy. Nobody ever told me that they could say that he did this and that and I think he works with this guy and they move so much in the market.

(b) Ambiguity, Uncertainty, and Complacency

It is common for dealers to be constantly on their guard and to suspect they are being watched or followed without having any concrete evidence. Suspicion alone, however, is typically not enough to get them to cease trafficking since some degree of suspicion and paranoia is considered normal and healthy. The police are skilled in conducting surveillance and targets will have a difficult time verifying that they are being watched. Suspects reported feeling as though they were being followed, but found nothing to verify their concerns. Since the situation is ambiguous and without clear evidence, they are reluctant to give up the money. Two offenders remark:

A month before the arrest I had a bad feeling. I started to see the same people in the same place and thought we were being followed. It was a feeling that something was happening. I told my friend and he said that he had a bad feeling too. We both commented that we would see each other in jail. Neither of us wanted to quit without good reason. There was nothing we could put our fingers on.

There were a number of suspicious incidents and strange occurrences that made me feel I was being followed. Nothing concrete.

The elaborate security precautions and strategies used to insulate themselves from the crime eventually give some dealers a false sense of security, leading them to become complacent and drop their guard.

I was careful and I used anti-surveillance strategies so I wasn't too concerned that they might get on to me, but it's like having an alarm system and a guard dog in your house—you think you're safe from a B-and-E. You begin to get complacent because of all the security around you.

This offender eventually discovered he was under police surveillance, but it was too late for him to avoid arrest and conviction.

At first I wasn't sure, then I set up a test and I caught someone following me. I went up to the guy and threw it into his face. I did it on impulse. It was my reaction to finding out they were following me—not the smartest thing to do. In hindsight, I don't want to comment on what I hypothetically should have done.

I decided I had to finish what I had started and I did and boom!—they took me down the next day. It was a big surprise when I was arrested so quickly after me making them. I never expected them to act so quickly. I can only speculate they had their meeting and said: "We have to take him now because he's onto us."

My arrest was uneventful. They hit three or four places simultaneously and got my co-accused and searched my personal residence at the same time. I had $9,000 cash on my person and they got over 50 grand from my residence and they seized that. They had over 3 feet of wiretap material at my trial.

Some offenders appear to become complacent and engage in activities they know are dangerous or indiscreet. For example, dealers will occasionally break their own rules and talk on the telephone, carry drugs on their person, store drugs in their home, or make similar indiscretions.

> You get to a point where you think you're untouchable because you've done it so many times and you never get caught. I would sometimes carry the drugs on me and I never did this when I started out. You begin to think other people are stupid.

Vigilance and patience allows the police to take advantage of these mistakes or security lapses and gain the evidence needed to convict.

(c) Ego and Overconfidence

Drug dealers also become overconfident over time and several reported that their ego and self-confidence made them believe they could outsmart the police. In one case, the 45-year-old subject stated that he knew that he was under surveillance, but continued trafficking in cocaine because he thought he was clever enough to avoid arrest.

> I knew the police had been following me and I was always giving them the slip. I kept seeing the same faces and I kept slipping away. And when they arrested me, this one officer busted through the door and threw me to the floor, and I remember him saying, "I've finally got you." That one comment expressed his eight months of tailing

me and his frustration. The evidence from the discovery showed me that there were times they had me set up and I got away.

Even after being arrested, this offender still gloats over his ability to outmanoeuvre the police and operate under their noses. He seems to miss the point that although he won some battles, he certainly lost the war. Another offender boasted about how he made police surveillance officers feel like "idiots" by setting a trap for them.

> I figured that my phones were bugged, so I decided to test them. I had a friend that was going to the states and he drives a truck. I called up another friend and said, "I've got 10 coming across the border and it's going to be in this truck." I found out later that his truck was ripped apart and they kept it for hours. They must have felt like idiots. I knew they were on to me, but I just wanted to make sure. I can't remember the little things that pointed me to them now, but you can always tell.

This man also continued trafficking for several months after this incident despite knowing that he was under surveillance. He admits that his ego got in the way of his better judgment. Another dealer, aware of police interest in him, blamed overconfidence for his downfall.

> I did not underestimate police capability. I overestimated my own abilities. I figured that if I touch nothing and I am smart enough, they can't get me.

Many subjects in this study admit that they knew or suspected that they were under surveillance, but continued dealing nonetheless. They believed that because they were careful and clever, the police would never obtain the hard evidence needed to convict them. A 35-year-old cocaine distributor explains why he continued dealing while knowing the police were onto him.

> I was under surveillance for a long time and one reason I didn't care is because I had nothing on me. What are they going to see or do? There was nothing incriminating they could observe. I knew I was under surveillance, but I figured that I could still operate. The only thing that they could ever get me for is what they got me for and that was conspiracy. They had nothing but bits and pieces, but they still convicted me.
>
> One of my distributors is a woman in her fifties. People call her "Grandma." She was telling me certain things about these buyers she had. They were from out of town. They wanted to deal in a parking lot. They don't care how much they pay per ounce. They will pay maximum dollar. That is the RCMP's MO! I tell her this, but she is not listening. I warned her and told her because I had the vibes. The police transmit certain things. They have behaviours I watch for and they watch for certain things.
>
> One day we're in a restaurant—just me and her. A couple comes in and sits down two tables away from us. They have a certain age—late twenties to early thirties. I said to her, "That couple are the police." She could not believe me. My father comes in and starts talking to this couple. He knew her and had past dealings. I ask my dad who she is and he knew her and she was an RCMP constable.
>
> They try not to make eye contact, but can't help themselves. Their training comes through. My gut instinct was right. That sixth sense is part of day-

to-day dealing. I ended up talking to the officer and told her to stop with the games.
>
> I know they are onto me, but I figured that I could still operate with them on me. It's a cat-and-mouse game and with my ego complex, I figured I could outwit them. I know they are there and I'll be careful. I planned to get some money together and get out for a while, but I never did that.

Some dealers are so confident that they will even taunt the police. Several dealers reported knowing associates who did so, but only three subjects in this study admitted to making this mistake.

> When you operate for a long time, you can get to feeling confident. I had friends who openly taunt police. It's not smart to make a mockery of the police. Cops are like other people and if you are flaunting it in their face, they'll move you to the top of their list.

(d) Underestimating the Police

The lack of appreciation of law-enforcement capabilities will often lull otherwise cautious dealers into a false sense of security. Whereas some dealers underestimate their opponents, others simply lack knowledge about police investigative tactics. The fact that many of the offenders in this study have little or no experience with the police or the criminal justice system leads them to make mistakes that result in their arrest. Several dealers fail to appreciate police resources and determination until it is too late.

> I personally didn't think the police would go to the effort that they did. I didn't stop to think how big we had become or realize the stage that I was in at the time. I didn't know they would spend all that money to catch me.
>
> To their credit, the cops are very patient and very relentless. They took

the time they needed and they got us. It took them a lot of work.

(e) Greed

Greed is a common factor that leads dealers to take action they consider risky. In one case, Canada Customs officers became suspicious after X-raying three cardboard boxes containing wooden statues sent from Thailand to a business address on Avenue Road in Toronto. The RCMP removed 4 kilograms of heroin, replaced it with another substance, and had Customs call up the business to pick up the packages. The offender showed up later that day and signed for the boxes using false ID and driving a rented van. An RCMP surveillance team began following him, and he explains what happened next.

I picked up some wooden deer sculptures from Thailand at the Customs office. When I left there, I thought I was being followed. There's a lot of little subconscious things that you pick up on and it feeds it into your brain. I had experience with surveillance before and when I confirmed that I was under surveillance, I went to Yorkdale Mall and parked the van and left it unlocked in the parking lot and went into the mall and took the subway downtown. I abandoned the van and went and had lunch at a restaurant.

The next morning I started thinking that I should get these antiques, so I arranged for the rental company to pick up the van where I had left it. The rental company sent a tow truck to pick up the van and kept the boxes in their office. I got a taxi driver to go and pick up the boxes and take them to an appraiser. Then I had another taxi pick them up and drop them off at another address. The next day I picked up the boxes and I was arrested when I ran

a stoplight. The cops said that I was trying to make an escape. I was charged with conspiracy to import heroin and my co-accused was the guy I picked it up from. The guy that gave me the stuff on consignment was never found.

Because he was under surveillance, this suspect decided to walk away from the van and abandon the heroin. He reasoned that the police would not be able to identify him and that he would be safe from arrest. In fact, the surveillance team was unable to follow him on the subway and he made good his escape. Officers maintained surveillance on the van, however, in the hope that he would return. The subject allowed greed to cloud his judgment—the heroin was worth several hundred thousand dollars—and he returned to the van the next day and was arrested.

How the Police Use Conspiracy Laws

RCMP drug investigators realize from decades of experience that higher-level drug traffickers are careful and cautious and that their modus operandi makes it difficult to catch them in possession of illicit drugs. It has already been noted that dealers seldom place themselves in contact with the drugs and insulate themselves through a layer of workers and associates. The main characteristic of drug trafficking that makes dealers vulnerable is their involvement with others. Drug traffickers associate and communicate with other dealers in order to conduct drug transactions, which leaves them open to criminal conspiracy charges. The majority of offenders in this sample (40/70, 57.1%) were convicted of conspiracy to traffic and/or import drugs. The remainder were convicted of importing (15/70, 21.4%), possession for the purposes of trafficking (10/70, 14.3%), and cultivation or manufacturing (5/70, 7.1%). Many conclude that their biggest mistake in getting caught was their lack of appreciation for and understanding of conspiracy laws.

> Conspiracy is a charge where a lot of it can be by association. They may not even have you on the tapes, but it takes more than one person to conspire. Your name is mentioned and that can be good enough.

> I was convicted for conspiracy because they could never catch me with anything on me. I was unaware of conspiracy laws and did not know how dangerous they could be.

> If there was one big mistake that I made, it would have been related to conspiracy laws and not realizing that all of the little fragments together can be woven and made into a case. They had no hard evidence, but they don't need it.

> One thing that I didn't know much about was the law on conspiracy. I do now. I used to think that it was hard to convict on conspiracy laws. The laws mean that they can say what they want. They can present a theory and twist things around to fit their theory.

The lack of appreciation of police capabilities, along with a lack of understanding of conspiracy laws, often lulls otherwise cautious dealers into a false sense of security. Because higher-level drug traffickers must operate with distributors and others to move and sell their product, they engage in a conspiracy, which in law involves an agreement by two or more people to commit a criminal offence. Conviction does not require proof of an overt act—only that there was an agreement to engage in a criminal enterprise.

The charge of conspiracy is presented to the court as a theory that explains the various actions and statements of different suspects whom the Crown alleges are connected together in a criminal enterprise. The web of conspiracy often extends through various layers of offenders, many of whom may never have met one another. The Crown's case must show, therefore, how accused people are linked through their interactions with intermediaries. Although some dealers are occasionally caught in possession of illicit drugs, most are cautious enough to avoid making this kind of mistake. The charge of conspiracy thus relies on evidence that links the higher-level dealer to others on whom the police have hard evidence. Conspiracy laws are enabling in the sense that they allow the prosecution to use fragments of information to draw inferences that the accused were involved in a criminal enterprise. Evidence gained from wiretaps and physical surveillance is introduced to link offenders to one another and outline the role each played in the conspiracy.

The charge of conspiracy relies on evidence demonstrating that suspects have interacted together, communicated, planned, and agreed to carry out certain criminal activites. Because the evidence gathered often involves communications that are fragmentary and ambiguous, the Crown presents a theory to explain their case. In practice, the Crown will introduce testimony, transcripts, and/or photographs that prove that the co-accused knew and interacted with one another. Much of the evidence in drug conspiracies is based on wiretaps in which the accused are alleged to have used coded messages. Police will introduce a witness officer, who interprets the code and testifies that the accused were involved in a criminal enterprise. In one case, for example, the accused told an associate over the phone that he hadn't eaten lately and had lost 10 pounds. The police witness alleged that the "10 pounds" referred to a recent police seizure of 10 kilos of cocaine that the dealer had lost. In a particularly obvious case, a lower-level supplier received a call from a dealer complaining that he was "three eggs short of 16." The police told the jury that "eggs" referred to ounces of cocaine. The offender comments:

> It sounded really bad when they played the tapes in court. We sounded very guilty. The Crown asked the jury, "How do you buy your eggs?" I wasn't surprised they found us guilty.

Police testimony about codes is difficult to refute since the officer is presented as an expert witness and the conversations often make little sense. In addition, drug seizures and other evidence will be used to corroborate the charges. A number of subjects complained that police interpretations of the alleged codes are sometimes in error or exaggerated.

> Once they had me on a tap saying that my uncle was coming into town and I had to pick him up. In fact, my uncle did come into town, but the officer at the disclosure said in court that "uncle" meant cocaine and I was going to pick up drugs.

> We used code words for the drugs, but one RCMP officer said that he identified eight or nine code words. That just wasn't true. I'm not bitter with the police, but they do inflate.

> I found out in disclosure that the cops had duplicates of all of our pagers. When I used mine, I would always signal that it was me calling by signing Star 25. After the 2.5 kilos of cocaine was seized, the police said that my Star 25 sign was referring to the cocaine. They didn't mention that I always used

that signature to indicate my identity.

> A vivid example happened with my friend's partner. He's talking to his brother on the phone. In Cuba, the slang term for a penny is kilo. The brother said, "You haven't given me a kilo," meaning that you haven't given me a cent. They told the jury that kilo was cocaine. I found that dishonest because they knew that he meant it was a cent. They represent the law and truth and they should be truthful.

> They had me talking to a friend about marijuana and they took that as I was talking about cocaine. I wanted 10 for $2,900 and that cannot be cocaine at that price.

Police also use photographs of dealers together, recordings of conversations, and observations of suspicious behaviours to draw inferences that the accused are involved in a criminal enterprise. The various pieces of evidence are woven together to present a picture of a drug conspiracy. Charts are used to show the court how each of the co-accused operated in the distribution chain. One dealer described his case:

> They had photos of me meeting my supplier at the airport and at some restaurants and all over the city. They identified him as a high-ranking Colombian drug trafficker who had served time in the U.S. for cocaine smuggling. I was made to look guilty by association.

Defence attorneys complain that conspiracy laws allow the police to make allegations with little or no evidence and create a reverse onus on the accused to prove that their actions are not criminally motivated. Since the Crown's theory contends that the various behaviours and statements represent criminal actions and intent, the defence must produce a theory that offers a different and more benign conclusion. This is often a difficult challenge.

> We argued that there were three other theories that could explain the calls, but the jury chose to believe the RCMP interpretations. I found out that with conspiracy laws, you have to prove yourself innocent.

> The telephone is a bad thing to use. I learned it the hard way too. I tried to talk by code, but you find out that it sounds the same in court.

> I listened to the wiretaps in court and the conversations didn't make sense unless you're talking about drugs.

One suspect in this study was acquitted in a conspiracy case several years earlier by offering a theory about his conversations that raised a reasonable doubt with the jury.

> It was a strip bar business and we talked about girls and parties and made it sound like it was our business we were talking about. And we used a code. In 1995 I was talking about selling a Corvette for 40 grand. The cops said I was selling a kilo of cocaine for 40 grand. It came to court and I beat it because that was the value of the car and we could show that.

Money-Laundering Activities

People involved in the illicit drug trade collect their payments in cash and must find a way to convert this money into legitimate income.

Money laundering is the process by which one conceals the existence, illegal source, or illegal application of income, and then disguises that income to make it appear legitimate. One form of money laundering involves the conversion of one currency to another. Drug traffickers in Canada often must convert their illegal cash income into foreign currencies in order to pay suppliers in other countries. In most cases, the currency of choice is the U.S. dollar because it is accepted worldwide. Cocaine dealers in Canada, for instance, receive payments in Canadian dollars, but are required to convert some of this into U.S. dollars to pay their suppliers south of the border. Currency exchanges are regulated by the *Proceeds of Crime (Money Laundering) Act*, which requires that cash transactions over $10,000 be accompanied by a declaration identifying the client and the source of the income. Higher-level drug traffickers often exchange hundreds of thousands of dollars on a regular basis and understandably wish to remain anonymous. They seek to exchange funds as discreetly as possible and in a manner that minimizes the possibility of tracing the transaction to its origin.

A common method of exchanging currencies is through the use of "smurfs" (money exchangers), who visit numerous financial institutions, exchanging amounts less than $10,000 at a time. Smurfs are typically paid employees or independent people who provide this service on a commission basis. A more preferred method used by higher-level dealers is to find a currency exchange or employees of a financial institution who will illegally convert large amounts of cash without the required documentation. This service is typically provided at one or two percentage points above the prevailing rate.

Money laundering also includes methods that recirculate illegal income in a manner that allows it to appear legitimate. It is common for dealers to make large cash purchases of real estate, automobiles, yachts, and other luxury items with the co-operation of vendors or sales agents. A highly effective and popular laundering technique is to purchase or invest in legitimate businesses. This not only provides a legitimate front for the dealer—that of a businessperson—it also allows him or her to launder illicit income through the company. On occasion, the business may also be used as a means to move or smuggle drugs. Businesses that generate large quantities of cash are preferred vehicles for money-laundering purposes.

Canada Customs

Canada Customs plays a large part in the law-enforcement effort against illicit drug dealing by acting as gatekeepers against smugglers who attempt to import drugs into the country. Border crossings and international airports are the territory of Customs agents who are trained to identify suspected couriers and inspect cargo that may contain illicit drugs. Customs agents work in co-operation with the RCMP, are occasionally involved in police investigations, and share information and intelligence. The legal mandate of Customs agents requires a distinct division of labour between themselves and the RCMP. Once Customs officers have intercepted a drug shipment and/or a smuggler, they will hand the case over to the RCMP, who will arrest and question the suspect, undertake any further investigation, and prepare the legal documents for court.

The RCMP will routinely pass on information about suspected drug smugglers, couriers, vehicles, and modes of entry to Customs officials. The Mounties may also provide the names of higher-level drug traffickers and their associates for Customs to red flag whenever they cross the border. One offender in this sample was suspected of using his cousin to

courier drugs across the border. The RCMP passed on the cousin's name and licence plate number and three months later, an alert Customs agent conducted a thorough search of the vehicle and discovered 15 kilos of cocaine hidden in a false section of the gas tank.

Occasionally the RCMP will request that Customs allow a drug smuggler and/or a cache of illicit drugs to pass so that the police can follow the suspect and/or cargo to its source. In one case, Customs discovered 4 kilos of heroin in the suitcase of a passenger who was in transit between Hong Kong and Montreal with a stopover in Vancouver. They notified the RCMP, who asked them to allow the suitcase and passenger to clear Customs. A police surveillance team uncovered the suspect's Canadian distributors, who were later arrested in Montreal.

On occasion, police may be reluctant to make an arrest so as not to compromise an ongoing investigation. By asking Customs to step in, the arrest and/or seizure can appear to be serendipitous and not raise suspicions. At the very least, the dealers will be unsure whether or not the police are on their tail. An example of one such incident occurred in the "Eyespy" currency-exchange sting in Vancouver. The operation lasted four years and the police delayed most arrests until the exchange was shut down. In one instance, however, surveillance officers observed a dealer hand over several hundred thousand dollars in U.S. currency to two Mexican-American citizens from California. The money was believed to be payment for cocaine that had been delivered two weeks earlier. The two Americans drove to the border where an alerted Customs agent searched their vehicle and discovered the cash. Although neither man was charged, the money was seized for a violation of currency laws. The drug syndicate continued to operate, allowing the RCMP to gather further evidence to make their case.

The RCMP Money-Exchange Sting in Montreal and Vancouver

The International Monetary Centre

In September 1990, the RCMP opened a currency-trading office operated by undercover officers in downtown Montreal. From an earlier investigation, the police learned that higher-level drug traffickers were illegally converting millions of dollars in Canadian funds into U.S. currency through a currency exchange in downtown Montreal in order to purchase drugs from suppliers south of the border. In order to flush out traffickers, the Mounties set up their own currency exchange in Montreal using undercover officers posing as corrupt businessmen. The aim was to videotape criminal transactions, place suspects under surveillance, identify accomplices and suppliers, and gather the evidence required to arrest and convict higher-level drug traffickers.

The Montreal exchange was named the International Monetary Center Inc., and operated in the central business district from September 1990 until August 30, 1994. During its four years in business, the exchange took in $141.5 million in known and suspected drug money and handed out the equivalent in U.S. funds or bank drafts. The exchange charged clients known to be involved in illegal dealings a premium of 1% or 2% per currency transaction above prevailing market rates. This helped the business make $2.5 million of profit, most of which was used to cover operational costs and launch other investigations. The Mounties also seized $16.5 million Can. in cash and property under *Proceeds of Crime* legislation.

From the start, the RCMP were unprepared for the number of higher-level drug traffickers who used their facility. A lack of resources left the task force understaffed and underfunded and unable to pursue most of the criminal syndicates who became their clients. Although the sting resulted in the arrest of 57 individuals on money-laundering and drug charges, the operation uncovered so many drug traffickers that the police were able to investigate only two of 25 criminal organizations that it supplied with U.S. currency. A total of $125 million of the $141.5 million in suspected drug money was not recovered.

The RCMP found that cocaine sold in the Montreal area generated Canadian currency that was exchanged into U.S. dollars and smuggled out of the country. Much of it was laundered through offshore banks and dummy offshore companies with the assistance of the undercover officers staffing the covert operation. The money then made its way up a chain of distributors, eventually reaching the source country and Colombian drug cartels. Critics in the media and Parliament charged that the massive movement of money by the RCMP helped expand the clandestine drug pipeline between Colombia's cocaine cartels and organized criminal syndicates in Canada. Frustrated by the shortage of personnel, one RCMP investigator complained to his supervisors on October 16, 1992, writing: "Without the necessary resources, it seems like our undercover officers are simply offering a money laundering service for drug traffickers." He requested a transfer and began working in British Columbia where he helped set up the "Eyespy" operation.

The Vancouver "Eyespy" Sting

From July 1993 to January 1996, the RCMP operated a currency exchange in the main business district of downtown Vancouver known as the Pacific Rim International Currency Exchange. The sting was code-named the "Eyespy" operation and was the biggest money-laundering and drug investigation in B.C. history. "Eyespy" led to charges against 90 suspects in B.C., Alberta, and 30 people in the U.S. Before setting up the "Eyespy" project, a member of the RCMP Vancouver Proceeds of Crime Unit visited the covert money exchange in Montreal to obtain ideas on how to operate the Vancouver sting and organize surveillance.

The "Eyespy" project had a number of objectives: (1) to identify criminal organizations involved in the sale of illicit drugs or other contraband through the exchange of monies for these organizations; (2) to disrupt criminal organizations by gathering evidence to support cases of money laundering, drug trafficking, importing, and possession of the proceeds of crime; and (3) to identify assets purchased with funds derived from criminal activities and facilitate the seizure of illegally obtained monies, narcotics, and other contraband.

Like the Montreal sting, undercover Mounties in Vancouver posed as corrupt businessmen in order to attract criminals seeking illegal currency exchanges. Whereas almost all the transactions in Montreal involved the exchange of Canadian currency into U.S. dollars, approximately 30% of the illicit money traded in Vancouver were U.S. funds exchanged for Canadian currency. These transactions reflect the fact that cocaine dealers in Canada receive payment in Canadian dollars but need U.S. money to pay their American suppliers. B.C. marijuana growers and dealers, on the other hand, ship high-grade marijuana into the U.S., receive payment in U.S. funds, and exchange it into Canadian dollars to cover their expenses at home. The RCMP report that a pound of marijuana sells for $3,000 Can. wholesale in B.C., but is worth $5,000 to $6,000 Can. in Washington state and as much as $7,500 Can. in California.

The nature of these currency exchanges indicates that although the province of British Columbia produces marijuana that is sold in the United States, the U.S. acts as a transit country in which cocaine is smuggled into Canada. According to RCMP investigations, most of the cocaine sold in Canada is imported from Colombia through Mexico and the U.S. Although U.S. government officials and politicians complain about the flow of high-grade B.C. marijuana into the U.S.—even going as far as to threaten to declare Canada a source country—these data indicate that in monetary terms, the flow of drugs into Canada from the U.S. is much greater. In addition, the marijuana shipped into the U.S. is a far less dangerous and addictive drug than the cocaine smuggled into Canada.

The "Eyespy" project was initiated by the RCMP Vancouver Proceeds of Crime Section in conjunction with the Drug Section, the U.S. Drug Enforcement Administration (DEA), and the United States Customs Service. Other branches of the RCMP and various municipal police services also aided in the investigation. Those charged included career criminals with records of violence, along with successful businesspeople with families, legitimate enterprises, and homes in respectable neighbourhoods. Among the latter group were stock promoters, fish and mushroom exporters, trucking firm owners and drivers, the owner of a courier company, and the owner of a luxury car dealership who provided expensive vehicles to drug dealers in cash transactions and helped launder drug money.

The Vancouver business laundered $40 million in its two-and-a-half years of operation. The RCMP used the *Proceeds of Crime* legislation to seize $2.5 million in cash and millions of dollars in assets from drug dealers. Police also seized 800 kilograms of cocaine valued at approximately $24–$28 million Can. at wholesale prices along with an additional 220 kilograms of marijuana.

The RCMP set up their storefront exchange in the Vancouver downtown business area close to other exchanges and banks. The task force rented a suite in an adjacent hotel to maintain direct observations of people entering and leaving the business. Two undercover

NEWS RELEASE
Royal Canadian Mounted Police/Gendarmerie royale du Canada
96-01-24

Major Money Laundering Undercover Operation Terminated
Vancouver, B.C., January 24, 1996

Project "Eyespy," a 42-month undercover operation directed at money laundering and related criminal offences culminated this date with the arrests of numerous persons in British Columbia, Ontario, Alberta and the United States for a variety of criminal offences.

The undercover operation consisted of the operation of an actual business engaged in foreign currency dealing. The business, Pacific Rim International Currency Exchange, was located at 818 Burrard Street in downtown Vancouver. The business was established specifically for this investigation and was staffed entirely with undercover members of the RCMP. In addition to developing evidence in support of money laundering charges, the operation was intended to initiate drug seizures and prosecutions for related offences.

Approximately 1100 criminal charges, primarily money laundering and drug trafficking charges against 90 persons, have been initiated in Canada; the laundering charges involve approximately $40 million of suspected criminal proceeds. Thirty persons have been arrested in the U.S.; charges include drug trafficking, money laundering and currency violations, smuggling and kidnapping. Investigations related to this operation have resulted in the seizure of approximately 1,800 lbs of cocaine and 490 lbs of marijuana, as well as the seizure of a number of weapons and approximately $2.5 million cash. Additional charges and seizures are anticipated in the future.

The operation was initiated by RCMP Vancouver Proceeds of Crime Section, in conjunction with RCMP Vancouver Drug Section, the U.S. Drug Enforcement Administration and the United States Customs Service. Also assisting were the Vancouver Police Department, Delta Police Department, New Westminster Police Department, Canada Customs, Coordinated Law Enforcement Unit, RCMP Detachments at Richmond, Burnaby, North Vancouver, Coquitlam, Surrey and Langley, and RCMP in Alberta, Manitoba, and Ontario.

The operation was terminated at 0830 hrs, January 24, 1996, with approximately 130 police personnel conducting coordinated searches and arrests in the following locations: **British Columbia**: Vancouver, Victoria, Surrey, Delta, Richmond, Langley, North Vancouver, Bridal Falls, Kelowna, Penticton, Vernon; **Alberta**: Calgary, Grand Prairie; **Ontario**: Toronto; **Washington** and **Oregon** states.

OTTAWA CITIZEN
Thursday, June 11, 1998

How the RCMP Helped "Push" $2 Billion Worth of Cocaine

For four years, the Mounties laundered drug money for the mob, for bikers, for the Colombian drug cartels, and for transient dealers on Montreal's streets. Few of the deals were ever investigated. Andrew McIntosh reports.

Andrew McIntosh
The Ottawa Citizen

An undercover RCMP currency exchange operating in Montreal between 1990 and 1994 facilitated efforts by Colombian drug traffickers and Canadian crime mobs to import and sell close to 5,000 kilograms of cocaine on the streets of central Canada, internal RCMP documents show.

The covert police company, known as the Montreal International Currency Center Inc., took in $141.5 million Can. in known and suspected drug money and handed out the equivalent in U.S. cash or bank drafts in U.S. dollars, for 25 criminal organizations during its four years in business.

The RCMP estimated this gave the drug traffickers in Canada enough currency to buy 5,000 kilos of cocaine from Colombian drug cartels and have it shipped back to Canada in boats, planes or by other means.

The Montreal Urban Community Police drug squad, using average market prices for cocaine between 1990 and 1994, estimates that 5,000 kilos of cocaine, once divided and cut into quarter-gram portions by traffickers, would have represented approximately $2 billion in sales made on the street.

But during the four-year stint running an undercover outpost in the global drug trade, the RCMP investigated members of only two of the 25 drug and money-laundering organizations that it supplied with U.S. currency, the RCMP documents show.

A *Citizen* investigation has revealed that the undercover unit had neither enough manpower nor the financial and technical resources needed to properly investigate more. As the RCMP-run currency exchange immersed itself in the world of cocaine cartels, biker gangs and organized crime, it became clear that the understaffed police unit was quickly in over its head.

One criminal outfit led by Montreal lawyer Joe Lagana, whose members had laundered $93 million in drug money through the RCMP covert currency exchange, saw its members investigated, charged and convicted. But less than one quarter of the $93 million was recovered by the RCMP. Other organizations that exchanged about $40 million were not charged.

Frustrated by the chronic manpower and other resource shortages as the covert operation progressed, one incensed RCMP investigator, Const. Mike Cowley, complained in writing to his superiors on Oct. 16, 1992. "Without the necessary resources, it seems like our undercover officers are simply offering a money laundering service for drug traffickers," he wrote. A short time later, Const. Cowley asked to be taken off the covert RCMP operation, which is known inside the force and the dusty RCMP file room as "Operation 90-26C" and was code named "Operation Contract." Const. Cowley was reassigned. He was not disciplined for making his remarks.

RCMP Staff Sgt. Yvon Gagnon, who oversaw the covert operation, told the *Citizen* in a recent interview that Const. Cowley's observation about the problems plaguing the Montreal operation was accurate. "He was right," Sgt. Gagnon said. "We kept asking for resources and we didn't get them. We hoped that somebody at headquarters would be reading the reports and begin to understand what was going on."

Frustrated officers asked their bosses for permission to seek help from the Canadian Security Intelligence Service or other police forces after files on suspects began piling up, but the requests were denied, documents show.

The covert RCMP operation was so short-staffed, officers were unable to even identify a group of people who had exchanged $7.2 million of the $141.5 million in suspected drug money.

When the operation ended on Aug. 30, 1994, police seized $16.5 million in cash and properties that the suspects had acquired with the drug money. But $125 million of the $141.5 million in known and suspected drug money exchanged by the covert Mountie company in Montreal had vanished and could not be traced or seized by police.

The money was laundered through offshore banks and dummy offshore companies and directed back to Colombian drug czars—all with the assistance of the undercover officers staffing the covert RCMP currency exchange.

"And it served to buy and import more drugs," according to retired RCMP corporal Andre Moisan, who worked on the covert operation for two years. Mr. Moisan said federal Justice department officials and members of the government were deeply disturbed and fearful about the potential socio-political fallout should the dark side of the operation become known.

"Justice Canada was freaked out by this," Mr. Moisan said. "The sums were enormous. Cash was coming in (to the currency exchange) so fast and the amounts were so large, it would make you fall off your chair. Imagine you're the fourth manager below the deputy minister and you receive this report from the RCMP while the operation is ongoing," he added.

"The report says, 'We've got this (currency exchange) operation in Montreal. We've moved over $100 million through it.' They say: 'What?' 'Yeah,' you say, 'Nobody's been arrested, nobody's been charged. We don't know where we're going with this. But perhaps we should put some men on this and start investigating,'" he said. "You tell them, 'We've identified 25 criminal organizations but we'll only be able to investigate one or two. The rest of the information will have to be banked when the operation ends.' What would you do in you were told this? You'd start freaking out," Mr. Moisan added. "The government was really afraid of getting into trouble when they found all this out," said Mr. Moisan, who now works at a Montreal investment firm.

The government had a trump card. It knew lower-ranking Mounties were handcuffed and could not expose their own ongoing operation. "We couldn't say a word. The lives of the undercover officers (working at the company under assumed identities) were on the line," Mr. Moisan said.

The currency exchange created by the RCMP was opened in September 1990. It operated from chic, street-level premises which were rented in a building at the corner of Maisonneuve Boulevard

West and Peel Street in Montreal, one of the busiest business districts in Quebec's largest city.

The operation ended on Aug. 30, 1994, when Mounties arrested 57 people and Crown prosecutors laid a slew of money laundering and drug charges.

The RCMP held a splashy news conference and officers declared "Operation Contract" an unprecedented, successful policing effort, saying they had cracked the biggest money laundering racket in Canadian history.

Mr. Lagana was their biggest catch: he worked with and laundered drug money for reputed mob kingpin Vito Rizzuto. He was sentenced to 13 years in jail, but was released after only 2 years in jail under a non-violent offender program.

But more than 5,000 pages of government documents about the covert operation—including four years' worth of secret RCMP investigation reports, other internal RCMP memoranda and sworn affidavits which officers used to obtain telephone wiretaps in 1994—show the probe had a much darker side.

The massive movement of money helped expand the clandestine drug pipeline between Colombia's cocaine cartels and Canadian biker and Italian mafia gangs which import, distribute and sell cocaine to users and addicts in Canada. In 1992 and 1993 alone, the covert RCMP operation helped move over $94.7 million in drug money directly and indirectly to Colombia.

Here's how it worked. The drug traffickers in Canada sold cocaine. Pushers working on the streets, in their homes or in bars, taverns or other businesses controlled by criminal organizations, made sales by the ounce. Criminal organizations gathered the Canadian cash they received from selling the drugs and took it to the RCMP-run currency exchange counter. The drug traffickers asked that the Canadian money be exchanged into U.S. money or bank drafts in U.S. dollars. Then they'd take their money and leave the country.

The traffickers or the couriers working for them would travel to Colombia with the U.S. cash or bank drafts. Sometimes, they would ask the RCMP currency exchange to wire the U.S. funds to overseas bank accounts. The bank drafts, made payable to phony names, were cashed in offshore bank accounts opened by dummy corporations controlled by the traffickers. The money was then secretly moved back to cocaine producers in Cali and Medellin, Colombia, for the purchase of more cocaine.

The RCMP currency exchange "clients," or the couriers working for them, often travelled between Montreal and Colombia, carrying U.S. cash and cheques in their luggage while under RCMP surveillance, even as they drove to and from Canadian airports without being arrested.

As the money exchanged by the covert RCMP company flowed into Colombia to purchase more and more cocaine, that country's then-president, Cesar Gaviria, was desperately struggling to bring drug lord Pablo Escobar and his acolytes to justice and stop a horrific wave of cocaine-world bombings and murders.

Back in Canada, the covert RCMP operation was repeatedly undermined: by a chronic shortage of both police manpower and technical resources, such as specialized computers needed to perform wiretap operations; by missed drug seizures, caused by the understaffing and lack of equipment; by policing mistakes; and by internal security breaches by two or more corrupt RCMP officers, according to an investigation by *The Citizen*.

operators acting as businessmen worked in the exchange (referred to as "the covert premises," "the business," "the store," "the storefront") and maintained contact with the cover and surveillance teams in the covert field office in the hotel across the street. The close proximity of the field office provided security for the undercover officers in the storefront and a staging area for surveillance of suspects leaving the store. The field office was close enough for visual surveillance, and cameras in the hotel room and within the store recorded all transactions and suspects. The task force kept surveillance teams ready to mobilize as required. Although they did not expect any violence, the RCMP made contingency plans to prevent or minimize the possibility of a robbery. The risk of a holdup was a concern because the exchange often had several hundred thousand dollars at hand. Fortunately, no violent incidents occurred during the investigation and subsequent arrests and prosecutions.

To attract business, the RCMP placed low-profile advertisements in flyers and newspapers in the downtown area. They also relied on their proximity to four other exchanges and several bank outlets known to be used by money-laundering rings. Based on their experience from the Montreal sting, investigators assumed that it would take five or six months to become known in the underworld. They also knew that higher-level drug dealers hired "smurfs" to move from one financial institution to another, exchanging relatively small amounts of cash. Under the *Proceeds of Crime Act* (Bill C-9, Money Laundering), transactions over $10,000 Can. require clients to declare their of source of funds. To avoid this, smurfs will visit several exchanges a day, changing $8,000 or $9,000 at each outlet.

Surveillance soon revealed that smurfs would visit as many as a dozen financial institutions each week and that some dealers employed several smurfs to exchange their funds. Police also discovered that some

suspects—subordinate smurfs—would hand over the laundered money to a person who acted as a handler or coordinator. The RCMP learned that the majority of smurfs are paid a percentage of the money exchanged—usually 1% or 2%—by their employers while others work on a commission basis. Some independent smurfs were observed delivering money to several different and unrelated criminals. These "smurfs-for-hire" were intimately familiar with the currency-exchange rates because these made a difference in the profit they made from the conversion. One female smurf who worked for an organization with Colombian connections converted $4 million Can. at the Vancouver exchange in one year.

The task force found it relatively easy to differentiate between legitimate clients and money launderers. Tourists, for example, would typically cash several hundred dollars in travellers' cheques, whereas smurfs would appear on a weekly basis, exchanging $5,000 to $10,000 in cash. As one investigator states, "You can tell the difference between middle-age Japanese tourists and a 21-year-old man who comes walking in with a wad of $7,000 in twenties." Other suspicious behaviours included: a large number of small bills; unorthodox packaging of money; the money smells of marijuana or mothballs; suspects display several packets of cash in precounted amounts, but trades only one bundle at the storefront, saving others to be traded at other institutions; suspects conduct multiple transactions, sometimes within the same day; suspects request to do several transactions under $10,000 instead of one large transaction; suspects are observed with other known smurfs; suspects state that they are exchanging the money for someone else or that they have several clients; and suspects admit or even brag about the criminal activity.

After two or three visits in which someone would exchange cash amounts under the

$10,000 limit, undercover officers in the exchange would approach the client and let it be known that they were willing to exchange larger amounts at higher rates. The suspects would typically ask: "What about the forms?" to which the officers replied: "For an extra 1% or 2%, we can overlook the forms." Although some smurfs turned down the offer and continued to exchange amounts under $10,000 with various money exchanges around Vancouver, the vast majority accepted the deal and began exchanging large amounts of cash on a weekly basis. The higher commission led the Vancouver RCMP exchange sufficient profit over its two-and-a-half years of operation to cover expenses, including rental fees for the hotel room and business office, telephone, leased equipment, parking, and other incidentals. All salaries were paid out of RCMP operating budgets.

On several occasions, clients voiced their suspicions and asked investigators if they were undercover officers. This question was posed most often when smurfs were first offered the opportunity to exchange cash under the table, but also when the Montreal sting operation was reported in the newspapers. All suspects appeared to accept assurances that the business owners were not the police. One officer commented:

> There is a myth that cops can't lie and if bad guys ask us if we're cops, we have to tell them the truth. Many criminals believe that police officers can't lie to them. We would tell them not to come back if they didn't believe us. It was rare that the person did not come back.

Undercover officers in the storefront attempted to portray themselves as crooked businessmen and used various strategies to give their performance credibility. They would inform clients that large amounts of currency brought in before 10:00 a.m. would be exchanged by 4:00 in the afternoon, and transactions above $200,000 would require 24 hours. The delay provided sufficient time to prepare the surveillance team and helped portray the officers as credible businesspeople. Very few businesses carry large amounts of cash and the 24-hour time delay was meant to allay suspicions. It was common for smurfs and traffickers to trust the exchange personnel with hundreds of thousands of dollars since receipts for cash were not given.

The RCMP used other strategies to persuade suspects they were illegitimate businessmen. In particular, smurfs were told to be cautious with whom they discussed business and were warned that they would lose their privileges if they attracted police attention. As far as the task force was aware, no suspects discovered that the exchange was a police sting until after their arrest.

Once a smurf entered the business to make an exchange, undercover operators would press a button under the counter to alert the cover team. The surveillance squad would then follow and photograph suspects moving from one exchange to another and attempt to link them to accomplices and automobiles. Typically, suspects would visit three or four money exchanges and banks per day and sometimes meet up with two or three others smurfs who were doing the same work. The suspects would finish their day's work, return to their car, and drive away. On an average day, three or four smurfs would visit the Vancouver exchange. Approximately 430 people were identified as money launderers and about half were judged to be low- to mid-level traffickers who exhanged the money themselves. The other suspects were smurfs employed by higher-level drug traffickers determined to keep a distance from high-risk activities.

The law requires that people exchanging over $1,000 Can. provide identification, so most smurfs would display their driver's licences. This enabled the RCMP to identify money exchangers immediately and begin their investigation. Only rarely did a suspect provide false ID. The RCMP task force and surveillance squad would videotape the transactions, photograph suspects and their accomplices, record licence plate numbers, and follow targets to their destination. The main goal was to identify higher-level dealers before passing the file to the RCMP Vancouver Drug Section. Smurfs often made the job of the surveillance team relatively easy by driving directly to the person who supplied them with the cash. Others would wait a day or two before handing over the laundered money.

Most employers were higher-level drug dealers and these "bosses" became the main targets for the Vancouver Drug Squad. The RCMP's goal was to trace the money to drug traffickers, gather evidence of trafficking and money laundering, lay criminal charges, and begin seizures under the *Proceeds of Crime Act*. Once the surveillance team identified a suspected drug dealer, the Drug Squad would check their files and other sources to determine whether or not they had any information on him or her. In some cases, the target was identified as a known trafficker or as a person engaged in some type of enterprise crime. All higher-level traffickers uncovered in this and the Montreal sting were men, although some used women to help exchange the money. Most of the evidence on dealers was obtained through physical and electronic surveillance.

In order to streamline the investigation and save time, officers attempted to flush out higher-level dealers and engage them in illegal activities. They would approach the smurf and tell him or her that they wanted to meet the main man or boss of the operation in order to discuss some business items. The police assured the smurf that they were not attempting an "end run" and that they would continue to deal with the smurf as an intermediary. Without this assurance, the smurf might be unwilling to make the introduction out of concern that he or she could be circumvented and lose the commission. The officers used the threat of ending the business relationship as leverage to arrange the meeting, stating they were getting nervous by the large amounts of cash being exchanged and wanted to meet the boss in order to satisfy their concerns that proper precautions were in place. Although some dealers were concerned about revealing their identity, most eventually met with the undercover officers. Several offenders caught up in the sting and interviewed for this study stated that they let their guard down in part because the meeting was set up to discuss financial matters rather than drug dealing and they felt less threatened by this agenda. In some cases, dealers were too cautious and/or suspicious to meet with the officers and moved their business elsewhere.

The RCMP arranged meetings with higher-level dealers in part to speed up the investigation. There was so much illegal business that they did not have the surveillance personnel to follow and identify all of the players and obtain the evidence necessary for a conviction. Arranging meetings in which dealers made incriminating statements or agreed to sell drugs helped generate evidence that could prove that the money was obtained illegally through drug trafficking.

After some initial trepidation, several dealers decided to meet with exchange personnel. Meetings took place in hotel lobbies, restaurants, and bars, and were videotaped for evidence purposes. During the meetings, dealers often relaxed and made incriminating statements to undercover officers, which were used to gain authorization for electronic surveillance and as evidence in court. In some cases, the police arranged drug purchases from dealers, telling them they wanted an ounce or two to get their girlfriends high. Some dealers became so trusting that they would routinely meet in hotel lobbies and pass over a gym bag or briefcase full of money and pick up their exchange the following day. Several traffickers didn't even bother to count the money, trusting the exchange to do that task for them. One dealer paid his smurf a $10,000 finder's fee for introducing him to the officers and showed up carrying a hockey bag with $980,000 in Canadian currency. The police exchanged his money and placed him under physical and electronic surveillance. Within a few weeks, they arrested one of his couriers with 30 kilos of cocaine and charged him with conspiracy to traffick in narcotics. The investigating officer described him this way:

> He is a mid-level dealer and no rocket scientist. He's just a big pleasant guy who had the connections. He was a quick file. He had a car coming back with 30 or more kilos of cocaine that was seized. There was also a large cash seizure in that investigation. He was arrested and granted bail and rearrested and charged months later.

Although the police postponed making their arrests until the investigation was completed, there were several occasions in which they moved to intercept large quantities of drugs. In one case, the RCMP arrested three men as they unloaded 45 kilos of cocaine from a truck that had just crossed into Canada from the U.S. The suspects were charged and released on bail. This was done in order to avoid a discovery hearing, which would have required the Mounties to reveal their evidence and the existence of the covert money exchange. The offenders and their employer, a high-level drug smuggler, were rearrested a year later when the currency exchange sting was completed. In cases where there were drug or cash seizures or early arrests, the task force took steps to ensure that the bust was not attributed to the money exchange.

The "Eyespy" project ended January 24, 1996, when 130 police personnel coordinated

searches and arrested 120 people in several provinces and U.S. states. Many of those arrested were smurfs or small-time money exchangers on individual contracts. Others were large-scale drug importers, growers, distributors, and dealers. Most of the charges related to money laundering and drug trafficking. Other charges included currency violations, smuggling, and kidnapping. During the investigation, police uncovered several hydroponic grow houses, seized four handguns, and investigated five murders. All five victims were suspected of having been killed because of conflicts in the drug trade. The prosecutions that resulted from the "Eyespy" investigation took several years to complete, and some appeals made it to the Supreme Court of Canada.

The "Eyespy" sting uncovered one alcohol and cigarette smuggler who laundered $6 million Can. in 12 months. The Customs and Excise Section of the RCMP investigated, arrested, and prosecuted the suspect. This 42-year-old man was the only one of 430 identified targets who was not involved in drug-trafficking violations under *The Controlled Drugs and Substances Act*. Most suspects were involved in the cocaine business and about one-third sold or cultivated marijuana. Surprisingly, no higher-level heroin dealers were arrested in this sting operation even though the province of British Columbia and the city of Vancouver have the most serious heroin problem in the country. The RCMP speculate that they failed to attract heroin traffickers because higher-level dealers are mostly Asian. Although the Pacific Rim International Currency Exchange was a fully functional exchange and dealt in all currencies, including those of Asian countries, police intelligence indicate that Asian dealers use currency exchanges within the Asian community. The fact that the RCMP storefront business was the only exchange in the city run by Caucasian males may also have made Asian heroin dealers uneasy and suspicious.

Despite having learned from the Montreal currency exchange sting and despite having thoroughly planned their investigation, the "Eyespy" task force soon found that the number of suspects that emerged overwhelmed the personnel assigned to the task. The project generated so much intelligence and so many targets that the Drug Squad was unable to pursue each and every drug-dealing syndicate. The sting uncovered a new drug-dealing group almost every week, many of whom exchanged over $100,000 a month. Investigators estimate that it would have taken all the resources of the Drug Squad and more to handle the traffic that was generated.

Because personnel and financial resources were limited, the task force targeted those cases in which arrests and convictions were reasonably assured. Focusing on targets that were easiest to apprehend helped to ensure the largest number of arrests and the greatest disruption to the drug supply possible. This meant, however, that the most cautious and insulated dealers were likely overlooked. In some cases, the money was followed to a location, but there was insufficient time or resources to determine how it was transferred up the organization. In other instances, suspected drug dealers were so surveillance conscious that it was not possible to follow the money through the completed laundering cycle—the surveillance had to be discontinued to avoid detection or it was detected and had to be called off. Other suspects made too few visits to the covert premises and on those occasions when they came into the store, surveillance could not be mounted because of a lack of personnel.

Summary

As a federal police force with a mandate to pursue higher-level drug traffickers, the RCMP have developed co-operative working relationships with provincial and municipal police services, Immigration Canada, Canada Customs, and foreign law-enforcement agencies such as the U.S. Customs Service and the Drug Enforcement Agency. The RCMP also maintain liaisons with financial institutions to monitor large and suspicious currency exchanges and transfers, and with laboratory and drug companies to investigate suspicious purchases.

Drug investigations are by necessity proactive and the RCMP actively pursue dealers involved in large-scale organized criminal syndicates. Investigative techniques typically involve the use of agents/informants, physical and electronic surveilllance, undercover work, and sting operations. A frequent point of entry is through an informant/agent who identifies dealers and provides the information necessary to plan and launch an investigation and obtain authorizations for electronic surveilllance. Whereas informants have a privilege in law that allows their identities to be protected, agents actively assist the police and/or act under their direction and are compellable witnesses in court. Police are under moral and legal obligations to prevent any possible retribution against informants and agents. The Source Witness-Protection Program has been established to provide for the security of those who assist in criminal investigations.

The RCMP have developed a specialized Operations Undercover Techniques Course that trains undercover officers and their supervisors. Before an operator goes undercover, a new identity and cover story are constructed and the officer enters the field with a task force that acts as his or her cover team. The operator meets regularly with cover team members, follows their instruction, and is monitored, advised, and supervised throughout the investigation. The RCMP report that most higher-level traffickers avoid using violence. Nonetheless, undercover work is potentially dangerous and all safety precautions are taken to protect operators from harm. Only one RCMP undercover officer has died on assignment, and his death was largely accidental.

Most RCMP investigators view the constraints imposed by legislation and case law as necessary protections in a democratic society in which privacy and civil liberties are among our highest values. They point out, however, that legal constraints require them to spend more time and resources on each case, which significantly decreases efficiency. Costly and time-consuming legal impediments result in fewer drug traffickers being investigated and convicted. RCMP officers interviewed for this study view the existing laws—conspiracy laws in particular—as sufficiently enabling to allow them to do their jobs. The largest impediment to investigations of higher-level traffickers, in their opinion, are insufficient personnel and financial resources for costly investigations that include physical and electronic surveillance, agents, undercover officers, and a cover team to support operators in the field. The police report that there is no shortage of known or suspected traffickers. Budget constraints, however, force investigators to be selective in choosing their targets. The Montreal and Vancouver currency-exchange investigations illustrate the problem—both stings identified far more suspects than either task force was able to target.

The small size of drug trafficking crews has implications for law-enforcement policies and strategies since small criminal syndicates are difficult to identify and infiltrate, and the large number of these enterprises requires tremendous resources that the police often do not have. With so many groups operating, the success of a police investigation in shutting down one syndicate is likely to have a very small impact on the overall supply of drugs on the market.

Most higher-level drug traffickers are convicted of conspiracy to traffick or import narcotics. Dealers are vulnerable to conspiracy laws because trafficking requires that players communicate, interact, plan, and undertake illegal actions with one another. The charge of conspiracy is presented in court as a theory that explains the various actions and statements of different suspects whom the Crown alleges are connected together in a criminal enterprise. Evidence of association, planning, distribution, and/or money laundering are used to show how accused people—some of whom never interact—are linked to one another through intermediaries. Physical surveillance and wiretap evidence, corroborated by drug seizures and the testimony of agents and undercover officers, are presented in court to prove that offenders engage together in a conspiracy to market illicit drugs. Traffickers and their lawyers complain that conspiracy laws create a reverse onus that requires them to prove that their actions are not criminally motivated. The effectiveness of conspiracy legislation is evidenced by the fact that 57.1% (40/70) of higher-level dealers in this sample were convicted of this offence. Offenders cite their lack of appreciation for and understanding of conspiracy laws as the major reason for their arrest and conviction.

RCMP drug investigators are realistic in their expectations and know that law-enforcement efforts can have only limited success in combatting higher-level drug trafficking. The demand for illicit drugs is high and profits are so attractive that there are many people willing to step in and fill the void whenever certain players are arrested and taken out of the game. Many investigators take the view that law enforcement deters many would-be dealers, keeps drug usage and trafficking within tolerable limits, and removes the more violent offenders from the trade.

CHAPTER 8

Higher-Level Drug Trafficking in Canada
Social Policy Implications

The present study has examined the characteristics of higher-level drug traffickers, their motivation and modus operandi, the risks and rewards involved in this activity, and the legislation and law-enforcement strategies used to combat organized criminal syndicates. This chapter discusses the implications of these findings for government and law-enforcement drug policies.

Drug Trafficking Research and Social Policy Implications

A Summary of the Findings

Most higher-level drug dealers operate in small groups based on friendship and ethnic loyalty; maintain a low profile to avoid detection; do not normally corrupt law enforcement; and are typically non-violent. The present sample consists of middle-age male offenders with strong family ties, many of whom have ethnic connections with source countries. Most subjects had been dealing drugs for several years, had realized huge profits, and were arrested after lengthy and proactive criminal investigations. Dealers experience upward social mobility, and many own legitimate businesses and live otherwise conforming, law-abiding lives. The study describes how industriousness, discipline, and skills acquired from legitimate employment or business help make illegitimate businesses efficient and successful. Drug selling requires entrepreneurship, the ability to collaborate with others, and a reputation for trustworthiness in order to secure and retain clients. The illicit side of the enterprise requires secrecy, caution, and a sophisticated modus operandi.

Motivation, Deterrence, and Policy Implications

To consider the policy implications of higher-level drug trafficking, it is helpful to revisit the motivational components that fuel this criminal endeavour. Research indicates that the majority of retail drug sellers are themselves users and motivated by a need to support an expensive drug habit. Higher-level dealers, on the other hand, are typically non-users and are driven instead by greed and the promise of great wealth. It appears from these and other findings (e.g., Reuter, MacCoun, & Murphy, 1990) that upper-level traffickers carefully consider the advantages and disadvantages of drug dealing and make rational and relatively well-informed choices before they take up this illegal venture. Subjects perceive quite accurately that trafficking yields much higher profits than legitimate employment or business and they assume, with some degree of validity, that risks are relatively low. After all, this is a consensual activity that takes place between associates who know and trust one another. Most eventually intend to retire from crime at some future time and live off their investments. Power, status, and a luxurious lifestyle, however, seduce many to continue in this activity even after they have made their fortunes. Overall, it appears that offenders perceive trafficking as a low-risk, high-reward activity and make rational and well-informed choices. This does not bode well for law enforcement and makes the task of deterring would-be dealers very difficult.

A common liberal political/economic strategy for dealing with social problems advocates increasing job opportunities for the disadvantaged. This long-term proposal is not likely to have much effect on higher-level traffickers since most come from solid working- or middle-class backgrounds and have ample job opportunities. Legitimate employment cannot possibly offer returns that compare with those available in the drug trades. For most, their involvement in crime is not due to poverty or the shortage of legitimate opportunities, so an improved economy will have little effect on people motivated by greed. There is the possibility, however, that job-creation strategies could diminish the demand for drugs among the underclass and thus have an indirect impact on drug distribution.

The Risks Involved in Higher-Level Trafficking: Policy Implications

The Risk of Apprehension

Deterrence theory suggests that by increasing the risks of arrest, conviction, and imprisonment, society can deter would-be offenders from committing their crimes.

It is difficult to determine if the risk of apprehension for higher-level drug dealing in Canada is high or low since there are no reliable data to indicate how many dealers are caught as opposed to the number who go undetected. Even if it is possible to increase the risk of arrest, this in itself is unlikely to deter offenders if they perceive the risk to be low. The motivation of higher-level dealers is based on a subjective appraisal of risk versus reward and not on an objective assessment of the danger of apprehension. For deterrence to work, society would somehow have to convince would-be dealers that risks are indeed high, but it is difficult to say how this can be accomplished.

The present study suggests that dealers perceive the risk as moderate to low and deem the potential rewards worth pursuing. In addition, subjects developed a modus operandi they believed to be effective against law enforcement, asset seizure, and the threat of violence. From a social policy perspective, risks may deter some would-be offenders, but for those willing to take the risk, legal sanctions can be viewed as an entry barrier to competitors. This helps to ensure that profit margins remain high and serves as an incentive for risk takers to enter the market.

The Risk of Forfeiture of Offence-Related Property

A major policy initiative aimed at deterring economic crimes is evident in federal government legislation that facilitates the seizure of assets accumulated through crime. Higher-level drug traffickers now face an increased risk of losing money and property through proceeds of crime legislation. In 1989, the federal government of Canada enacted Bill C-61 in an effort to strip drug dealers and other criminals of assets accumulated through crime. Sec. 462.31(1) of the *Criminal Code* and sec. 8 and 9 of the *Controlled Drugs and Substances Act* make it an offence punishable by up to 10 years imprisonment for using, possessing, or transferring property obtained through crime and/or for laundering the proceeds of crime. Both the *Controlled Drugs and Substances Act* (sec. 11–23) and the *Criminal Code of Canada* (sec. 462.3–462.5, 489, 490) incorporate provisions for the pre-trial search and seizure and post-conviction forfeiture of any offence-related property and proceeds of crime.

Although these laws give the courts significant powers to punish dealers financially, they do not appear to play an important role in the prosecution of drug traffickers. As discussed in Chapter 2, only five subjects in this study were convicted under money-laundering legislation and only 16/70 (22.8%) report losing money or property through the proceeds of crime. Higher-level drug dealers are acutely aware of these laws and take precautions against losing their gains. Many transfer their money outside the country and use the assistance of lawyers, bankers, and/or accountants to protect their assets. Even the

money and property seized represent a small percentage of accumulated wealth. It appears that proceeds of crime and money-laundering legislation are not significant deterrents for higher-level drug traffickers since few (5/70, 7.1%) are convicted under these provisions, the majority (54/70, 77.1%) do not suffer forfeitures, and those who do (16/70, 22.8%) usually have most of their assets safely hidden away.

The Risk of Injury or Death

Research on drug trafficking indicates that most violence is found at the retail or street level. The risk of injury or death does not appear to be a deterrent to higher-level drug dealers since violence at this level is relatively uncommon. Offenders know that death or injury is possible, take precautions, and see the risks as remote. Even the more criminally-oriented dealers attempt to conduct business with as little conflict as possible and avoid situations in which violence could occur.

The basic assumption behind deterrence theory is that people will not engage in criminal activities if the risks of apprehension and punishment are great. What are risks to some people, however, may be perceived as opportunities to others. Increasing success in capturing and imprisoning dealers may temporarily diminish supply, but it will have little effect on demand. This will likely increase the cost that buyers must pay for their drugs and translates into higher profits for those willing to enter or stay in the game.

Entry into Drug Trafficking: Opportunity and Policy Implications

The present study demonstrates that entry into higher-level trafficking is largely dependent on illegitimate opportunity. In particular, connections within one's ethnic community and in source countries afford many dealers with the chance to import, purchase, or distribute high-quality drugs at low prices. Many immigrant groups have strong links with producing countries because they speak the same language and have close friendship and kinship ties. These connections give them a competitive advantage in the drug-trafficking world.

Opportunity is also tied into business connections and experiences. The majority of subjects owned small businesses prior to dealing and for many, these commercial enterprises provided an entry into higher-level trafficking through contacts in source countries, a sense of entrepreneurship, and valuable knowledge in importing, sales, and distribution. Business experience is used for criminal purposes and translates into an opportunity structure for higher-level drug trafficking.

Recent strategies used to combat crime attempt to construct barriers that impede access to illegitimate opportunities. These programs are typically crime specific and often aim to make the target less attractive and more difficult to attack. With respect to robbery, "target-hardening" techniques include better lighting, video cameras, trained staff, and secure drop safes for excess cash. Higher-level drug trafficking, however, is a crime with no clear target since buyers and sellers are willing participants. Limiting opportunity for participating in this activity is almost impossible when these opportunities are imbedded in ethnic, family, and friendship relations, and/or in the structure and functioning of one's business. One method of decreasing opportunity is to increase border security. Since most illicit drugs enter Canada from other countries, increased inspections of people and cargo will intercept more product and increase the risk of apprehension. This may diminish opportunities for drug importation, but will undoubtedly slow down the flow of people and goods across the busiest trading border in the world. Economic and political considerations make the proposal unfeasible.

Structure and Organization of Higher-Level Drug Trafficking: Policy Implications

The data from this study suggest that the illicit drug trade in Canada, with the exception of perhaps a few groups such as outlaw motorcycle gangs, is characterized by open competition among a large number of small criminal networks that operate in tight-knit groups based on friendship, ethnic, and/or kinship ties. Higher-level drug trafficking does not appear to be dominated by drug cartels that secure geographic territories and control the importation, manufacturing, and distribution of narcotics. Most higher-level drug traffickers deal with very few people as a safety measure against police practices. In particular, smaller groups can better protect themselves against the police use of informants, surveillance, and undercover agents. Dealers realize that, as far as the drug-distribution business is concerned, smaller is safer.

It can be argued that police efforts to combat higher-level drug trafficking have a direct impact on the size of these groups. Given the fact that drug investigations require a huge expenditure of time and resources, police will understandably target larger rather than smaller organizations. In this way, they obtain "more bang for the buck" as measured by the number of arrests, the quantity of drugs seized, and disruptions to the illicit market. In addition, large syndicates are more easily identified and infiltrated by the police than smaller crews. The result of effective law enforcement, therefore, is to fragment the drug market into a large number of small independent criminal enterprises.

The size of drug-trafficking crews will in turn have implications for law-enforcement policies and strategies since small criminal syndicates are difficult to locate and infiltrate and the large number of these enterprises require greater police resources. Ironically, police success against large syndicates creates an even more difficult challenge for law enforcement. With so many groups operating, the arrest of the members of one group will have little effect on the overall supply of drugs since other dealers will quickly move in to fill the void. In addition, effective policing makes the business more profitable for offenders clever or lucky enough to avoid detection and arrest. Many drug officers concede that the most law enforcement is able to accomplish is to minimize violence and keep a lid on drug sales and consumption.

On the plus side, it appears that with the exception of some outlaw motorcycle gangs, the police have been able to target and effectively remove the most violent criminal organizations. Higher-level dealers realize that violence attracts police attention, so the best way to run their illicit business is to keep a low profile and to avoid conflicts and violent confrontations.

There was very little evidence of corruption of public officials in this or other studies of higher-level drug trafficking. Because dealers operate in relatively small secret networks, they are unlikely to have the financial resources and close contacts required to access and corrupt public officials or law-enforcement personnel. Drug syndicates in Canada rely on trust, secrecy, and caution rather than corruption to conduct their illicit business and protect themselves from arrest. Consequently, there are no policy implications related to this issue.

Overall, it is clear that the drug industry is highly profitable and relatively simple to organize and run. The high demand for drugs and lure of huge profits make it difficult for law enforcement to deter people from trafficking in drugs. Consequently, policy initiatives that rely solely or exclusively on law-enforcement agencies are unlikely to have more than a small impact on the sale, consumption, or distribution of narcotics in Canada.

Personal Characteristics of Offenders: Implications for Sentencing, Imprisonment, and Parole

Most of the drug traffickers in this study come from stable families, have middle- or working-class backgrounds, and report extensive employment and business experience. Less than one-third of the sample (20/70, 28.6%) have lengthy criminal records while the majority (50/70, 71.4%) live relatively law-abiding lives apart from their involvement in the drug trade. The average age is 40 years, and two-thirds of subjects (47/70, 67%) are married or live in common-law relationships and report strong family ties. Most dealers have relatively pro-social values, are non-violent, present themselves as successful businessmen, and live in middle-class or upscale neighbourhoods. Partners and associates have similar backgrounds and lifestyles and typically do not use illicit drugs.

From a sociological perspective, most of the subjects in this study are good candidates for rehabilitative programs. Strong family bonds provide incentives to go straight while their work and business skills afford them opportunities for gainful employment after their release from prison. In general, the personal and background characteristics of higher-level drug traffickers indicate that they are at low risk to reoffend. This suggests that sentencing policy should reflect rehabilitative goals and make limited use of incarceration. The average sentence for the men in this study, however, is seven years. It appears that judges and Crown attorneys emphasize other principles of sentencing including denunciation, deterrence, and incapacitation.

At the correctional level, however, the rehabilitative potential of these offenders is recognized and most gain early release from prison. The *Corrections and Conditional Release Act* grants accelerated parole to non-violent inmates serving their first sentence in a federal penitentiary. The majority of men in this study (50/70, 71.4%) fit the businessman drug-trafficker profile and lead relatively law-abiding lives apart from drug-dealing offences. Thus, most of them qualify for this program and serve only one-sixth of their sentence in a prison. The remaining time is served under supervision in the community where they can be gainfully employed and maintain family relationships. It should be noted, however, that the wealth to be gained in the drug game is a powerful incentive to reoffend. A significant proportion of the men in this sample return to drug dealing after their release from prison as evidenced by the fact that 38% (19/50) of businessmen dealers have previously been convicted for drug-trafficking offences. Similarly, an analysis of the 1978 Rand inmate survey showed that offenders who achieved higher earnings were more likely to be recidivists three years later (Robitaille, 2001).

The Liberalization/Prohibition Debate

The debate over Canadian drug policies has been ongoing for several decades. The conflicting demands made on the federal government during the late 1960s regarding drug legislation led to the formation of the five-member Le Dain Commission of Inquiry into the Non-Medical Use of Drugs (see Cook, 1970). The commissioners reached consensus on the importance of education, treatment, and rehabilitiation, but there was less agreement on the need for law reform and the role of legal sanctions in combatting drug usage. Both the *Cannabis* report and the *Final Report* contained a majority and two minority reports on the subject of appropriate legal controls. One minority report, for instance, recommended the elimination of criminal controls for simple possession of amphetamines, opiate narcotics, cocaine, and marijuana; another minority report recommended that all legal penalties be retained for these drugs; and, the majority supported the abolition of the offence for cannabis only. Since the Le Dain Commission submitted its report in 1972, the federal government has vacillated back and forth, occasionally announcing plans to decriminalize marijuana, but later retreating from making any legal reform in a process referred to as "the saga of promise, hesitation, and retreat" (Giffen, Endicott, & Lambert, 1991:571; see also Giffen & Lambert, 1988; Fischer et al., 2003). In May 2003, the federal Justice minister tabled Bill C-38, the *Amendment Act to the Contraventions Act* and the *Controlled Drugs and Substances Act*, which would reform certain cannabis-possession offences that are currently governed by criminal law into non-criminal contraventions under the *Contraventions Act* punishable by limited fines only. The legislation was delayed and was not put to a vote in Parliament because of the June 2004 national election.

The debate over how society should regulate psychoactive and habit-forming substances—particularly heroin, cocaine, and marijuana—tends to fall into two polar extremes: the conservative side, which supports harsh prohibitionism, and the liberal side, which proposes sweeping legalization. The prohibitionists have been the clear winners in this controversy since most countries in the world prohibit and punish possession and trafficking of a variety of drugs. Nonetheless, the debate continues with more and more proponents campaigning for a relaxation of the prohibition against the use of certain drugs. A recent conference in Albuquerque, New Mexico, sponsored by the Lindesmith Centre and the Drug Policy Foundation, for instance, saw speaker after speaker argue that current punitive drug policies did more harm than good (*The Economist*, 2001:15).

Prohibitionists support strict legal penalties against currently illicit drugs and attribute the widespread availability and use of drugs to ineffective law enforcement and soft penalties. Consequently, many would like to see greater resources given to the police and harsher penalties for drug-related offences. People who propose a more liberal approach argue that prohibitionist policies do more harm than good and are largely to blame for the disease and violent crime that are related to drug usage. They would like to see our drug laws reformed and replaced with a system of regulations similar to the way in which society deals with tobacco, alcohol, and prescription drugs.

The following is a summary of the legalization debate and the key arguments that distinguish both sides. The reader should keep in mind that many of the proponents on both sides employ one-sided arguments to further their aims and are quite selective in highlighting the particular dimensions of harm that serve their rhetorical purposes.

The Prohibitionist Model: Arguments against Legalization

Prohibitionists have both moral and practical reasons for opposing the liberalization of drug laws. On the one hand, they condemn drug use as immoral behaviour and oppose decriminalization or legalization because they believe such a move endorses drug usage and sends the wrong message to the public. On the practical side, prohibitionists argue that any liberalization in drug laws will lead to an increase in the number of drug users and/or addicts along with an increase in drug-related crime, family conflicts, and a variety of social and health problems.

From their perspective, prohibitionism symbolically condemns drug usage as immoral and harmful, makes drugs less accessible, and deters many from using drugs. Prohibitionists admit that although law enforcement cannot eliminate illicit drugs, it at least keeps a lid on the problem and leads to less usage and fewer drug-related problems. By offering some degree of deterrence, prohibition sends out the message that drug usage is wrong, is punishable by legal sanctions, and discourages an unknown number of people from experimenting with drugs. Prohibitionists argue that if drug use were legalized, the number of drug users would rise. For one thing, the stigma attached to these drugs would be reduced; the price would drop significantly; availability would increase; quality would be regulated; there would be no fear of arrest; and industry advertising and marketing could lead target audiences to experiment with these substances. The result is likely to be more users and more addicts.

The Liberalization Model: Arguments in Favour of Legalization

Reformers acknowledge that on the surface, it seems paradoxical to argue that we can decrease the problems associated with drug use by legalizing the very behaviour that is problematic. Even people who acknowledge that our present policies are largely ineffective wonder whether it would be right to add to the list of harmful substances that are legally available (*The Economist*, 2001:11). For one thing, no one knows how demand may respond to lower prices and the legalization of drugs.

Advocates of the liberalization model argue, however, that there are complex and unintended costs of prohibitionist policies— increased crime and corruption, disease, financial costs, the harm done by the criminal justice system, racial tension and disparity, and the loss of civil liberties—and that these harms grossly outweigh the benefits society gains from banning drugs. There is also the argument that prohibitionism is ineffective in dealing with drug usage and drug trafficking. Law-enforcement efforts to stem the flow of drugs by pursuing traffickers are doomed because drugs are too profitable and whenever the police arrest one dealer, the void is filled by another. Although law-enforcement agencies have developed innovative ways to convict drug dealers, the best they are able to do is to keep a lid on the market. After all, the real problem is demand. Drugs offer a pleasurable experience and as long as there is high demand and high profits, people will be willing to traffick despite vigilant law enforcement and harsh penalties.

Critics of present policies argue that the war on drugs has led to an erosion of civil liberties because drug investigations require informants, wiretaps, and undercover tactics that are highly proactive and intrusive in the lives of citizens. One of the more serious victims of the war on drugs are justice systems throughout the world. Numerous countries fill their jails with drug users whose behaviour is no more threatening than that of people who drink alcohol. Unfortunately, many emerge from prison more harmed and more dangerous than when they go in, and this in itself engenders disrespect for the law and the justice system.

Prohibitionist policies are also criticized for being divisive and racist since the damage inflicted falls disproportionately on poor countries and on poor people of minority status in rich countries. In the United States, for example, thousands of young Blacks and Hispanics are imprisoned for minor drug offences. Although Blacks make up only 12% of the general population, they constitute

two-thirds of admissions to state prisons for drug offences. A similar disproportion exists for Hispanics, who represent 10% of the population but constitute 25% of all those sent to prison for drug offences. It is not surprising that these laws have increased suspicion in the Black community that drug enforcement is an instrument of continuing White oppression (Reuter, 1997:268).

Even taking into account economic factors, prohibitionism is extremely expensive and wasteful. In the U.S., for instance, drug control is estimated to cost between $30–35 billion annually (*The Economist*, 2001; Reuter, 1997:264)—money that critics argue could be better spent on employment, education, and treatment programs. There is also a huge loss of potential revenue since all drug profits are funnelled into the hands of dealers. This is money that could otherwise be taxed and used as government revenues as is done with other vices such as gambling, tobacco, and alcohol.

The liberalization model is a less moralistic approach because it accepts drug usage without moral condemnation. Instead, liberal social policy advocates a utilitarian and pragmatic approach to the drug problem that emphasizes practical and effective measures to reduce the harm now being imposed on society. This harm-reduction model focuses on reducing health problems, violence, and the harsh legal penalties used to punish drug users, and brings with it a more humanitarian and therapeutic perspective. The liberal perspective views drug use and addiction as a lifestyle choice and/or a public health problem rather than a crime. A harm-reduction model stresses the need for a shift in resources away from enforcement and toward prevention, education, and treatment and supports initiatives such as methadone programs, needle-exchange centres, and prescription heroin.

Drug-Specific Legal Reform

The prohibition/liberalization debate has tended to ignore the differences between the current illicit substances and treat them in a similar fashion. Before drug laws are liberalized, however, it is no doubt wise to first evaluate each type of drug, consider their effects and potential for harm, and develop drug-specific regulations.

> Just as legal drugs are available through different channels—caffeine from any cafe, alcohol only with proof of age, Prozac only on prescription—so the drugs that are now illegal might one day be distributed in different ways, based on knowledge about their potential for harm. Moreover, different countries should experiment with different solutions. (*The Economist*, 2001:12)

Based on their potential for harm, marijuana, heroin, cocaine, and designer drugs should all have different regulations. Marijuana is likely to have the least restrictive controls since it is non-addictive and has relatively few health concerns. Many otherwise law-abiding and productive citizens use marijuana recreationally and there is widespread support for the decriminalization or legalization of this substance.

Advocates of drug policy reform are frequently categorized into two camps: decriminalizers support the legal ban on the sale of current illicit substances, but favour a reduction in criminal sanctions for possession of small amounts of drugs; legalizers, on the other hand, propose making the sale and use of illicit drugs legal while at the same time maintaining some government regulation and control. The legalization position places less restrictions on who can use, sell, or administer drugs, but there are restrictions nonetheless.

MacCoun, Reuter, and Schelling (1996) make the point:

> With the exception of some libertarians, no one seriously advocates relaxing the drug laws so that the currently illicit substances would be as freely available as peanut butter or gasoline, regulated only for purity, quality, and safety. Everyone seems to agree that children, at least, should not be able to buy cocaine at the local candy store. Thus "legalization," taken literally, is not under discussion. Indeed even for the presently legal drugs ... there is some age restrictions. (MacCoun, Reuter, & Schelling, 1996:332)

In general, reformers argue that present illicit drugs should be regulated in a manner similar to alcohol and tobacco, and argue that liberalizing drug laws will significantly reduce the black market for drugs, drug-related crime and violence, the potential for the corruption of officials, wasted expenditures on the criminal justice system, and the unnecessary suffering that a punitive prohibitionist policy inflicts on so many users and other minor offenders. Legalization will allow society to regulate drug sales and gain control over a problem that has resisted being controlled through coercive means.

Besides making the case that liberalization will have practical benefits for society, reformers present moral and philosophical arguments based on their concern for justice, compassion, and freedom. They condemn the fact that so many young people and members of minority groups are brutally punished for minor offences. They also criticize the laws as hypocritical and unjust because society tolerates other harmful substances such as alcohol and tobacco. Reformists further argue that democratic societies should maximize the freedom of its citizens, including the freedom to engage in behaviour that may be harmful to oneself. *The Economist* quotes John Stuart Mill in support of their advocacy of drug law reform.

> The principles were set out, a century and a half ago, by John Stuart Mill, a British liberal philosopher, who urged that the state had no right to intervene to prevent individuals from doing something that harmed them, if no harm was thereby done to the rest of society. "Over himself, over his own body and mind, the individual is sovereign," Mill famously proclaimed. This is a view that The *Economist* has always espoused, and one to which most democratic governments adhere, up to a point. They allow the individual to undertake all manner of dangerous activities unchallenged, from mountaineering to smoking to riding bicycles through city streets. Such pursuits alarm insurance companies and mothers, but are rightly tolerated by the state. (*The Economist*, 2001)

Reformists also argue that a regulated and legal market gives society greater control over drug usage and is the most effective way of minimizing the danger and harm associated with this activity. Through regulations, society can control the strength and the quality of drugs sold, exclude purchases by minors, and oversee health-related issues. Removal of the ban on drugs would make it easier to treat the problems of addiction and prevent the spread of diseases such as AIDS and hepatitis. What is envisioned is a system of laws and regulations similar to those that govern the sale and distribution of alcohol and tobacco.

Many use the experience with Prohibition in the U.S. during the years 1919–1932 to attack the present prohibitionist policy on drug usage. During the 13 years that the sale of alcohol was prohibited in the U.S., the illegal market flourished and gave rise to violent organized crime and the widespread corruption of law enforcement. One lesson that should be learned from the "Great Experiment" with alcohol prohibition is that banning drugs is not the best way to protect society from harm. The war on drugs has had a negative effect on countries throughout the world and a devastating impact in developing countries such as Colombia where the very foundations of democracy have come under attack by drug-fuelled conflicts.

Summary

In July 2002, England announced plans to liberalize drug policy regarding the use of marijuana so that possession of small quantities will no longer be treated as a crime. The country is also reviving a decades-old policy that allows medical practitioners to prescribe heroin to addicts. These changes have brought Britain into line with a number of other European countries, including Italy, Spain, Portugal, Switzerland, the Netherlands, and Belgium, which have begun to decriminalize various drugs.

Whereas the U.S. public tend to view illegal drug usage as a crime that needs to be solved by punishment, European nations generally see drug usage primarily as a lifestyle choice and/or health problem that requires a more therapeutic approach. Several European countries support treatment of addicts and other pragmatic policies such as needle-exchange programs aimed at reducing the spread of HIV. Despite an increasing tolerance of drug usage, Western European countries remain firmly prohibitionist when it comes to drug trafficking. Drug-trafficking laws are harsh, vigorously enforced, and courts issue relatively punitive sentences.

Even though the actual changes in British law are rather timid, some political commentators believe that Britain's move to decriminalize marijuana is significant because it represents "the largest crack that has yet appeared in the prohibitionist dam" (Gwynne Dyer, *Kitchener Waterloo Record*, July 13, 2002). Dyer calls the war on drugs "one the most spectacularly counter-productive activities human beings have ever engaged in." From a global perspective, the main engine of the "war on drugs" and the major source of prohibitionist sentiment is the United States. During the Cold War, the U.S. managed to enshrine its prohibitionist views in international law by a series of United Nations treaties that make it impossible for national legislatures to legalize the commonly used recreational drugs. Without the United States's agreement, countries can do little more than decriminalize the possession and use of some currently illicit drugs. Critics argue that the effects of America's misdirected policies spread across the world. Other rich countries that try to change their policies meet fierce American resistance; poor countries that ship drugs (as Latin American experience shows) come under huge pressure to prevent the trade, whatever the cost to civil liberties or the environment. At present, many countries are bound by a United Nations convention that hampers even the most modest moves toward liberalization, and that clearly needs amendment (Gwynne Dyer, *Kitchener Waterloo Record*, July 13, 2002; *The Economist*, 2001:12)

Many scholars contend that the problems associated with illicit drug usage have less to do with social policy than other societal problems. Social factors such as racism and discrimination, social inequality, poverty and unemployment, dysfunctional families, and weak informal social controls promote the use of illicit drugs and worsen the problems associated with their usage. Reuter makes the following suggestion:

> If policy is only moderately important in controlling drug use, then perhaps

we can mitigate the harshness of our policies with little risk of seeing an expansion of drug use and related problems. Reducing our drug *policy* problem (i.e., the adverse consequences of the policies themselves) is worth a good deal, though it would obviously be even more desirable if we could also reduce our drug problem. (Reuter, 1997:263)

Those who favour legalization have an uphill battle since they are dealing with people who see drug use as a moral issue. Some observers suggest that the two sides are so polarized that there is little common ground or chance for a reasonable compromise. Reuter comments on the low level of the debate that has taken place to date.

> I am struck by the lack of any nuanced debate about drug policy, beyond the ungrounded and polarizing legalization shouting match and the banal and marginal discussion of how the federal drug budget should be spent .... A society that deliberately averts its eyes from an honest assessment of a massive and frequently cruel intervention that sacrifices so many other goals for the one desideratum of drug abstinence can scarcely expect to find a well-grounded alternative. (Reuter, 1997:274)

Before any liberalization can take place, reformers must first engage the prohibitionists in a constructive dialogue on the relative advantages and disadvantages of control models that vary along a spectrum of restrictiveness. Only by discussing relevant issues is it possible for moderates on both sides to resolve their differences and agree upon drug policies acceptable to most people. Reformers must also engage government agencies and make them interested in assessing the consequences of a prohibition model and experiment with less harsh and innovative controls and regulations. It will be difficult to overcome the status quo and change the minds of people who see drug control as a moral crusade.

> To legalize will not be easy. Drug-taking entails risks, and societies are increasingly risk-averse. But the role of government should be to prevent the most chaotic drug-users from harming others—by robbing or by driving while drugged, for instance—and to regulate drug markets to ensure minimum quality and safe distribution. The first task is hard if law enforcers are preoccupied with stopping all drug use; the second impossible as long as drugs are illegal. A legal market is the best guarantee that drug-taking will be no more dangerous than drinking alcohol or smoking tobacco. And, just as countries rightly tolerate those two vices, so they should tolerate those who sell and take drugs. (*The Economist*, 2001:12)

The data generated in the present study has been used to discuss social policies relevant to illicit drug dealing and drug usage. It must be emphasized, however, that the research is based on a relatively small sample of captive subjects, has methodological shortcomings, and should be used with caution. Despite its limitations, it is hoped that this study, in conjunction with other research, can assist in the ongoing efforts by citizens and government officials to develop the most appropriate social policies for dealing with the problem of drug abuse and drug trafficking in Canada.

References

Abadinsky, H.
1990   *Organized Crime*, 3rd ed. Chicago: Nelson Hall.

Abell, P.
1991   *Rational Choice Theory*. Cambridge: Cambridge University Press.

Adler, P.A.
1985   *Wheeling and Dealing: An Ethnography of an Upper-Level Drug Dealing and Smuggling Community*. New York: Columbia University Press.

Adler, P.A. & P. Adler.
1982   Criminal Commitment among Drug Dealers. *Deviant Behavior* 3:117–135.
1983   Shifts and Oscillations in Deviant Careers: The Case of Upper-Level Drug Dealers and Smugglers. *Social Problems* 31:195–207.
1992   Relationships between Dealers: The Social Organization of Illicit Drug Transactions. *Sociology and Social Research* 67:261–277.

Agnew, R.
1992   Foundation for a General Strain Theory of Crime and Delinquency. *Criminology* 30:47–87.

Albini, J.
1971   *The American Mafia: Genesis of a Legend*. New York: Appleton, Crofts.

Altschuler, D.M. & P.J. Broustein.
1991   Patterns of Drug Trafficking, and Other Delinquency among Inner-City Adolescent Males in Washington, D.C. *Criminology* 29:589–621.

Arlacchi, P. & R. Lewis
1990   *Imprenditorialita illecita e droga. Il mercato dell'eroina a Verona*. Bologna: Il Mulino.

219

Atkyns, R.L. & G.J. Hanneman.
1974   Illicit Drug Distribution and Dealer Communication Behavior. *Journal of Health and Social Behavior* 15:36–43.

Barber, J.
1986   The New Drug Crusade. *Maclean's* (September 29):36–39.

Beare, M.E.
1996   *Criminal Conspiracies: Organized Crime in Canada.* Toronto: Nelson Canada.

Beare, M.E. & R.T. Naylor.
1999   *Major Issues Relating to Organized Crime within the Context of Economic Relationships.* Toronto: Nathanson Centre for the Study of Organized Crime.

Becchi, A.
1996   Italy: Mafia-Dominated Drug Market? In N. Dorn, J. Jepsen, & E. Savona (Eds.), *European Drug Policies and Enforcement*, pp. 119–130. London: Macmillan.

Becker, G.S.
1968   Crime and Punishment: An Economic Approach. *Journal of Political Economy* 76(2):169–217.

Bell, D.
1953   Crime as an American Way of Life. *Antioch Review* 13:131–154.

Bellah, R.N., R. Madsen, W.M. Sullivan, A. Swidler, & S.M. Tipton.
1985   *Habits of the Heart: Individualism and Commitment in American Life.* Berkeley: University of California Press.

Blackwell, J.S. & P.G. Ericson (Eds.).
1988a   The Le Dain Commission Recommendations. In J.S. Blackwell & P.G. Ericson (Eds.), *Illicit Drugs in Canada: A Risky Business,* pp. 336–344. Scarborough: Nelson Canada.
1988b   *Illicit Drugs in Canada: A Risky Business.* Scarborough: Nelson Canada.

Block, A.
1979   *East Side—West Side: Organizing Crime in New York 1939–1959.* Swansea: Christopher Davis.
1991   Organized Crime, Garbage, and Toxic Waste: An Overview. In A. Block (Ed.), *Perspectives on Organized Crime: Essays in Opposition*, pp. 79–101. Boston: Kluwer-Nijhoff Publishing.
1999   Bad Business: A Commentary on the Criminology of Organized Crime in the United States. In Tom Farer (Ed.), *Transnational Crime in the Americas.* New York: Routledge.

Blok, A.
1974   *The Mafia of a Sicilian Village 1860–1960: A Study of Violent Peasant Entrepreneurs.* Oxford: Basil Blackwell.

Blum, R.H.
1972   *The Dream Sellers.* San Francisco: Jossey-Bass.

Boyd, N.
1988   Canadian Punishment of Illegal Drug Use: Theory and Practice. In J.S. Blackwell & P.G. Ericson (Eds.), *Illicit Drugs in Canada: A Risky Business*, pp. 301–313. Scarborough: Nelson Canada.
1991   *High Society: Legal and Illegal Drugs in Canada.* Toronto: Key Porter Books.

Bueno de Mesquita, B. and L.E. Cohen.
1995   Self-interest, Equity, and Crime Control: A Game-Theoretic Analysis of Criminal Decision Making. *Criminology* 33:483–517.

Camp, G.M.
1968   *Nothing to Lose: A Study of Bank Robbery in America.* Ann Arbor, Michigan: Yale University Ph.D. Dissertation.

Carey, J.T.
1968   *The College Drug Scene.* Englewood Cliffs: Prentice-Hall.

Carpenter, C., B. Glassner, B.D. Johnson & J. Loughlin
1988   *Kids, Drugs, and Crime.* Lexington, MA: Lexington Books.

Carroll, J. & F. Weaver.
1986   Shoplifters' Perceptions of Crime Opportunities: A Process-Tracing Study. In D.B. Cornish & R.V. Clarke (Eds.), *The Reasoning Criminal: Rational Choice Perspectives on Offending,* pp. 19–38. New York: Springer-Verlag.

Chambliss, W.
1978   *On the Take.* Bloomington: University of Indiana.

Chin, K.L.
1996.   *Chinatowns Gangs: Extortion, Enterprise, and Ethnicity.* New York: Oxford University Press.

Cloward, R.
1959   Illegitimate Means, Anomie, and Deviant Behavior. *American Sociological Review* 24:164–176.

Cloward, R.A. & L.E. Ohlin.
1960   *Delinquency and Opportunity.* New York: Free Press.

Cohen, A.K.
1955   *Delinquent Boys: The Culture of the Gang.* Glencoe, IL: Free Press.

Comack, E.
1985   The Origins of Canadian Drug Legislation: Labelling Versus Class Analysis. In T. Fleming (Ed.), *The New Criminologies in Canada: State, Crime, and Control,* pp. 65–86. Toronto: Oxford University Press.

Commission of Inquiry into the Non-Medical Use of Drugs (The Le Dain Commission).
1970   *Interim Report.* Ottawa: Queen's Printer.
1972a   *Cannabis.* Ottawa: Information Canada.
1972b   *Treatment.* Ottawa: Information Canada.
1973   *Final Report.* Ottawa: Information Canada.

Cook, S.
1970   *Variations in Response to Illegal Drug Use.* Toronto: Addiction Research Foundation.

Cornish, D.B. & R.V. Clarke (Eds.).
1986a   *The Reasoning Criminal: Rational Choice Perspectives on Offending.* New York: Springer-Verlag.
1986b   Introduction. In D.B. Cornish & R.V. Clarke (Eds.), *The Reasoning Criminal: Rational Choice Perspectives on Offending,* pp. 1–16. New York: Springer-Verlag.
1987   Understanding Crime Displacement: An Application of Rational Choice Theory. *Criminology* 25:933–947.

Cressey, D.
1967   The Function and Structure of Criminal Syndicates. In President's Commission on Law Enforcement and the Administration of Justice, *The Challenge of Crime in a Free Society.* Washington: U.S. Government Printing Office.

1969   *Theft of Nation: The Structure and Operation of Organized Crime in America.* New York: Harper & Row.

1972   *Criminal Organization.* New York: Harper Torchbooks.

Curcione, N.
1997   Suburman Snowmen: Facilitating Factors in the Careers of Middle-Class Coke Dealers. *Deviant Behavior* 18:233–253.

Desroches, F.
2002 [1995] *Force and Fear: Robbery in Canada.* Toronto: Canadian Scholars' Press.

Dorn, N., K. Murji, & N. South.
1992   *Drug Markets and Law Enforcement.* London: Routledge.

Dorn, N. & N. South.
1990   Drug Markets and Law Enforcement. *British Journal of Criminology* 30:171–188.

Dubro, J.
1985   *Mob Rule: Inside the Canadian Mafia.* Toronto: Totem Books.

Durkheim, E.
1951 [1899] *Suicide.* New York: The Free Press.

The Economist.
2001   A Survey of Drugs (July 28): 11–12; *Special Report,* 1–16.

Edwards, A. & P. Gill.
2002   Crime as Enterprise? The Case of "Transnational Organized Crime." *Crime, Law & Social Change* 38:203–223.

Erickson, P.G.
1989   Living with Prohibition: Regular Cannabis Users, Legal Sanctions and Informal Controls. *International Journal of the Addictions* 24(3):175–188.

1990   Past, Current and Future Directions in Canadian Drug Policy. *International Journal of the Addictions* 25:247–266.

1992   Recent Trends in Canadian Drug Policy: The Decline and Resurgence of Prohibitionism. *Daedalus* 121:239–267.

1998   Recent Trends in Canadian Drug Policy: The Decline and Resurgence of Prohibitionism. In T.F. Hartnagel (Ed.), *Canadian Crime Control Policy,* pp. 212–230. Toronto: Harcourt Brace and Company.

Erickson, P.G., E. Adlaf, G. Murray, & R. Smart.
1987   *The Steel Drug: Cocaine in Perspective.* Lexington: Lexington Books, D.C. Heath.

Erickson, P.G. & Y.W. Cheung.
1992   Drug Crime and Legal Control: Lessons from the Canadian Experience. *Contemporary Drug Problems* (Summer):247–277.

Erickson, P.G. & G.F. Murray.
1986   Cannabis Criminals Revisited. *British Journal of Addiction* 81(1):81–85.

Erickson, P.G., D.M. Riley, Y.W. Chueng, & P. O'Hare (Eds.).
1997   *Harm Reduction: A New Direction for Drug Policies and Programs.* Toronto: University of Toronto Press.

Erickson, P.G. & R. Smart.
1988   The Le Dain Commission Recommendations. In Judith C. Blackwell & Patricia Ericson (Eds.), *Illicit Drugs in Canada: A Risky Business*, pp. 336–344. Scarborough: Nelson Canada.

Farer, F. (Ed.).
1999   *Transnational Crime in the Americas*. New York: Routledge.

Feeney, F.
1986   Robbers as Decision Makers. In D.B. Cornish & R.V. Clarke (Eds.), *The Reasoning Criminal: Rational Choice Perspectives on Offending*. New York: Springer-Verlag.

Feeney, F. & A. Weir.
1975   The Prevention and Control of Robbery. *Criminology* 13:102–105.

Fields, A.
1984   Slinging Weed: the Social Organization of Street Corner Marijuana Sales. *Urban Life* 13:247–270.
1986   Weedslingers: Young Black Marijuana Dealers. In George Beschner & Alfred Friedman (Eds.), *Teen Drug Use*, pp. 85–104. Lexington: Lexington Books.

Fijnaut, F.B., G. Bruinsma & H. van de Bunt.
1998   *Organized Crime in the Netherlands*. The Hague: Kluwer Law International.

Finckenauer, J. & E. Waring.
1998   *Russian Mafia in America*. Boston: Northeastern University Press.

Fischer, B., K. Ala-Leppilampi, E. Single & A. Robins.
2003   Cannabis Law Reform in Canada: Is the "Saga of Promise, Hesitation and Retreat" Coming to an End? *Canadian Journal of Criminology and Criminal Justice* 45:265–295.

Gabor, T., M. Baril, M.Cusson, D. Elie, M. Leblanc & A. Normandeau.
1987   *Armed Robbery: Cops, Robbers, and Victims*. Springfield: Charles C. Thomas Publisher.

Gambetta, D.
1993   *The Sicilian Mafia*. Boston: Harvard University Press.

Garcia Marquez, G.
1990   The Future of Colombia. *Granta* 31:86–89.

Giffen, P.J., S. Endicott & S. Lambert.
1991   *Panic and Indifference: The Politics of Canada's Drug Laws*. Ottawa: Canadian Centre on Substance Abuse.

Giffen, P.J. & S. Lambert.
1988   What Happened on the Way to Law Reform? In Judith C. Blackwell & Patricia Ericson (Eds.), *Illicit Drugs in Canada: A Risky Business*, pp. 345–369. Scarborough: Nelson Canada.

Glaser, D.
1985   The Criminal Law's Nemesis: Drug Control. *American Bar Foundation Research Journal*: 619–626.

Godson, R. & W.J. Olson.
1993   *International Organized Crime: Emerging Threat to U.S. Security*. Washington: National Strategy Information Center.

Goldstein, P.J.
1985   The Drugs/Violence Nexus: A Triapartite Conceptual Framework. *Journal of Drug Issues* 15:493–506.
1989   Drugs and Violent Crime. In Neil Alan Weiner & Marvin E. Wolfgang (Eds.), *Pathways to Criminal Violence*, pp. 16–48. Newbury Park: Sage Publications.

Goode, E.
1970   *The Marijuana Smokers*. New York: Basic Books Inc.

Gottfredson, M.R. & T. Hirschi.
1990   *A General Theory of Crime*. Palo Alto: Stanford University Press.

Green, M.
1979   A History of Canadian Narcotics Control: The Formative Years. *University of Toronto Faculty of Law Review* 37:42–79.

Hafley, S.R. & R. Tewksbury.
1995   The Rural Kentucky Marijuana Industry: Organization and Community Involvement. *Deviant Behavior: An Interdisciplinary Journal* 16:201–221.

Hagan, F.
1983   The Organized Crime Continuum: A Further Specification of a New Conceptual Model. *Criminal Justice Review* Spring(8):52–57.

Hagedorn, J.M.
1994   Homeboys, Dope Fiends, Legits, and New Jacks. *Criminology* 32(2): 197–219.

Handelman, S.
1995   *Comrade Criminal: Russia's New Mafia*. New Haven: Yale University Press.

Haran, J.F. & J.M. Martin.
1977   The Imprisonment of Bank Robbers: The Issue of Deterrence. *Federal Probation* 41:27–30.

Hawkins, G.
1969   God and the Mafia. *Public Interest* Winter(14):24–51.

Hirschi, T.
1969   *Causes of Delinquency*. Berkeley: University of California Press.
1986   On the Compatibility of Rational Choice and Social Control Theories of Crime. In D.B. Cornish & R.V. Clarke (Eds.), *The Reasoning Criminal: Rational Choice Perspectives on Offending*, pp. 105–118. New York: Springer-Verlag.

Hobbs, D.
1998a   Debate: There Is Not a Global Crime Problem. *International Journal of Risk, Security and Crime Prevention* 3(2):133–137.
1998b   Going Down the Global: The Local Context of Organized Crime. *The Howard Journal* 37(4):407–422.

Holzman, H.
1983   The Serious Habitual Property Offender as 'Moonlighter': An Empirical Study of Labor Force Participation Among Robbers and Burglars. *Journal of Criminal Law and Criminology* 73:1174–92.

Ianni, F.J.
1974   *Black Mafia: Ethnic Succession in Organized Crime*. New York: Simon & Schuster.

Ianni, F.J. & E. Reuss-Ianni.
1972   *A Family Business: Kinship and Social Control in Organized Crime*. New York: Russel Sage Foundation.

Jacobs, B.A.
1999   *Dealing Crack: The Social World of Streetcorner Selling*. Boston: Northeastern University Press.

Jankowski, M.S.
1991   *Islands in the Street: Gangs and American Urban Society*. Berkeley: University of California Press.

Jenkins, P. & G. Potter.
1987   The Politics and Mythology of Organized Crime: A Philadelphia Case-Study. *Journal of Criminal Justice* 15:473–484.

Johnson, B.D., P. Goldstein, E. Preeble, J. Schmeidler, D. Lipton, B. Spunt & T. Miller
1985   *Taking Care of Business: The Economics of Crime by Heroin Abusers*, pp. 56–78. Lexington, MA: Lexington.

Johnson, B.D., A. Hamid & H. Sanabria
1992   Emerging Models of Crack Distribution. In T. Mieczkowski (Ed.), *Drugs, Crime and Social Policy*, pp. 56–78. Boston: Allyn and Bacon.

Johnson, B., A. Golub & J. Fagan.
1995   Careers in Crack, Drug Use, Drug Distribution, and Non-Drug Criminality. *Crime and Delinquency* 41:275–295.

Johnson, B.D., M.A. Kaplan & J. Schmmeidler.
1990   Days with Drug Distribution: Which Drugs? How Many Transactions? With What Returns? In Ralph Weisheit (Ed.), *Drugs, Crime, and the Criminal Justice System*, pp. 193–214. Cincinnati: Anderson Publishing Co.

Kefauver Senate Investigating Commission.
1951   United States Congress, Senate Special Committee to Investigate Organized Crime and Interstate Commerce.
1951a   *Third Interim Report*. Washington: U.S. Government Printing Office.

Kenny, D.J. & J.O. Fiuckenauer.
1995   *Organized Crime in America*. Belmont: Wadsworth.

Korf, D.J. and M. de Kort.
1990   *Drugshandel en Drugsbestrijiding*. Amsterdam: Criminologisches Institut "Bonger," University van Amsterdam.

Langer, J.
1977   Drug Entrepreneurs and the Dealing Culture. *Social Problems* 24:377–386.

Lee, R.W.
1999   Transnational Organized Crime: An Overview. In Tom Farer (Ed.), *Transnational Crime in the Americas*. New York: Routledge.

Letkemann, P.
1973   *Crime as Work*. Englewood Cliffs: Prentice-Hall Inc.

Lewis, R.
1994   Flexible Hierarchies and Dynamic Disorders. In J. Strang & M. Gossup (Eds.), *Heroin Addiction and Drug Policy: The British System*, pp. 42–54. Oxford: Oxford University Press.

Lieb, J. & S. Olson.
1976   Prestige, Paranoia, and Profit: On Becoming a Dealer of Illicit Drugs in a University Community. *Journal of Drug Issues* 6: 356-367.

Maas, P.
1968   *The Valachi Papers*. New York: Bantam Books.

MacCoun, R.J., J.P. Kahan, J. Gillespie & J. Rhee.
1993   A Content Analysis of the Drug Legalization Debate. *Journal of Drug Issues* 23(4):615–629.

MacCoun, R. & P. Reuter.
1992   Are the Wages of Sin $30 an Hour? Economic Aspects of Street-Level Drug Dealing. *Crime and Delinquency* 38:477–491.

MacCoun, R., P. Reuter & T. Schelling.
1996   Assessing Alternative Drug Control Regimes. *Journal of Policy Analysis and Management* 15(3):330–352.

Maher, L.
1997   *Sexed Work: Gender, Race, and Resistance in a Brooklyn Drug Market*. Oxford: Clarendon Press.

Maher, L. & K. Daly.
1996   Women in the Street-Level Drug Economy: Continuity or Change? *Criminology* 34:465–491.

Maltz, M.
1976   On Defining Organized Crime. *Crime and Delinquency* 22:338–346.

Martin's Annual Criminal Code.
2002   Aurora, Ontario: Canada Law Books Inc.

Matsueda, R.S., R. Gartner, I. Piliavin & M. Polakowski.
1992   The Prestige of Criminal and Conventional Occupations: A Subcultural Model of Criminal Activity. *American Sociological Review* 57:752–770.

Matza, D.
1964   *Delinquency and Drift*. New York: Wiley.
1969   *Becoming Deviant*. Englewood Cliffs: Prentice-Hall.

McCarthy, B. & J. Hagan.
2001   When Crime Pays: Capital, Competence, and Criminal Success. *Social Forces* 79(3):1035–1059.

McCarthy, B., J. Hagan & L.E. Cohen.
1998   Uncertainty, Cooperation, and Crime: Understanding the Decision to Co-offend. *Social Forces* 77:154184.

Merton, R.K.
1938   Social Structure and Anomie. *American Sociological Review* 3:672–682.
1968   *Social Theory and Social Structure*, 2nd ed. New York: Free Press.

Mieczkowski, T.
1986   Geeking Up and Throwing Down: Heroin Street Life in Detroit. *Criminology* 25:645–666.
1988   Studying Heroin Retailers: A Research Note. *Criminal Justice Review* 13:39–44.
1990   Drugs, Crime, and the Failure of American Organized Crime Models. *International Journal of Comparative and Applied Criminal Justice* 14(1):97–106.
1994   The Experiences of Women Who Sell Crack: Some Descriptive Data from the Detroit Crack Ethnography Project. *The Journal of Drug Issues* 24:227–248.

Moore, W.
1974   *The Effective Regulation of an Illicit Market in Heroin.* Lexington: Lexington Books.

Morselli, C.
2001   Structuring Mr. Nice: Entrepreneurial Opportunities and Brokerage Positioning in the Cannabis Trade. *Crime, Law, & Social Change* 35:203–244.
2003a   Contacts, Opportunities, and Crime: Relational Foundations of Criminal Enterprise. *Research in Profile: Just Research.* Department of Justice Canada 8:14–17.
2003b   Career Opportunities and Network-Based Privileges in the Cosa Nostra. *Crime, Law, & Social Change* 39:383–418.

Morselli, C. & P. Tremblay.
2004   Criminal Achievement, Offender Networks, and the Benefits of Low Self-Control, *Criminology* 42:773–804.

Murphy, E.F.
1922   *The Black Candle.* Toronto: Thomas Allen.

Murphy, S., D. Waldorf & C. Reinarman.
1990   Drifting into Dealing: Becoming a Cocaine Seller. *Qualitative Sociology* 13:321–343.

Naylor, R.T.
1995   From Cold War to Crime War: The Search for a New National Security Threat. *Transnational Organized Crime* 1(4):37–56.
2002   *Wages of Crime: Black Markets, Illegal Finance, and the Underworld Economy.* Kingston: McGill-Queen's University Press.

Padilla, F.
1992   *The Gang as an American Enterprise.* New Brunswick: Rutgers University Press.

Paoli, L.
1999   Organized Crime in Italy. In Cliomedia (Ed.), *The Mafia: 150 Years of Facts, Stories, and Faces.* Torino: Cliomedia.
2000   *Pilot Project to Describe and Analyze Local Drug Markets—First Phase Final Report: Illegal Drug Markets in Frankfurt and Milan.* Lisbon: EMCDDA at <http://www.emcdda.org>.
2002   The Paradoxes of Organized Crime. *Crime, Law & Social Change* 37:51–97.

Pennsylvania Crime Commission.
1991   *Organized Crime in Pennsylvania: A Decade of Change, 1990 Report.* Commonwealth of Pennsylvania.

Polsky, N.
1967   *Hustlers, Beats, and Others.* Chicago: Aldine.

Potter, G.
1993   *Criminal Organizations: Vice Racketeering and Politics in an American City.* Prospects Heights: Waveland Press.

Preble, E. & J.J. Casey.
1969   Taking Care of Business: The Heroin User's Life on the Street. *International Journal of the Addictions* 4:1–24.

Rawlinson, P.
1998   Mafia, Media and Myth: Representations of Russian Organized Crime. *The Howard Journal* 37(4):346–358.

Redlinger, L.
1975   Marketing and Distributing Heroin. *Journal of Psychedelic Drugs* 7:331–353.

Reuter, P.
1978   Fact, Fancy, and Organized Crime. *Public Interest* 2:45–67.
1983   *Disorganized Crime: The Economics of the Visible Hand*. Cambridge: The MIT Press.
1984   *Disorganized Crime: Illegal Markets and the Mafia*. Cambridge: The MIT Press.
1985   *The Organization of Illegal Markets: An Economic Analysis*. Washington: National Institute of Justice.
1993   Prevalence Estimation and Policy Formulation. *The Journal of Drug Issues* 23(2):167–184.
1995   The Decline of the American Mafia. *Public Interest* 120:89–99.
1997   Why Can't We Make Prohibition Work Better? Some Consequences of Ignoring the Unattractive. *Proceedings of the American Philosophical Society* 141(3):262–275.

Reuter, P. & J. Haaga.
1989   *The Organization of High-Level Drug Markets: An Exploratory Study*. Santa Monica: Rand Corporation.

Reuter, P., R. MacCoun & P. Murphy.
1990   *Money from Crime: A Study of the Economics of Drug Selling in Washington, D.C.* Santa Monica: Rand Corporation, Drug Policy Research Center.

Robitaille, Clement.
2001   Gains Criminals et Facteurs Individuels de Reussite: Une Re-Analyse du Sondage de 1978 de la Rand Corporation. Master's Dissertation, School of Criminology, University of Montreal.

Sacco, V.
1986   An Approach to the Study of Organized Crime. In Robert A. Silverman & James J. Teevan, Jr. (Eds.), *Crime in Canadian Society*, 3rd ed. Toronto: Butterworth.

Schelling, T.
1984   *Choice and Consequence*. Cambridge: Harvard University Press.

Shaw, C.R. & H.D. McKay.
1972 [1942] *Juvenile Delinquency of Urban Areas*. Chicago: The University of Chicago Press.

Simon, H.A.
1957   *Models of Man*. New York: Wiley.

Skinner, J.
1963   Writs of Assistance. *University of Toronto Faculty of Law Review* 21:26–44.

Small, S.
1978   Canadian Narcotics Legislation, 1908–1923: A Conflict Model Interpretation. In W.K. Greenaway & S.L. Brickley (Eds.), *Law and Social Control in Canada*. Scarborough: Prentice-Hall.

Smart, R. & A. Osborne.
1986   *Northern Spirits*. Toronto: ARF Books.

Smart, R.G., E.M. Adlaf & G.W. Walsh.
1992   Adolescent Drug Sellers: Trends, Characteristics and Profiles. *British Journal of Addictions* 87:1561–1570.

Smith, D.C., Jr.
1976   Mafia: The Prototypical Alien Conspiracy. *The Annals of the American Academy* January(423): 75–88.

Solomon, R.R.
1988a   Canada's Drug Legislation. In J.S. Blackwell & P.G. Ericson (Eds.), *Illicit Drugs in Canada: A Risky Business*. Scarborough: Nelson Canada.
1988b   The Noble Pursuit of Evil: Arrest, Search, and Seizure in Canadian Drug Law. In J.S. Blackwell and P.G. Ericson (Eds.), *Illicit Drugs in Canada: A Risky Business*. Scarborough: Nelson Canada.

Solomon, R.R. & M. Green.
1988   The First Century: The History of Non-medical Opiate Use and Control Policies in Canada, 1870–1970. In P.G. Blackwell (Eds.), *Illicit Drugs in Canada: A Risky Business*. Scarborough: Nelson Canada.

Solomon, R. & T. Madison.
1977   The Evolution of Non-Medical Opiate Use in Canada 1870–1929. *Drug Forum* 5(3): 239–249.

Sorfleet, P.
1976   Dealing Hashish: Sociological Notes on Trafficking and Use. *Canadian Journal of Criminology* 18:123–151.

Statutes of Canada.
The Opium and Drug Act, SC 1911, c. 17.
Narcotic Control Act, SC 1985, c. N-1.
Food and Drugs Act, RSC 1985, c. F-27
Corrections and Conditional Release Act, 1992
Witness Protection Program Act, SC, 1996
Controlled Drugs and Substances Act, 1996
Proceeds of Crime (Money Laundering) Act, 1993
Criminal Code of Canada, 2005

Sterling, C.
1994   *Thieves' World*. New York: Simon & Schuster.

Sutherland, E.H.
1947   *The Principles of Criminology*, 4th ed. Philadelphia: Lippincott.

Sykes, G. & D. Matza.
1957   Techniques of Neutralization: A Theory of Delinquency. *American Sociological Review* 22:664–670.

Trasov, G.E.
1962   History of the Opium and Narcotic Drug Legislation in Canada. *Criminal Law Quarterly* 4:274–282.

Tremblay, P. & C. Morselli.
2000   Patterns in Criminal Achievement: Wilson and Abrahamse Revisited. *Criminology* 38:633–657.

Tunnell, K.D.
1993   Inside the Drug Trade: Trafficking from the Dealer's Perspective. *Qualitative Sociology* 16:361–481.

United States Congress, Permanent Subcommittee on Investigations of the Senate Committee on Government Operations (McClellan Committee).
1960   *Gambling and Organized Crime.* Washington: U.S. Government Printing Office.

United States President's Commission on Law Enforcement and Administration of Justice.
1967   *Crime and Its Impact: Task Force Report.* Washington: U.S. Government Printing Office.

VanDuyne, P.C.
1996–1997. Organized Crime, Corruption, and Power. *Crime, Law, and Social Change* 20(3):201–206.

VanNostrand, L. & R. Tewksbury.
1999   The Motives and Mechanics of Operating an Illegal Drug Enterprise. *Deviant Behavior: An Interdisciplinary Journal* 20:57–83.

Waldorf, D.
1987   Business Practices and Social Organization of Cocaine Sellers. Presented at the American Society of Criminology, Montreal, Canada. November.

Waldorf, D., S. Murphy, C. Reinarman & B. Joyce.
1977   *An Ethnography of Cocaine Snorters.* Washington, DC: Drug Abuse Council.

Waldorf, D., C. Reinarman & S. Murphy.
1991   *Cocaine Changes: The Experience of Using and Quitting.* Philadelphia. Pa.: Temple University Press.

Weisheit, R.A.
1990   Domestic Marijuana Growers: Mainstreaming Deviance. *Deviant Behavior* 11:107–129.
1991a   Drug Use among Domestic Marijuana Growers. *Contemporary Drug Problems* 18:191–217.
1991b   The Intangible Rewards from Crime: The Case of Domestic Marijuana Cultivation. *Crime and Delinquency* 37:506–527.

Williams, Phil.
1998   The Nature of Drug Trafficking Networks. *Current History* (April):154–159.

Williams, Phil & Roy Godson.
2002   Anticipating Organized and Transnational Crime. *Crime, Law, and Social Change* 37:311–355.

Wilson, J.Q. & A. Abrahamse.
1992   "Does Crime Pay?" *Justice Quarterly* 9:359–377.

Case References

Beaver v. R. (1957) 118 CCC 129, 26 CR 193 (SCC)
Bisaillon v. Keable (1983) 2 SCR 60
Fuller v. R. (1975) 2 SCR 121
Guimond v. R. (1979) 44 CCC (2d) 481, 26 NR 91 (SCC) (7:2)
Kowbel v. R. (1954) 110 CCC 47, 18 CR 380 (SCC) (4:1)
Marshall v. R. (1969) 5 CRNS 348 (Alta. CA)
McGee v. R. (1978) 3 CR (3d) 371 (Que. CA)

R. v. Addison ex p. Mooney (1970) 1 CCC 127 (1969) 2 OR 674 (CA)

R. v. Arason (1993) 78 CCC (3d) 1 (BCCA)

R. v. Arnold (1989) 9 WCB (2d) 258 (BCCA)

R. v. Baron and Wertman (1976) 31 CCC (2d) 525, 73 DLR (3d) 213 (Ont. CA)

R. v. Beaulne (1979) 50 CCC (2d) 524 (Ont. CA)

R. v. Bell (1983) 8 CCC (3d) 97 (SCC)

R. v. Caccamo (1973) 2 OR 367 (CA), aff'd (1976) 1 SCR 786

R. v. Caldwell (1972) 19 CRNS 293 (Alta. CA)

R. v. Chambers (1985) 20 CCC (3d) 440 (Ont. CA)

R. v. Champagne (1969) 8 CRNS 245 (B.C. CA)

R. v. Davies (1982) 1 CCC (3d) 299 (Ont. CA)

R. v. Douglas (1974) 18 CCC (2d) 189 (Ont. CA)

R. v. Drysdale (1978) 41 CCC (2d) 238, 22 NBR (2d) 86 (SC App. Div.)

R. v. Fahlman (1968) 5 CRNS (B.C. Co. Ct.)

R. v. Garofoli (1990) 2 SCR 1421

R. v. Gauvreau (1982) 35 OR (2d) 388 (CA)

R. v. Harvey (1969) 1 NBR (2d) 587 (CA)

R. v. Khela (1991) 68 CCC (3d) 83–94 (CAQ)

R. v. Krueger (1966) 3 CCC 127 55 WWR 624 (Sask. CA)

R. v. Larson (1972) 6 CCC (2d) 145, 18 CRNS 149 (B.C. CA)

R. v. Leduc (1972) 5 NSR (2d) 82 (CA)

R. v. Leipert (1997) 1 SCR 281

R. v. Martin (1973) 21 CRNS 149 (Ont. HC)

R. v. Masters (1973) 12 CCC (2d) 573, aff'd (1974) 15 CCC (2d) 142 (Ont. CA)

R. v. McNamara et al. (No. 1) 1981, 56 CCC (2d) 193 (Ont. CA) (452-4)

R. v. Michel (1968) 2 OR 68 CA

R. v. O'Brien (1954) 110 CCC 1 (1954) SCR 666, 19 CR CR 371 (3:2)

R. v. Pearson (1992) 77 CCC (3d)

R. v. Scott (1990) 3 SCR 979

R. v. Sherman (1977) 36 CCC (2d) 207, 39 CRNS 255 (B.C. CA)

R. v. Smith (1973) 3 WWR 81 (B.C. CA)

R. v. Stinchcombe (1991) 3 SCR 326

R. v. Terrence (1983) 4 CCC (3rd) 193, 33 CR (3d) 193, [1983] 1 SCR 357 (t:0)

R. v. Thomas (1998) 124 CCC (3d) 178

R. v. Tokarek (1967) 58 WWR 691 (B.C. CA)

R. v. Underwood (1987) 3 WCB (2d) 139

R. v. Vautour (1970) 1 NBR (2d) 735 (CA)

R. v. Weselak (1972) 9 CCC (2d) 193

Index

233

DATE DUE